BEOWULF

THE DONALDSON TRANSLATION
BACKGROUNDS AND SOURCES
CRITICISM

D0010977

≫ A NORTON CRITICAL EDITION ≪

BEOWULF

THE DONALDSON TRANSLATION
BACKGROUNDS AND SOURCES
CRITICISM

≫ ≪

Edited by

JOSEPH F. TUSO

UNIVERSITY OF SCIENCE AND ARTS OF OKLAHOMA

≫ ≪

W · W · NORTON & COMPANY
NEW YORK · LONDON

W. W. Norton & Company, Inc., 500 Fifth Avenue, New York, N.Y. 10110

Library of Congress Cataloging in Publication Data
Beowulf. English.
  Beowulf: the Donaldson translation, backgrounds and sources, criticism.
  (A Norton critical edition)
  Bibliography: p.
  Includes index.
  1. Beowulf. 2. Anglo-Saxon poetry—Criticism and interpretation—Addresses, essays, lectures. I. Donaldson, Ethelbert Talbot. II. Tuso, Joseph F.
PR1583.D6   1975   829'.3   75-17991

PRINTED IN THE UNITED STATES OF AMERICA

4 5 6 7 8 9 0

ISBN 0-393-04413-0 CL
ISBN 0-393-09225-0 PBK

THIS BOOK IS DEDICATED TO

Lt. Col. Walton F. Dater, Jr. (1932–1974)

Warrior—Scholar—Friend

—he wæs manna mildust ond monðwærust—

Contents

Abbreviations

ABC	*An Anthology of Beowulf Criticism*
ARV	*Journal of Scandinavian Folklore*
BP	*The Beowulf Poet*
EETS	Early English Text Society
ELH	*Journal of English Literary History*
ES	*English Studies*
JEGP	*Journal of English and Germanic Philology*
MÆ	*Medium Ævum*
MHRA	Modern Humanities Research Association
MLA	Modern Language Association of America
MLN	*Modern Language Notes*
MLQ	*Modern Language Quarterly*
MLR	*Modern Language Review*
MP	*Modern Philology*
MS	Manuscript
Neophil	*Neophilologus* (Groningen)
NM	*Neuphilologische Mitteilungen*
OE	Old English
ON	Old Norse
OEL	*Old English Literature*
OEP	*Old English Poetry*
PBA	*Proceedings of the British Academy*
PMLA	*Publications of the Modern Language Association of America*
PQ	*Philological Quarterly* (Iowa City)
RES	*Review of English Studies*
rpt.	reprinted
Sewanee Rev.	*Sewanee Review*
SP	*Studies in Philology*
UTQ	*University of Toronto Quarterly*

Preface

This volume offers the beginning student E. Talbot Donaldson's excellent modern prose translation of *Beowulf*. Its acceptance by my students, by my colleagues throughout the country, as well as by numerous critics and scholars, renders any further comments on its quality unnecessary.

Backgrounds and Sources begins with Robert C. Hughes' history of the English language up to the time of *Beowulf's* composition. Stanley B. Greenfield's survey of the major Old English manuscripts and genres is followed by E. Talbot Donaldson's concise discussion of the major features of Old English poetry as seen in Cædmon's *Hymn*, a work that had a profound influence upon the diction of *Beowulf*. Readers interested in Old English poetry will find suitable references in the Selected Bibliography.

E. G. Stanley's discussion of the *Beowulf* manuscript, sources, and the poem's original audience lays the groundwork for the excerpt from Dorothy Whitelock's essay, which has been an influential modern approach to the milieu, social setting, and chronology of the poem's composition. Fr. Klaeber highlights the elements which the poet probably drew upon as he worked, and Chambers and Greenfield discuss two related works, the *Grettis saga* and the *Fight at Finnsburg*.

The section concludes with Klaeber's clarification of the historic details of the feud between the Danes and Heatho-Bards, C. L. Wrenn's thoughts on the historicity of the hero, and Ralph Arnold's survey of valuable archaeological evidence which establishes the physical layout and functions of early English royal halls.

The Criticism section begins with Donaldson's comments on theme, Germanic society, and fate. On the question of whether the poem's Christian elements are integral or later interpolations, Klaeber maintains that they are an essential part of *Beowulf* as we know it. No collection of essays on *Beowulf* would be complete without an excerpt from J. R. R. Tolkien's landmark essay, "*Beowulf*: The Monsters and the Critics," and so I include his witty, brilliant interpretation of the poem itself wherein he discusses sources, theme, style, structure, and the role of the monsters.

Kenneth Sisam's reasoned differences with Tolkien next lead us into R. E. Kaske's allegorical approach to *Beowulf*; his analysis convinces him that Beowulf is the ideal Christian hero. Margaret E. Goldsmith, on the other hand, while using an approach almost identical to Kaske's, concludes that Beowulf is predominantly a less than ideal Germanic hero. Alvin A. Lee uses a mythic approach to the poem's theme; John Leyerle provides an original and striking view of the structure of the work and the character of the hero, and oral-formulaic theory is defined by Cassidy and Ringler and rejected, at least in his own mind, by Paull F. Baum.

E. V. K. Dobbie's careful explanation of the relationships between Swedes and Geats is based solidly on the *Beowulf* text, and leads in to an analysis of the Battle of Ravenswood by Edward B. Irving, Jr. Irving places this part of the poem in its structural and thematic context, and also shows how it sharpens the characterization of Beowulf himself. The final selection by Frederick R. Rebsamen ends the essays as the poet himself ends *Beowulf*—elegiacally. The material in the Appendices will, I hope, be of use and interest, especially the Index of Proper Names, which I place last for convenient reference.

I am very grateful to all the contributors who have so generously permitted me to reprint their material in this volume. I have attempted to keep my own notes to a minimum. In the notes I abbreviate the titles of journals and substitute Arabic for Roman volume numbers. In most cases I omit lengthy Latin or Old English quotations, but in such instances Donaldson's or the author's modern English is always supplied. I have taken as few liberties as possible with the texts of the essays themselves. That the contributors and publishers allowed me a certain editorial latitude is a tribute to their desire to make this edition useful and readable for the audience for which it is intended.

I am especially grateful to E. Talbot Donaldson for allowing me to use his translation, extremely useful notes, and other material; for the valuable advice of Douglas R. Butturff, James L. Rosier, and Frederick R. Rebsamen in the early stages of my work, and for John Leyerle's help in preparing his article for reprinting. Special thanks must also go to Mr. Peter W. Phelps of W. W. Norton & Company, Inc., for his unflagging faith in this edition from the very outset, and to Thelma Sargent for her expert attention to detail in the preparation of my manuscript for publication.

Finally, I must thank my eldest daughter, Ann, for helping me proofread, my younger daughters Mary, Lisa, Kathleen, and Jody for staying out of my study while I was at work, and my wife, Jean—*næs hio hnah swa þeah, ne to gneað gifa*—who treated me with far more consideration than I deserved during the many months I obsessively spent weekends and evenings working on this edition.

JOSEPH F. TUSO

The Translation[†]

The chief purpose of this translation is to try to preserve for the reader what the translator takes to be the most striking characteristic of the style of the original: extraordinary richness of rhetorical elaboration alternating with—often combined with—the barest simplicity of statement. The effect of this, impressive though it is, is difficult to analyze; perhaps the principal thing it accomplishes is to keep us constantly aware that while the aspirations of the people concerned are high-heroic, the people themselves are merely people—men with almost all the limitations (Beowulf's great physical strength is an exception) of ordinary mortals. That is, men may rise to the heroism of the rhetorical style, but they are nevertheless always the human beings of the plain style. In order to try to reproduce this effect, it has seemed best to translate as literally as possible, confining oneself to the linguistic and intellectual structure of the original. It is perfectly true that a literal translation such as this is bound to result in a style of modern English prose that was never seen before on land or sea and is not apt to be again—a good example of what Ben Jonson would surely call "no language." But no received English style that I know, modern or archaic, sounds anything like *Beowulf*: there seems to be no accepted alternate to a literal rendering.

For a good many years prose translators of *Beowulf* chose to use a "heroic" style which at least sounded archaic, for it borrowed liberally from Milton, Pope, Shakespeare, and the King James Bible, as well as from later imitators of these. A good many serviceable translations were thus produced, but in general the homogeneousness of their style necessarily proved false to the original by elevating even its simplest statements into highly adorned ones: the hero can perform the commonest actions—like sitting down—only by means of an elaborate periphrasis. More recent translators have eschewed the artificiality of such style and have rendered the poem into what is called "modern colloquial English." This has resulted in bringing out very effectively the starker side of the poem, its understatements and its directness, but has also given the unfortunate impression that the heavily rhetorical side is excrescent and unnecessary: heaped-up epithets are reduced, like fractions to

† From *Beowulf*, a new prose translation by E. Talbot Donaldson, pp. xii–xv by E. T. Donaldson. Revised for this Edition in 1975. Copyright © 1966 by W. W. Norton & Company, Inc. Reprinted by permission of the publisher.

be simplified, to one or two terms, the "whale-road" is resolved into what it surely is, the sea, and "*þaet waes god cyning*" becomes, colloquially but rather donnishly, "He was an excellent king." Decorum expects translators to maintain a consistent point of view through their style, but the *Beowulf* poet (along with most great poets) forges a complex style that simultaneously discloses differing aspects of the same situation; lacking his vision and his language (not to mention his talent), we tend to emphasize one aspect at the expense of the other.

One sentence will illustrate the kind of difficulty the translator of *Beowulf* constantly encounters. It occurs during the hero's fight with Grendel's mother in her under-water hall. The sword Hrunting has failed him; he has grappled with the monster-woman and thrown her to the floor; then he himself stumbles and falls. At this point the poet says, "Ofsaet þa þone selegyst": "Then she sat upon the hall-guest." This is a reasonable action, for she is much bigger than he, and is preparing to stab him. Yet if one is using a consistently heroic style, the simple verb "sat"—especially in juxtaposition with the seemingly "epic" epithet "hall-guest"—will simply not do; in order to preserve the translator's and the hero's dignity, Grendel's mother must throw, hurl, fling, or otherwise precipitate herself upon her adversary. If, on the other hand, one is using the colloquial style, then "hall-guest" is an embarrassment, and one is apt to go through the (perfectly correct) semantic process of *hall-guest = hall-visitor* or *hall-stranger = visitor* or *stranger in the hall = intruder*. And "intruder" is in many ways quite satisfactory, but it lacks whatever potential for quick, grim humor the expression "hall-guest" has. Surely something specious has been added if Grendel's mother acts more dramatically than just sitting upon Beowulf, and something good has been lost if he becomes other than a hall-guest.

An honest translator must confess that while he has tried to avoid the defects of his predecessors, he has probably introduced defects of which they were free. My resolute avoidance of such terms as bill, buckler, and byrnie undoubtedly gives the impression that the poet's vocabulary was limited in words for sword, shield, and mail-shirt: actually it was so rich that bill, buckler, and byrnie lend only paltry, stopgap aid, and I have thought it better to make the poet monotonous than quaint. At times I have been guiltily aware that an Old English word might be more exactly translated by a polysyllabic Latinate synonym than by the word's modern English monosyllabic descendant which I have preferred, but one is so often absolutely compelled to use Latinisms that I have tried to avoid them whenever there was the slightest possibility of doing so. With words whose potential translations range from the colorless to the highly colored—such as "man: warrior: hero"—I have generally preferred the more modest of the alternates, though it might be argued that I have thus behaved anti-heroically. I am not sure that my feeling that *thou* and *thee* are inappropriate in a modern translation may not be idiosyncratic, but it has at least enabled me to evade such monstrosities as "thou achievedest." I am sorry we have lost the interjection "lo" from modern English: it is enormously useful, and hard to get around for Old English *hwaet*, though I have got around it when I could. While my translation is not intended to be in purely "natural" English, I have avoided unnatural expressions unless they performed some function in rendering the Old English style.

I cannot boast that I have been able to resolve with entire honesty every dilemma presented by the original. Like most translators, I have put in proper names in some places where the poet used only pronouns, have occasionally changed difficult constructions to easy ones, and have altered word order—and thus the poet's emphasis—in sentences where to preserve the literal would be to obscure the sense. I have also occasionally introduced glosses into the text. For instance, after the Danes and Geats have journeyed from Heorot to Grendel's mere and have found it boiling with blood —and Aeschere's head upon the shore—the poet says, "Again and again the horn sang its urgent war-song. The whole troop sat down." Seen from a realistic point of view, there is nothing surprising about this: the warriors have had a hard trip, and nothing is, for the moment, to be gained by remaining standing. Yet even one who believes that heroic warriors need not always be in furious motion experiences a sense of anticlimax here, and I have wilfully added a gloss: "The whole troop sat down to rest." A problem of a different sort, to be solved only by suppression of sense, occurs in the Danish coast-guard's speech to the arriving Geats. After marveling at their boldness and warlike appearance, he says to them (literally): "Hear my simple thought: haste is best to make known whence your comings are." The thought is, indeed, simple enough, but the expression is highly elaborate, a plain question put in a most formal way that shows at once respect for and defiance of the Geatish warriors. I know of no way to render such shades of meaning in modern English, and my translation makes of the coast-guard a plainer, blunter man than the poet probably conceived. In general I hope, however, that I have not played false too often, and that the reader unfamiliar with Old English may derive from this translation some real sense of the poem's extraordinary qualities. I have eschewed verse in the same hope, for I am persuaded that only a prose translation, made with no other end in mind than fidelity to the original, can bring out the distinctive qualities of the work.

To make it a modern poem is, inevitably, to make it a different poem. The author of one of the best verse translations of *Beowulf* emphasizes that "a creative re-creation [i.e., a poetic translation] is a creation"; no two creative artists can create the same thing. If, on the other hand, a verse translation does not try to be a poem in its own right, then it can only be versification, a literal rendering constantly distracted from literalism by the need to versify, as a more creative translation is constantly distracted from literalism by the translator's creativity. Rather than try to create a new and lesser poem for the reader, it seems better to offer him in prose the literal materials from which he can re-create the poem.

I should like to thank Miss Mary Carruthers for her great help in checking the translation, correcting errors, and suggesting improvements. To several of my friends who are enormously learned in Old English I am also much indebted for their patient kindness in answering my sometimes naïve questions, but since they did not see the manuscript, I shall not embarrass them by naming them. Two colleagues who did see the manuscript—William Wiatt of Indiana and Albert H. Marckwardt of Princeton—offered most helpful suggestions; I am grateful, both for those that I used and those that I didn't. I tried not to consult other translations during the course of my own work (except in the case of several venerable cruxes), but I was familiar with several of them—especially Clark Hall's—before I began, and I know that they often helped me when I was not aware of their doing so. The translation is based on F. Klaeber's third edition of the poem (1950); in general, the emendations suggested by J. C. Pope, *The Rhythm of Beowulf*, second edition (1966), have been adopted.

E. TALBOT DONALDSON

The Text of

Beowulf

Translated by E. Talbot Donaldson

Beowulf

[*Prologue: The Earlier History of the Danes*]

Yes, we have heard of the glory of the Spear-Danes' kings in the old days—how the princes of that people did brave deeds.

Often Scyld Scefing [1] took mead-benches away from enemy bands, from many tribes, terrified their nobles—after the time that he was first found helpless.[2] He lived to find comfort for that, became great under the skies, prospered in honors until every one of those who lived about him, across the whale-road, had to obey him, pay him tribute. That was a good king.

Afterwards a son was born to him, a young boy in his house, whom God sent to comfort the people: He had seen the sore need they had suffered during the long time they lacked a king. Therefore the Lord of Life, the Ruler of Heaven, gave him honor in the world: Beow[3] was famous, the glory of the son of Scyld spread widely in the Northlands. In this way a young man ought by his good deeds, by giving splendid gifts while still in his father's house, to make sure that later in life beloved companions will stand by him, that people will serve him when war comes. Through deeds that bring praise, a man shall prosper in every country.

Then at the fated time Scyld the courageous went away into the protection of the Lord. His dear companions carried him down to the sea-currents, just as he himself had bidden them do when, as protector of the Scyldings,[4] he had ruled them with his words —long had the beloved prince governed the land. There in the harbor stood the ring-prowed ship, ice-covered and ready to sail, a prince's vessel. Then they laid down the ruler they had loved, the ring-giver, in the hollow of the ship, the glorious man beside

1. The meaning is probably "son of Sceaf," although Scyld's origins are mysterious.
2. As is made clear shortly below, Scyld arrived in Denmark as a child alone in a ship loaded with treasures.
3. Although the manuscript reads "Beowulf," most scholars now agree that it should read "Beow." Beow was the grandfather of the Danish king Hrothgar.
4. I.e., the Danes ("descendants of Scyld").

the mast. There was brought great store of treasure, wealth from lands far away. I have not heard of a ship more splendidly furnished with war-weapons and battle-dress, swords and mail-shirts. On his breast lay a great many treasures that should voyage with him far out into the sea's possession. They provided him with no lesser gifts, treasure of the people, than those had done who at his beginning first sent him forth on the waves, a child alone. Then also they set a golden standard high over his head, let the water take him, gave him to the sea. Sad was their spirit, mournful their mind. Men cannot truthfully say who received that cargo, neither counsellors in the hall nor warriors under the skies.

(I.)⁵ Then in the cities was Beow of the Scyldings beloved king of the people, long famous among nations (his father had gone elsewhere, the king from his land), until later great Healfdene was born to him. As long as he lived, old and fierce in battle, he upheld the glorious Scyldings. To him all told were four children born ₍into the world, to the leader of the armies: Heorogar and Hrothgar and the good Halga. I have heard tell that [. . . was On]ela's queen,⁶ beloved bed-companion of the Battle-Scylfing.

[*Beowulf and Grendel*]

[THE HALL HEOROT IS ATTACKED BY GRENDEL]

Then Hrothgar was given success in warfare, glory in battle, so that his retainers gladly obeyed him and their company grew into a great band of warriors. It came to his mind that he would command men to construct a hall, a mead-building large[r] than the children of men had ever heard of, and therein he would give to young and old all that God had given him, except for common land and men's bodies.⁷ Then I have heard that the work was laid upon many nations, wide through this middle-earth, that they should adorn the folk-hall. In time it came to pass—quickly, as men count it—that it was finished, the largest of hall-dwellings. He gave it the name of Heorot,⁸ he who ruled wide with his words. He did not forget his promise: at the feast he gave out rings, treasure. The hall stood tall, high and wide-gabled: it would wait for the fierce flames of vengeful fire; ⁹

5. The numbering of sections is that of the manuscript, which makes, however, no provision for Section XXX.
6. The text is faulty, so that the name of Healfdene's daughter has been lost; her husband Onela was a Swedish (Scylfing) king.
7. Or "men's lives." Apparently slaves, along with public land, were not in the king's power to give away.
8. I.e., "Hart."
9. The destruction by fire of Heorot occurred at a later time than that of the poem's action, probably during the otherwise unsuccessful attack of the Heatho-Bard Ingeld on his father-in-law Hrothgar, mentioned in the next clause.

the time was not yet at hand for sword-hate between son-in-law and father-in-law to awaken after murderous rage.

Then the fierce spirit [1] painfully endured hardship for a time, he who dwelt in the darkness, for every day he heard loud mirth in the hall; there was the sound of the harp, the clear song of the scop.[2] There he spoke who could relate the beginning of men far back in time, said that the Almighty made earth, a bright field fair in the water that surrounds it, set up in triumph the lights of the sun and the moon to lighten land-dwellers, and adorned the surfaces of the earth with branches and leaves, created also life for each of the kinds that move and breathe.—Thus these warriors lived in joy, blessed, until one began to do evil deeds, a hellish enemy. The grim spirit was called Grendel, known as a rover of the borders, one who held the moors, fen and fastness. Unhappy creature, he lived for a time in the home of the monsters' race, after God had condemned them as kin of Cain. The Eternal Lord avenged the murder in which he slew Abel. Cain had no pleasure in that feud, but He banished him far from mankind, the Ruler, for that misdeed. From him sprang all bad breeds, trolls and elves and monsters—likewise the giants who for a long time strove with God: He paid them their reward for that.

(II.) Then, after night came, Grendel went to survey the tall house—how, after their beer-drinking, the Ring-Danes had disposed themselves in it. Then he found therein a band of nobles asleep after the feast: they felt no sorrow, no misery of men. The creature of evil, grim and fierce, was quickly ready, savage and cruel, and seized from their rest thirty thanes. From there he turned to go back to his home, proud of his plunder, sought his dwelling with that store of slaughter.

Then in the first light of dawning day Grendel's war-strength was revealed to men: then after the feast weeping arose, great cry in the morning. The famous king, hero of old days, sat joyless; the mighty one suffered, felt sorrow for his thanes, when they saw the track of the foe, of the cursed spirit: that hardship was too strong, too loathsome and long-lasting. Nor was there a longer interval, but after one night Grendel again did greater slaughter—and had no remorse for it—vengeful acts and wicked: he was too intent on them. Thereafter it was easy to find the man who sought rest for himself elsewhere, farther away, a bed among the outlying buildings—after it was made clear to him, told by clear proof, the hatred of him who now controlled the hall.[3]

---

1. I.e., Grendel.
2. The "scop" was the Anglo-Saxon minstrel, who recited poetic stories to the accompaniment of a harp.
3. I.e., Grendel.

Whoever escaped the foe held himself afterwards farther off and more safely. Thus Grendel held sway and fought against right, one against all, until the best of houses stood empty. It was a long time, the length of twelve winters, that the lord of the Scyldings suffered grief, all woes, great sorrows. Therefore, sadly in songs, it became well-known to the children of men that Grendel had fought a long time with Hrothgar, for many half-years maintained mortal spite, feud, and enmity—constant war. He wanted no peace with any of the men of the Danish host, would not withdraw his deadly rancor, or pay compensation: no counselor there had any reason to expect splendid repayment at the hands of the slayer.[4] For the monster was relentless, the dark death-shadow, against warriors old and young, lay in wait and ambushed them. In the perpetual darkness he held to the misty moors: men do not know where hell-demons direct their footsteps.

Thus many crimes the enemy of mankind committed, the terrible walker-alone, cruel injuries one after another. In the dark nights he dwelt in Heorot, the richly adorned hall. He might not approach the throne, [receive] treasure, because of the Lord; He had no love for him.[5]

This was great misery to the lord of the Scyldings, a breaking of spirit. Many a noble sat often in council, sought a plan, what would be best for strong-hearted men to do against the awful attacks. At times they vowed sacrifices at heathen temples, with their words prayed that the soul-slayer[6] would give help for the distress of the people. Such was their custom, the hope of heathens; in their spirits they thought of Hell, they knew not the Ruler, the Judge of Deeds, they recognized not the Lord God, nor indeed did they know how to praise the Protector of Heaven, the glorious King. Woe is him who in terrible trouble must thrust his soul into the fire's embrace, hope for no comfort, not expect change. Well is the man who after his death-day may seek the Lord and find peace in the embrace of the Father.

[THE COMING OF BEOWULF TO HEOROT]

(III.) So in the cares of his times the son of Healfdene constantly brooded, nor might the wise warrior set aside his woe. Too harsh, hateful and long-lasting was the hardship that had come upon the people, distress dire and inexorable, worst of night-horrors.

4. According to old Germanic law, a slayer could achieve peace with his victim's kinsmen only by paying them *wergild, i.e.,* compensation for the life of the slain man.
5. Behind this obscure passage seems to lie the idea that Grendel, unlike Hrothgar's thanes, could not approach the throne to receive gifts from the king, having been condemned by God as an outlaw.
6. I.e., the Devil. Despite this assertion that the Danes were heathen, their king, Hrothgar, speaks consistently as a Christian.

A thane of Hygelac,[7] a good man among the Geats, heard in his homeland of Grendel's deeds: of mankind he was the strongest of might in the time of this life, noble and great. He bade that a good ship be made ready for him, said he would seek the war-king over the swan's road,* the famous prince, since he had need of men. Very little did wise men blame him for that adventure, though he was dear to them; they urged the brave one on, examined the omens. From the folk of the Geats the good man had chosen warriors of the bravest that he could find; one of fifteen he led the way, the warrior sought the wooden ship, the sea-skilled one the land's edge. The time had come: the ship was on the waves, the boat under the cliff. The warriors eagerly climbed on the prow—the sea-currents eddied, sea against sand; men bore bright weapons into the ship's bosom, splendid armor. Men pushed the well-braced ship from shore, warriors on a well-wished voyage. Then over the sea-waves, blown by the wind, the foam-necked boat traveled, most like a bird, until at good time on the second day the curved prow had come to where the seafarers could see land, the sea-cliffs shine, towering hills, great headlands. Then was the sea crossed, the journey at end. Then quickly the men of the Geats climbed upon the shore, moored the wooden ship; mail-shirts rattled, dress for battle. They thanked God that the wave-way had been easy for them.

Then from the wall the Scyldings' guard who should watch over the sea-cliffs saw bright shields borne over the gangway, armor ready for battle; strong desire stirred him in mind to learn what the men were. He went riding on his horse to the shore, thane of Hrothgar, forcefully brandished a great spear in his hands, with formal words questioned them: "What are you, bearers of armor, dressed in mail-coats, who thus have come bringing a tall ship over the sea-road, over the water to this place? Lo, for a long time I have been guard of the coast, held watch by the sea so that no foe with a force of ships might work harm on the Danes' land: never have shield-bearers more openly undertaken to come ashore here; nor did you know for sure of a word of leave from our warriors, consent from my kinsmen. I have never seen a mightier warrior on earth than is one of you, a man in battle-dress. That is no retainer made to seem good by his weapons—unless his appearance belies him, his unequalled form. Now I must learn your lineage before you go any farther from here, spies on the Danes' land. Now you far-dwellers, sea-voyagers, hear what I think: you must straightway say where you have come from."

---

7. I.e., Beowulf the Geat, whose king was Hygelac.

* A kenning or truncated metaphor; the "swan's road" is the sea. *Ed.*

(IV.) To him replied the leader, the chief of the band un-locked his word-hoard: "We are men of the Geatish nation and Hygelac's hearth-companions. My father was well-known among the tribes, a noble leader named Ecgtheow. He lived many winters before he went on his way, an old man, from men's dwellings. Every wise man wide over the earth readily remembers him. Through friendly heart we have come to seek your lord, the son of Healfdene, protector of the people. Be good to us and tell us what to do: we have a great errand to the famous one, the king of the Danes. And I too do not think that anything ought to be kept secret: you know whether it is so, as we have indeed heard, that among the Scyldings I know not what foe, what dark doer of hateful deeds in the black nights, shows in terrible manner strange malice, injury and slaughter. In openness of heart I may teach Hrothgar remedy for that, how he, wise and good, shall overpower the foe—if change is ever to come to him, relief from evil's distress—and how his surging cares may be made to cool. Or else ever after he will suffer tribulations, con-straint, while the best of houses remains there on its high place."

The guard spoke from where he sat on his horse, brave officer: "A sharp-witted shield-warrior who thinks well must be able to judge each of the two things, words and works. I understand this: that here is a troop friendly to the Scyldings' king. Go forward, bearing weapons and war-gear. I will show you the way; I shall also bid my fellow-thanes honorably to hold your boat against all enemies, your new-tarred ship on the sand, until again over the sea-streams it bears its beloved men to the Geatish shore, the wooden vessel with curved prow. May it be granted by fate that one who behaves so bravely pass whole through the battle-storm."

Then they set off. The boat lay fixed, rested on the rope, the deep-bosomed ship, fast at anchor. Boar-images [8] shone over cheek-guards gold-adorned, gleaming and fire-hardened—the war-minded boar held guard over fierce men. The warriors hastened, marched together until they might see the timbered hall, stately and shining with gold; for earth-dwellers under the skies that was the most famous of buildings in which the mighty one waited—its light gleamed over many lands. The battle-brave guide pointed out to them the shining house of the brave ones so that they might go straight to it. Warrior-like he turned his horse, then spoke words: "It is time for me to go back. The All-Wielding Father in His grace keep you safe in your undertakings. I shall

8. Carved images of boars (sometimes represented as clothed like human war-riors) were placed on helmets in the belief that they would protect the wearer in battle.

go back to the sea to keep watch against hostile hosts."

(V.) The road was stone-paved, the path showed the way to the men in ranks. War-corselet shone, hard and hand-wrought, bright iron rings sang on their armor when they first came walking to the hall in their grim gear. Sea-weary they set down their broad shields, marvelously strong protections, against the wall of the building. Then they sat down on the bench—mail-shirts, warrior's clothing, rang out. Spears stood together, sea-men's weapons, ash steel-gray at the top. The armed band was worthy of its weapons.

Then a proud-spirited man [9] asked the warriors there about their lineage: "Where do you bring those gold-covered shields from, gray mail-shirts and visored helmets, this multitude of battle-shafts? I am Hrothgar's herald and officer. I have not seen strangers—so many men—more bold. I think that it is for daring—not for refuge, but for greatness of heart—that you have sought Hrothgar." The man known for his courage replied to him; the proud man of the Geats, hardy under helmet, spoke words in return: "We are Hygelac's table-companions. Beowulf is my name. I will tell my errand to Healfdene's son, the great prince your lord, if, good as he is, he will grant that we might address him." Wulfgar spoke—he was a man of the Wendels, his bold spirit known to many, his valor and wisdom: "I will ask the lord of the Danes about this, the Scyldings' king, the ring-giver, just as you request—will ask the glorious ruler about your voyage, and will quickly make known to you the answer the good man thinks best to give me."

He returned at once to where Hrothgar sat, old and hoary, with his company of earls. The man known for his valor went forward till he stood squarely before the Danes' king: he knew the custom of tried retainers. Wulfgar spoke to his lord and friend: "Here have journeyed men of the Geats, come far over the sea's expanse. The warriors call their chief Beowulf. They ask that they, my prince, might exchange words with you. Do not refuse them your answer, gracious Hrothgar. From their war-gear they seem worthy of earls' esteem. Strong indeed is the chief who has led the warriors here."

(VI.) Hrothgar spoke, protector of the Scyldings: "I knew him when he was a boy. His father was called Ecgtheow: Hrethel of the Geats [1] gave him his only daughter for his home. Now has his hardy offspring come here, sought a fast friend. Then, too, seafarers who took gifts there to please the Geats used to say that he has in his handgrip the strength of thirty men, a man

---

9. Identified below as Wulfgar.
1. Hrethel was the father of Hygelac and Beowulf's grandfather and guardian.

famous in battle. Holy God of His grace has sent him to us West-Danes, as I hope, against the terror of Grendel. I shall offer the good man treasures for his daring. Now make haste, bid them come in together to see my company of kinsmen. In your speech say to them also that they are welcome to the Danish people."

Then Wulfgar went to the hall's door, gave the message from within: "The lord of the East-Danes, my victorious prince, has bidden me say to you that he knows your noble ancestry, and that you brave-hearted men are welcome to him over the sea-swells. Now you may come in your war-dress, under your battle helmets, to see Hrothgar. Let your war-shields, your wooden spears, await here the outcome of the talk."

Then the mighty one rose, many a warrior about him, a company of strong thanes. Some waited there, kept watch over the weapons as the brave one bade them. Together they hastened, as the warrior directed them, under Heorot's roof. The war-leader, hardy under helmet, advanced till he stood on the hearth. Beowulf spoke, his mail-shirt glistened, armor-net woven by the blacksmith's skill: "Hail, Hrothgar! I am kinsman and thane of Hygelac. In my youth I have set about many brave deeds. The affair of Grendel was made known to me on my native soil: sea-travelers say that this hall, best of buildings, stands empty and useless to all warriors after the evening-light becomes hidden beneath the cover of the sky. Therefore my people, the best wise earls, advised me thus, lord Hrothgar, that I should seek you because they know what my strength can accomplish. They themselves looked on when, bloody from my foes, I came from the fight where I had bound five, destroyed a family of giants, and at night in the waves slain water-monsters, suffered great pain, avenged an affliction of the Weather-Geats on those who had asked for trouble—ground enemies to bits. And now alone I shall settle affairs with Grendel, the monster, the demon. Therefore, lord of the Bright-Danes, protector of the Scyldings, I will make a request of you, refuge of warriors, fair friend of nations, that you refuse me not, now that I have come so far, that alone with my company of earls, this band of hardy men, I may cleanse Heorot. I have also heard say that the monster in his recklessness cares not for weapons. Therefore, so that my liege lord Hygelac may be glad of me in his heart, I scorn to bear sword or broad shield, yellow wood, to the battle, but with my grasp I shall grapple with the enemy and fight for life, foe against foe. The one whom death takes can trust the Lord's judgment. I think that if he may accomplish it, unafraid he will feed on the folk of the Geats in the war-hall as he has often done on the flower of men. You will not need to hide my head [2]

---

2. I.e., "bury my body."

if death takes me, for he will have me blood-smeared; he will
bear away my bloody flesh meaning to savor it, he will eat
ruthlessly, the walker alone, will stain his retreat in the moor; no
longer will you need trouble yourself to take care of my body. If
battle takes me, send to Hygelac the best of war-clothes that protects
my breast, finest of mail-shirts. It is a legacy of Hrethel, the
work of Weland.³ Fate always goes as it must."

(VII.) Hrothgar spoke, protector of the Scyldings: "For deeds
done, my friend Beowulf, and for past favors you have sought
us. A fight of your father's brought on the greatest of feuds.
With his own hands he became the slayer of Heatholaf among
the Wylfings. After that the country of the Weather-Geats might
not keep him, for fear of war. From there he sought the folk of
the South-Danes, the Honor-Scyldings, over the sea-swell. At that
time I was first ruling the Danish people and, still in my youth,
held the wide kingdom, hoard-city of heroes. Heorogar had died
then, gone from life, my older brother, son of Healfdene—he
was better than I. Afterwards I paid blood-money to end the feud;
over the sea's back I sent to the Wylfings old treasures; he ⁴
swore oaths to me.

"It is a sorrow to me in spirit to say to any man what Grendel
has brought me with his hatred—humiliation in Heorot, terrible
violence. My hall-troop, warrior-band, has shrunk; fate has swept
them away into Grendel's horror. (God may easily put an end
to the wild ravager's deeds!) Full often over the ale-cups warriors
made bold with beer have boasted that they would await with
grim swords Grendel's attack in the beer-hall. Then in the morning
this mead-hall was a hall shining with blood, when the day
lightened, all the bench-floor blood-wet, a gore-hall. I had fewer
faithful men, beloved retainers, for death had destroyed them.
Now sit down to the feast and unbind your thoughts, your famous
victories, as heart inclines."

[THE FEAST AT HEOROT]

Then was a bench cleared in the beer-hall for the men of the
Geats all together. Then the stout-hearted ones went to sit down,
proud in their might. A thane did his work who bore in his
hands an embellished ale-cup, poured the bright drink. At times a
scop sang, clear-voiced in Heorot. There was joy of brave men,
no little company of Danes and Weather-Geats.

(VIII.) Unferth spoke, son of Ecglaf, who sat at the feet of
the king of the Scyldings, unbound words of contention—to

---

3. The blacksmith of the Norse gods.   Wylfings Hrothgar had settled.
4. Ecgtheow, whose feud with the

him was Beowulf's undertaking, the brave seafarer, a great vex-
ation, for he would not allow that any other man of middle-
earth should ever achieve more glory under the heavens than
himself: "Are you that Beowulf who contended with Breca, com-
peted in swimming on the broad sea, where for pride you explored
the water, and for foolish boast ventured your lives in the deep?
Nor might any man, friend nor enemy, keep you from the
perilous venture of swimming in the sea. There you embraced the
sea-streams with your arms, measured the sea-ways, flung forward
your hands, glided over the ocean; the sea boiled with waves,
with winter's swell. Seven nights you toiled in the water's power.
He overcame you at swimming, had more strength. Then in the
morning the sea bore him up among the Heathoraemas; from
there he sought his own home, dear to his people, the land of
the Brondings, the fair stronghold, where he had folk, castle, and
treasures. All his boast against you the son of Beanstan carried
out in deed. Therefore I expect the worse results for you—though
you have prevailed everywhere in battles, in grim war—if you
dare wait near Grendel a night-long space."

Beowulf spoke, the son of Ecgtheow: "Well, my friend Unferth, drunk with beer you have spoken a great many things
about Breca—told about his adventures. I maintain the truth that
I had more strength in the sea, hardship on the waves, than
any other man. Like boys we agreed together and boasted—we
were both in our first youth—that we would risk our lives in the
salt sea, and that we did even so. We had naked swords, strong
in our hands, when we went swimming; we thought to guard
ourselves against whale-fishes. He could not swim at all far from
me in the flood-waves, be quicker in the water, nor would I move
away from him. Thus we were together on the sea for the time
of five nights until the flood drove us apart, the swelling sea,
coldest of weathers, darkening night, and the north wind battle-
grim turned against us: rough were the waves. The anger of the
sea-fishes was roused. Then my body-mail, hard and hand-linked,
gave me help against my foes; the woven war-garment, gold-
adorned, covered my breast. A fierce cruel attacker dragged me
to the bottom, held me grim in his grasp, but it was granted
me to reach the monster with my sword-point, my battle-blade.
The war-stroke destroyed the mighty sea-beast—through my hand.

(IX.) "Thus often loathsome assailants pressed me hard. I
served them with my good sword, as the right was. They had
no joy at all of the feast, the malice-workers, that they should
eat me, sit around a banquet near the sea-bottom. But in the
morning, sword-wounded they lay on the shore, left behind by
the waves, put to sleep by the blade, so that thereafter they

would never hinder the passage of sea-voyagers over the deep
water. Light came from the east, bright signal of God, the sea
became still so that I might see the headlands, the windy walls
of the sea. Fate often saves an undoomed man when his courage
is good. In any case it befell me that I slew with my sword
nine sea-monsters. I have not heard tell of a harder fight by
night under heaven's arch, nor of a man more hard-pressed in
the sea-streams. Yet I came out of the enemies' grasp alive, weary
of my adventure. Then the sea bore me onto the lands of the
Finns, the flood with its current, the surging waters.

"I have not heard say of you any such hard matching of
might, such sword-terror. Breca never yet in the games of war—
neither he nor you—achieved so bold a deed with bright swords
(I do not much boast of it), though you became your brothers'
slayer, your close kin; for that you will suffer punishment in hell,
even though your wit is keen. I tell you truly, son of Ecglaf, that
Grendel, awful monster, would never have performed so many
terrible deeds against your chief, humiliation in Heorot, if your
spirit, your heart, were so fierce in fight as you claim. But he has
noticed that he need not much fear the hostility, not much dread
the terrible sword-storm of your people, the Victory-Scyldings.
He exacts forced levy, shows mercy to none of the Danish
people; but he is glad, kills, carves for feasting, expects no
fight from the Spear-Danes. But I shall show him soon now the
strength and courage of the Geats, their warfare. Afterwards he
will walk who may, glad to the mead, when the morning light
of another day, the bright-clothed sun, shines from the south on the
children of men."

Then was the giver of treasure in gladness, gray-haired and
battle-brave. The lord of the Bright-Danes could count on help.
The folk's guardian had heard from Beowulf a fast-resolved
thought.

There was laughter of warriors, voices rang pleasant, words
were cheerful. Wealhtheow came forth, Hrothgar's queen, mindful
of customs, gold-adorned, greeted the men in the hall; and the
noble woman offered the cup first to the keeper of the land of
the East-Danes, bade him be glad at the beer-drinking, beloved
of the people. In joy he partook of feast and hall-cup, king
famous for victories. Then the woman of the Helmings went
about to each one of the retainers, young and old, offered them
the costly cup, until the time came that she brought the mead-
bowl to Beowulf, the ring-adorned queen, mature of mind. Sure
of speech she greeted the man of the Geats, thanked God that
her wish was fulfilled, that she might trust in some man for help
against deadly deeds. He took the cup, the warrior fierce in

battle, from Wealhtheow, and then spoke, one ready for fight—
Beowulf spoke, the son of Ecgtheow: "I resolved, when I set out
on the sea, sat down in the sea-boat with my band of men, that
I should altogether fulfill the will of your people or else fall
in slaughter, fast in the foe's grasp. I shall achieve a deed of
manly courage or else have lived to see in this mead-hall my
ending day." These words were well-pleasing to the woman, the
boast of the Geat. Gold-adorned, the noble folk-queen went to
sit by her lord.

Then there were again as at first strong words spoken in the
hall, the people in gladness, the sound of a victorious folk, until,
in a little while, the son of Healfdene wished to seek his evening
rest. He knew of the battle in the high hall that had been plotted
by the monster, plotted from the time that they might see the
light of the sun until the night, growing dark over all things, the
shadowy shapes of darkness, should come gliding, black under
the clouds. The company all arose. Then they saluted each other,
Hrothgar and Beowulf, and Hrothgar wished him good luck,
control of the wine-hall, and spoke these words: "Never before,
since I could raise hand and shield, have I entrusted to any
man the great hall of the Danes, except now to you. Hold now
and guard the best of houses: remember your fame, show your
great courage, keep watch against the fierce foe. You will not
lack what you wish if you survive that deed of valor."

[THE FIGHT WITH GRENDEL]

(X.) Then Hrothgar went out of the hall with his company
of warriors, the protector of the Scyldings. The war-chief would
seek the bed of Wealhtheow the queen. The King of Glory—
as men had learned—had appointed a hall-guard against Grendel; he had a special mission to the prince of the Danes: he kept
watch against monsters.

And the man of the Geats had sure trust in his great might,
the favor of the Ruler. Then he took off his shirt of armor, the
helmet from his head, handed his embellished sword, best of
irons, to an attendant, bade him keep guard over his war-gear.
Then the good warrior spoke some boast-words before he
went to his bed, Beowulf of the Geats: "I claim myself no
poorer in war-strength, war works, than Grendel claims himself.
Therefore I will not put him to sleep with a sword, so take
away his life, though surely I might. He knows no good tools
with which he might strike against me, cut my shield in pieces,
though he is strong in fight. But we shall forgo the sword in the

night—if he dare seek war without weapon—and then may wise
God, Holy Lord, assign glory on whichever hand seems good
to Him."

The battle-brave one laid himself down, the pillow received
the earl's head, and about him many a brave seaman lay down
to hall-rest. None of them thought that he would ever again seek
from there his dear home, people or town where he had been
brought up; for they knew that bloody death had carried off far
too many men in the wine-hall, folk of the Danes. But the Lord
granted to weave for them good fortune in war, for the folk of
the Weather-Geats, comfort and help that they should quite overcome their foe through the might of one man, through his sole
strength: the truth has been made known that mighty God has
always ruled mankind.

There came gliding in the black night the walker in darkness.
The warriors slept who should hold the horned house—all
but one. It was known to men that when the Ruler did not
wish it the hostile creature might not drag them away beneath
the shadows. But he, lying awake for the fierce foe, with heart
swollen in anger awaited the outcome of the fight.

(XI.) Then from the moor under the mist-hills Grendel came
walking, wearing God's anger. The foul ravager thought to catch
some one of mankind there in the high hall. Under the clouds
he moved until he could see most clearly the wine-hall, treasure-
house of men, shining with gold. That was not the first time that
he had sought Hrothgar's home. Never before or since in his
life-days did he find harder luck, hardier hall-thanes. The creature
deprived of joy came walking to the hall. Quickly the door gave
way, fastened with fire-forged bands, when he touched it with
his hands. Driven by evil desire, swollen with rage, he tore it
open, the hall's mouth. After that the foe at once stepped onto
the shining floor, advanced angrily. From his eyes came a light
not fair, most like a flame. He saw many men in the hall, a band
of kinsmen all asleep together, a company of war-men. Then
his heart laughed: dreadful monster, he thought that before the
day came he would divide the life from the body of every one
of them, for there had come to him a hope of full-feasting.
It was not his fate that when that night was over he should
feast on more of mankind.

The kinsman of Hygelac, mighty man, watched how the evil-
doer would make his quick onslaught. Nor did the monster mean
to delay it, but, starting his work, he suddenly seized a sleeping
man, tore at him ravenously, bit into his bone-locks, drank
the blood from his veins, swallowed huge morsels; quickly he
had eaten all of the lifeless one, feet and hands. He stepped

closer, then felt with his arm for the brave-hearted man on the bed, reached out towards him, the foe with his hand; at once in fierce response Beowulf seized it and sat up, leaning on his own arm. Straightway the fosterer of crimes knew that he had not encountered on middle-earth, anywhere in this world, a harder hand-grip from another man. In mind he became frightened, in his spirit: not for that might he escape the sooner. His heart was eager to get away, he would flee to his hiding-place, seek his rabble of devils. What he met there was not such as he had ever before met in the days of his life. Then the kinsman of Hygelac, the good man, thought of his evening's speech, stood upright and laid firm hold on him: his fingers cracked. The giant was pulling away, the earl stepped forward. The notorious one thought to move farther away, wherever he could, and flee his way from there to his fen-retreat; he knew his fingers' power to be in a hateful grip. That was a painful journey that the loathsome despoiler had made to Heorot. The retainers' hall rang with the noise—terrible drink [5] for all the Danes, the house-dwellers, every brave man, the earls. Both were enraged, fury-filled, the two who meant to control the hall. The building resounded. Then was it much wonder that the wine-hall withstood them joined in fierce fight, that it did not fall to the ground, the fair earth-dwelling; but it was so firmly made fast with iron bands, both inside and outside, joined by skillful smith-craft. There started from the floor—as I have heard say—many a mead-bench, gold-adorned, when the furious ones fought. No wise men of the Scyldings ever before thought that any men in any manner might break it down, splendid with bright horns, have skill to destroy it, unless flame should embrace it, swallow it in fire. Noise rose up, sound strange enough. Horrible fear came upon the North-Danes, upon every one of those who heard the weeping from the wall, God's enemy sing his terrible song, song without triumph—the hell-slave bewail his pain. There held him fast he who of men was strongest of might in the days of this life.

(XII.) Not for anything would the protector of warriors let the murderous guest go off alive: he did not consider his life-days of use to any of the nations. There more than enough of Beowulf's earls drew swords, old heirlooms, wished to protect the life of their dear lord, famous prince, however they might. They did not know when they entered the fight, hardy-spirited warriors, and when they thought to hew him on every side, to seek his soul, that not any of the best of irons on earth, no war-sword, would touch the evil-doer: for with a charm he had made

---

5. The metaphor reflects the idea that the chief purpose of a hall such as Heorot was as a place for men to feast in.

victory-weapons useless, every sword-edge. His departure to death
from the time of this life was to be wretched; and the
alien spirit was to travel far off into the power of fiends. Then he
who before had brought trouble of heart to mankind, committed
many crimes—he was at war with God—found that his body
would do him no good, for the great-hearted kinsman of Hygelac
had him by the hand. Each was hateful to the other alive. The
awful monster had lived to feel pain in his body, a huge wound
in his shoulder was exposed, his sinews sprang apart, his bone-
locks broke. Glory in battle was given to Beowulf. Grendel must
flee from there, mortally sick, seek his joyless home in the fen-
slopes. He knew the more surely that his life's end had come, the
full number of his days. For all the Danes was their wish fulfilled
after the bloody fight. Thus he who had lately come from far
off, wise and stout-hearted, had purged Heorot, saved Hrothgar's
house from affliction. He rejoiced in his night's work, a deed to
make famous his courage. The man of the Geats had fulfilled his
boast to the East-Danes; so too he had remedied all the grief, the
malice-caused sorrow that they had endured before, and had had
to suffer from harsh necessity, no small distress. That was clearly
proved when the battle-brave man set the hand up under the
curved roof—the arm and the shoulder: there all together was
Grendel's grasp.

[CELEBRATION AT HEOROT]

(XIII.) Then in the morning, as I have heard, there was many
a warrior about the gift-hall. Folk-chiefs came from far and near
over the wide-stretching ways to look on the wonder, the footprints of the foe. Nor did his going from life seem sad to any of
the men who saw the tracks of the one without glory—how,
weary-hearted, overcome with injuries, he moved on his way from
there to the mere [6] of the water-monsters with life-failing
footsteps, death-doomed and in flight. There the water was boiling
with blood, the horrid surge of waves swirling, all mixed with
hot gore, sword-blood. Doomed to die he had hidden, then, bereft
of joys, had laid down his life in his fen-refuge, his heathen soul:
there hell took him.

From there old retainers—and many a young man, too—
turned back in their glad journey to ride from the mere, high-
spirited on horseback, warriors on steeds. There was Beowulf's
fame spoken of; many a man said—and not only once—that,
south nor north, between the seas, over the wide earth, no other
man under the sky's expanse was better of those who bear shields,

6. Lake.

more worthy of ruling. Yet they found no fault with their own dear lord, gracious Hrothgar, for he was a good king. At times battle-famed men let their brown horses gallop, let them race where the paths seemed fair, known for their excellence. At times a thane of the king, a man skilled at telling adventures, songs stored in his memory, who could recall many of the stories of the old days, wrought a new tale in well-joined words; this man undertook with his art to recite in turn Beowulf's exploit, and skillfully to tell an apt tale, to lend words to it.

He spoke everything that he had heard tell of Sigemund's valorous deeds, many a strange thing, the strife of Waels's son,[7] his far journeys, feuds and crimes, of which the children of men knew nothing—except for Fitela with him, to whom he would tell everything, the uncle to his nephew, for they were always friends in need in every fight. Many were the tribes of giants that they had laid low with their swords. For Sigemund there sprang up after his death-day no little glory—after he, hardy in war, had killed the dragon, keeper of the treasure-hoard: under the hoary stone the prince's son had ventured alone, a daring deed, nor was Fitela with him. Yet it turned out well for him, so that his sword went through the gleaming worm and stood fixed in the wall, splendid weapon: the dragon lay dead of the murdering stroke. Through his courage the great warrior had brought it about that he might at his own wish enjoy the ring-hoard. He loaded the sea-boat, bore into the ship's bosom the bright treasure, offspring of Waels. The hot dragon melted.

He was adventurer most famous, far and wide through the nations, for deeds of courage—he had prospered from that before, the protector of warriors—after the war-making of Heremod had come to an end, his strength and his courage.[8] Among the Jutes Heremod came into the power of his enemies, was betrayed, quickly dispatched. Surging sorrows had oppressed him too long: he had become a great care to his people, to all his princes; for many a wise man in former times had bewailed the journey of the fierce-hearted one—people who had counted on him as a relief from affliction—that that king's son should prosper, take the rank of his father, keep guard over the folk, the treasure and stronghold, the kingdom of heroes, the home of the Scyldings. The kinsman of Hygelac became dearer to his friends, to all mankind: crime took possession of Heremod.

Sometimes racing their horses they passed over the sand-covered ways. By then the morning light was far advanced, hastening on.

7. Waels was Sigemund's father.
8. Heremod was an unsuccessful king of the Danes, one who began brilliantly but became cruel and avaricious, ulti- mately having to take refuge among the Jutes, who put him to death. His reputation was thus overshadowed by that of Sigemund.

Many a stout-hearted warrior went to the high hall to see the strange wonder. The king himself walked forth from the women's apartment, the guardian of the ring-hoards, secure in his fame, known for his excellence, with much company; and his queen with him passed over the path to the mead-hall with a troop of attendant women.

(XIV.) Hrothgar spoke—he had gone to the hall, taken his stand on the steps, looked at the high roof shining with gold, and at Grendel's hand: "For this sight may thanks be made quickly to the Almighty: I endured much from the foe, many griefs from Grendel: God may always work wonder upon wonder, the Guardian of Heaven. It was not long ago that I did not expect ever to live to see relief from any of my woes—when the best of houses stood shining with blood, stained with slaughter, a far-reaching woe for each of my counselors, for every one, since none thought he could ever defend the people's stronghold from its enemies, from demons and evil spirits. Now through the Lord's might a warrior has accomplished the deed that all of us with our skill could not perform. Yes, she may say, whatever woman brought forth this son among mankind—if she still lives —that the God of Old was kind to her in her child-bearing. Now, Beowulf, best of men, in my heart I will love you as a son: keep well this new kinship. To you will there be no lack of the good things of the world that I have in my possession. Full often I have made reward for less, done honor with gifts to a lesser warrior, weaker in fighting. With your deeds you yourself have made sure that your glory will be ever alive. May the Almighty reward you with good—as just now he has done."

Beowulf spoke, the son of Ecgtheow: "With much good will we have achieved this work of courage, that fight, have ventured boldly against the strength of the unknown one. I should have wished rather that you might have seen him, your enemy brought low among your furnishings. I thought quickly to bind him on his deathbed with hard grasp, so that because of my hand-grip he should lie struggling for life—unless his body should escape. I could not stop his going, since the Lord did not wish it, nor did I hold him firmly enough for that, my life-enemy: he was too strong, the foe in his going. Yet to save his life he has left his hand behind to show that he was here—his arm and shoulder; nor by that has the wretched creature bought any comfort; none the longer will the loathsome ravager live, hard-pressed by his crimes, for a wound has clutched him hard in its strong grip, in deadly bonds. There, like a man outlawed for guilt, he shall await the great judgment, how the bright Lord will decree for him."

Then was the warrior more silent in boasting speech of warlike deeds, the son of Ecglaf,[9] after the nobles had looked at
the hand, now high on the roof through the strength of a man,
the foe's fingers. The end of each one, each of the nail-places,
was most like steel; the hand-spurs of the heathen warrior were
monstrous spikes. Everyone said that no hard thing would hurt
him, no iron good from old times would harm the bloody battle-
hand of the monster.

(XV.) Then was it ordered that Heorot be within quickly
adorned by hands. Many there were, both men and women, who
made ready the wine-hall, the guest-building. The hangings on the
walls shone with gold, many a wondrous sight for each man who
looks on such things. That bright building was much damaged,
though made fast within by iron bonds, and its door-hinges sprung;
the roof alone came through unharmed when the monster, outlawed for his crimes, turned in flight, in despair of his life. That
is not easy to flee from—let him try it who will—but driven by
need one must seek the place prepared for earth-dwellers, soul-
bearers, the sons of men, the place where, after its feasting, one's
body will sleep fast in its death-bed.

Then had the proper time come that Healfdene's son should go
to the hall; the king himself would share in the feast. I have
never heard that a people in a larger company bore themselves
better about their treasure-giver. Men who were known for courage
sat at the benches, rejoiced in the feast. Their kinsmen, stout-
hearted Hrothgar and Hrothulf, partook fairly of many a mead-
cup in the high hall. Heorot within was filled with friends: the
Scylding-people had not then known treason's web.[1]

Then the son of Healfdene gave Beowulf a golden standard to
reward his victory—a decorated battle-banner—a helmet and mail-
shirt: many saw the glorious, costly sword borne before the warrior. Beowulf drank of the cup in the mead-hall. He had no need
to be ashamed before fighting men of those rich gifts. I have not
heard of many men who gave four precious, gold-adorned things
to another on the ale-bench in a more friendly way. The rim
around the helmet's crown had a head-protection, wound of wire,
so that no battle-hard sharp sword might badly hurt him when
the shield-warrior should go against his foe. Then the people's
protector commanded eight horses with golden bridles to be led
into the hall, within the walls. The saddle of one of them stood
shining with hand-ornaments, adorned with jewels: that had been
the war-seat of the high king when the son of Healfdene would

9. I.e., Unferth, who had taunted
Beowulf the night before.
1. A reference to the later history of
the Danes, when, after Hrothgar's death,
his nephew Hrothulf apparently drove
his son and successor Hrethric from
the throne.

join sword-play: never did the warfare of the wide-known one fail when men died in battle. And then the prince of Ing's friends [2] yielded possession of both, horses and weapons, to Beowulf: he bade him use them well. So generously the famous prince, guardian of the hoard, repaid the warrior's battle-deeds with horses and treasure that no man will ever find fault with them—not he that will speak truth according to what is right.

(XVI.) Then further the lord gave treasure to each of the men on the mead-bench who had made the sea-voyage with Beowulf, gave heirlooms; and he commanded that gold be paid for the one whom in his malice Grendel had killed—as he would have killed more if wise God and the man's courage had not forestalled that fate. The Lord guided all the race of men then, as he does now. Yet is discernment everywhere best, forethought of mind. Many a thing dear and loath he shall live to see who here in the days of trouble long makes use of the world.

There was song and music together before Healfdene's battle-leader, the wooden harp touched, tale oft told, when Hrothgar's scop should speak hall-pastime among the mead-benches . . . [of] Finn's retainers when the sudden disaster fell upon them. . . .[3]

The hero of the Half-Danes, Hnaef of the Scyldings, was fated to fall on Frisian battlefield. And no need had Hildeburh [4] to praise the good faith of the Jutes: blameless she was deprived of her dear ones at the shield-play, of son and brother; wounded by spears they fell to their fate. That was a mournful woman. Not without cause did Hoc's daughter lament the decree of destiny when morning came and she might see, under the sky, the slaughter of kinsmen—where before she had the greatest of world's joy. The fight took away all Finn's thanes except for only a few, so that he could in no way continue the battle on the field against Hengest, nor protect the survivors by fighting against the prince's thane. But they offered them peace-terms,[5] that they should clear

2. Ing was a legendary Danish king, and his "friends" are the Danes.

3. The lines introducing the scop's song seem faulty. The story itself is recounted in a highly allusive way, and many of its details are obscure, though some help is offered by an independent version of the story given in a fragmentary Old English lay called *The Fight at Finnsburg*.

4. Hildeburh, daughter of the former Danish king Hoc and sister of the ruling Danish king Hnaef, was married to Finn, king of the Jutes (Frisians). Hnaef with a party of Danes made what was presumably a friendly visit to Hidleburh and Finn at their home Finnsburg, but during a feast a quarrel broke out between the Jutes and the

Danes (since the scop's sympathies are with the Danes, he ascribes the cause to the bad faith of the Jutes), and in the ensuing fight Hnaef and his nephew, the son of Finn and Hildeburh, were killed, along with many other Danes and Jutes.

5. It is not clear who proposed the peace terms, but in view of the teller's Danish sympathies, it was probably the Jutes that sought the uneasy truce from Hengest, who became the Danes' leader after Hnaef's death. The truce imposed upon Hengest and the Danes the intolerable condition of having to dwell in peace with the Jutish king who was responsible for the death of their own king.

another building for them, hall and high seat, that they might have control of half of it with the sons of the Jutes; and at givings of treasure the son of Folcwalda [6] should honor the Danes each day, should give Hengest's company rings, such gold-plated treasure as that with which he would cheer the Frisians' kin in the high hall. Then on both sides they confirmed the fast peace-compact. Finn declared to Hengest, with oaths deep-sworn, unfeigned, that he would hold those who were left from the battle in honor in accordance with the judgment of his counselors, so that by words or by works no man should break the treaty nor because of malice should ever mention that, princeless, the Danes followed the slayer of their own ring-giver, since necessity forced them. If with rash speech any of the Frisians should insist upon calling to mind the cause of murderous hate, then the sword's edge should settle it.

The funeral pyre was made ready and gold brought up from the hoard. The best of the warriors of the War-Scyldings [7] was ready on the pyre. At the fire it was easy to see many a blood-stained battle-shirt, boar-image all golden—iron-hard swine—many a noble destroyed by wounds: more than one had died in battle. Then Hildeburh bade give her own son to the flames on Hnaef's pyre, burn his blood vessels, put him in the fire at the shoulder of his uncle. The woman mourned, sang her lament. The warrior took his place.[8] The greatest of death-fires wound to the skies, roared before the barrow. Heads melted as blood sprang out—wounds opened wide, hate-bites of the body. Fire swallowed them—greediest of spirits—all of those whom war had taken away from both peoples: their strength had departed.

(XVII.) Then warriors went to seek their dwellings, bereft of friends, to behold Friesland, their homes and high city.[9] Yet Hengest stayed on with Finn for a winter darkened with the thought of slaughter, all desolate. He thought of his land, though he might not drive his ring-prowed ship over the water—the sea boiled with storms, strove with the wind, winter locked the waves in ice-bonds—until another year came to men's dwellings, just as it does still, glorious bright weather always watching for its time. Then winter was gone, earth's lap fair, the exile was eager to go, the guest from the dwelling: [yet] more he thought of revenge for his wrongs than of the sea-journey—if he might bring about a fight where he could take account of the sons of the Jutes with his iron. So he made no refusal of the world's

---

6. I.e., Finn.
7. I.e., Hnaef.
8. The line is obscure, but it perhaps means that the body of Hildeburh's son

was placed on the pyre.
9. This seems to refer to the few survivors on the Jutish side.

custom when the son of Hunlaf [1] placed on his lap Battle-Bright, best of swords: its edges were known to the Jutes. Thus also to war-minded Finn in his turn cruel sword-evil came in his own home, after Guthlaf and Oslaf complained of the grim attack, the injury after the sea-journey, assigned blame for their lot of woes: breast might not contain the restless heart. Then was the hall reddened from foes' bodies, and thus Finn slain, the king in his company, and the queen taken. The warriors of the Scyldings bore to ship all the hall-furnishings of the land's king, whatever of necklaces, skillfully wrought treasures, they might find at Finn's home. They brought the noble woman on the sea-journey to the Danes, led her to her people.

The lay was sung to the end, the song of the scop. Joy mounted again, bench-noise brightened, cup-bearers poured wine from wonderful vessels. Then Wealhtheow came forth to walk under gold crown to where the good men sat, nephew and uncle: their friendship was then still unbroken, each true to the other. [2] There too Unferth the spokesman sat at the feet of the prince of the Scyldings: each of them trusted his spirit, that he had much courage, though he was not honorable to his kinsmen at sword-play. Then the woman of the Scyldings spoke:

"Take this cup my noble lord, giver of treasure. Be glad, gold-friend of warriors, and speak to the Geats with mild words, as a man ought to do. Be gracious to the Geats, mindful of gifts [which] [3] you now have from near and far. They have told me that you would have the warrior for your son. Heorot is purged, the bright ring-hall. Enjoy while you may many rewards, and leave to your kinsmen folk and kingdom when you must go forth to look on the Ruler's decree. I know my gracious Hrothulf, that he will hold the young warriors in honor if you, friend of the Scyldings, leave the world before him. I think he will repay our sons with good if he remembers all the favors we did to his pleasure and honor when he was a child."

Then she turned to the bench where her sons were, Hrethric and Hrothmund, and the sons of the warriors, young men together. There sat the good man Beowulf of the Geats beside the two brothers.

(XVIII.) The cup was borne to him and welcome offered

---

1. The text is open to various interpretations. The one adopted here assumes that the Dane Hunlaf, brother of Guthlaf and Oslaf, had been killed in the fight, and that ultimately Hunlaf's son demanded vengeance by the symbolical act of placing his father's sword in Hengest's lap, while at the same time Guthlaf and Oslaf reminded Hengest of the Jutes' treachery. It is not clear whether the subsequent fight in which Finn was killed was waged by the Danish survivors alone, or whether the party first went back to Denmark and then returned to Finnsburg with reinforcements.

2. See section XV, note 1, above.

3. The text seems corrupt.

in friendly words to him, and twisted gold courteously bestowed on him, two arm-ornaments, a mail-shirt and rings, the
largest of necklaces of those that I have heard spoken of on
earth. I have heard of no better hoard-treasure under the heavens
since Hama carried away to his bright city the necklace of the
Brosings,[4] chain and rich setting: he fled the treacherous hatred
of Eormenric, got eternal favor. This ring Hygelac of the Geats,[5]
grandson of Swerting, had on his last venture, when beneath his
battle-banner he defended his treasure, protected the spoils of
war: fate took him when for pride he sought trouble, feud
with the Frisians. Over the cup of the waves the mighty prince
wore that treasure, precious stone. He fell beneath his shield; the
body of the king came into the grasp of the Franks, his breast-
armor and the neck-ring together. Lesser warriors plundered the
fallen after the war-harvest: people of the Geats held the place
of corpses.

The hall was filled with noise. Wealhtheow spoke, before the
company she said to him: "Wear this ring, beloved Beowulf,
young man, with good luck, and make use of this mail-shirt from
the people's treasure, and prosper well; make yourself known
with your might, and be kind of counsel to these boys: I shall
remember to reward you for that. You have brought it about
that, far and near, for a long time all men shall praise you, as
wide as the sea surrounds the shores, home of the winds. While
you live, prince, be prosperous. I wish you well of your treasure.
Much favored one, be kind of deeds to my son. Here is each
earl true to other, mild of heart, loyal to his lord; the thanes are
at one, the people obedient, the retainers cheered with drink do
as I bid."

Then she walked to her seat. There was the best of feasts, men
drank wine. They did not know the fate, the grim decree made
long before, as it came to pass to many of the earls after evening
had come and Hrothgar had gone to his chambers, the noble one
to his rest. A great number of men remained in the hall, just as
they had often done before. They cleared the benches from the
floor. It was spread over with beds and pillows. One of the beer-
drinkers, ripe and fated to die, lay down to his hall-rest. They
set at their heads their battle-shields, bright wood; there on the
bench it was easy to see above each man his helmet that towered
in battle, his ringed mail-shirt, his great spear-wood. It was their

4. The Brisings' (Brosings') necklace
had been worn by the goddess Freya.
Nothing more is known of this story of
Hama, who seems to have stolen the
necklace from the famous Gothic king
Eormenric.

5. Beowulf is later said to have presented the necklace to Hygelac's queen,
Hygd, though here Hygelac is said to
have been wearing it on his ill-fated
expedition against the Franks and
Frisians, into whose hands it fell at his
death.

custom to be always ready for war whether at home or in the field, in any case at any time that need should befall t eir liege lord: that was a good nation.

[GRENDEL'S MOTHER'S ATTACK]

(XIX.) Then they sank to sleep. One paid sorely for his evening rest, just as had often befallen them when Grendel guarded the gold-hall, wrought wrong until the end came, death after misdeeds. It came to be seen, wide-known to men, that after the bitter battle an avenger still lived for an evil space: Grendel's mother, woman, monster-wife, was mindful of her misery, she who had to dwell in the terrible water, the cold currents, after Cain became sword-slayer of his only brother, his own father's son. Then Cain went as an outlaw to flee the cheerful life of men, marked for his murder, held to the wasteland. From him sprang many a devil sent by fate. Grendel was one of them, hateful outcast who at Heorot found a waking man waiting his warfare. There the monster had laid hold upon him, but he was mindful of the great strength, the large gift God had given him, and relied on the Almighty for favor, comfort and help. By that he overcame the foe, subdued the hell-spirit. Then he went off wretched, bereft of joy, to seek his dying-place, enemy of mankind. And his mother, still greedy and gallows-grim, would go on a sorrowful venture, avenge her son's death.

Then she came to Heorot where the Ring-Danes slept throughout the hall. Then change came quickly to the earls there, when Grendel's mother made her way in. The attack was the less terrible by just so much as is the strength of women, the war-terror of a wife, less than an armed man's when a hard blade, forge-hammered, a sword shining with blood, good of its edges, cuts the stout boar on a helmet opposite. Then in the hall was hard-edged sword raised from the seat, many a broad shield lifted firmly in hand: none thought of helmet, of wide mail-shirt, when the terror seized him. She was in haste, would be gone out from there, protect her life after she was discovered. Swiftly she had taken fast hold on one of the nobles, then she went to the fen. He was one of the men between the seas most beloved of Hrothgar in the rank of retainer, a noble shield-warrior whom she destroyed at his rest, a man of great repute. Beowulf was not there, for earlier, after the treasure-giving, another lodging had been appointed for the renowned Geat. Outcry arose in Heorot: she had taken, in its gore, the famed hand. Care was renewed, come again on the dwelling. That was not a good bargain, that on both sides they had to pay with the lives of friends.

Then was the old king, the hoary warrior, of bitter mind when he learned that his chief thane was lifeless, his dearest man dead. Quickly Beowulf was fetched to the bed-chamber, man happy in victory. At daybreak together with his earls he went, the noble champion himself with his retainers, to where the wise one was, waiting to know whether after tidings of woe the All-Wielder would ever bring about change for him. The worthy warrior walked over the floor with his retainers—hall-wood resounded —that he might address words to the wise prince of Ing's friends, asked if the night had been pleasant according to his desires.

(XX.) Hrothgar spoke, protector of the Scyldings: "Ask not about pleasure. Sorrow is renewed to the people of the Danes: Aeschere is dead, Yrmenlaf's elder brother, my speaker of wisdom and my bearer of counsel, my shoulder-companion when we used to defend our heads in battle, when troops clashed, beat on boar-images. Whatever an earl should be, a man good from old times, such was Aeschere. Now a wandering murderous spirit has slain him with its hands in Heorot. I do not know by what way the awful creature, glorying in its prey, has made its retreat, gladdened by its feast. She has avenged the feud—that last night you killed Grendel with hard hand-grips, savagely, because too long he had diminished and destroyed my people. He fell in the fight, his life forfeited, and now the other has come, a mighty worker of wrong, would avenge her kinsman, and has carried far her revenge—as many a thane may think who weeps in his spirit for his treasure-giver, bitter sorrow in heart. Now the hand lies lifeless that was strong in support of all your desires.

"I have heard landsmen, my people, hall-counselors, say this, that they have seen two such huge walkers in the wasteland holding to the moors, alien spirits. One of them, so far as they could clearly discern, was the likeness of a woman. The other wretched shape trod the tracks of exile in the form of a man, except that he was bigger than any other man. Land-dwellers in the old days named him Grendel. They know of no father, whether in earlier times any was begotten for them among the dark spirits. They hold to the secret land, the wolf-slopes, the windy headlands, the dangerous fen-paths where the mountain stream goes down under the darkness of the hills, the flood under the earth. It is not far from here, measured in miles, that the mere stands; over it hang frost-covered woods, trees fast of root close over the water. There each night may be seen fire on the flood, a fearful wonder. Of the sons of men there lives none, old of wisdom, who knows the bottom. Though the heath-stalker, the strong-horned hart, harassed by hounds makes for the forest after long flight, rather will he give his life, his being, on the bank than save his head by entering. That is no pleasant place. From it the surging waves rise up black to the heavens when the wind stirs up awful storms, until the air becomes gloomy, the skies weep. Now once again is the cure in you alone. You do not yet know the land, the perilous place, where you might find the seldom-seen creature: seek if you dare. I will give you wealth for the feud, old treasure, as I did before, twisted gold—if you come away."

(XXI.) Beowulf spoke, the son of Ecgtheow: "Sorrow not, wise warrior. It is better for a man to avenge his friend than much mourn. Each of us must await his end of the world's life. Let him who may get glory before death: that is best for the warrior after he has gone from life. Arise, guardian of the kingdom, let us go at once to look on the track of Grendel's kin. I promise you this: she will not be lost under cover, not in the earth's bosom nor in the mountain woods nor at the bottom of the sea, go where she will. This day have patience in every woe—as I expect you to."

Then the old man leapt up, thanked God, the mighty Lord, that the man had so spoken. Then was a horse bridled for Hrothgar, a curly-maned mount. The wise king moved in state; the band of shield-bearers marched on foot. The tracks were seen wide over the wood-paths where she had gone on the ground, made her way forward over the dark moor, borne lifeless the best of retainers of those who watched over their home with Hrothgar. The son of noble forebears [6] moved over the steep rocky slopes, narrow paths where only one could go at a time, an unfamiliar trail, steep hills, many a lair of water-monsters. He went before with a few wise men to spy out the country, until suddenly he found mountain trees leaning out over hoary stone, a joyless wood: water lay beneath, bloody and troubled. It was pain of heart for all the Danes to suffer, for the friends of the Scyldings, for many a thane, grief to each earl when on the cliff over the water they came upon Aeschere's head. The flood boiled with blood—the men looked upon it—with hot gore. Again and again the horn sang its urgent war-song. The whole troop sat down to rest. Then they saw on the water many a snake-shape, strong sea-serpents exploring the mere, and water-monsters lying on the slopes of the shore such as those that in the morning often attend a perilous journey on the paths of the sea, serpents and wild beasts.

These fell away from the shore, fierce and rage-swollen: they had heard the bright sound, the war-horn sing. One of them a man of the Geats with his bow cut off from his life, his water-warring, after the hard war-arrow stuck in his heart: he was

6. I.e., Hrothgar.

weaker in swimming the lake when death took him. Straightway he was hard beset on the waves with barbed boar-spears, strongly surrounded, pulled up on the shore, strange spawn of the waves. The men looked on the terrible alien thing.

Beowulf put on his warrior's dress, had no fear for his life. His war-shirt, hand-fashioned, broad and well-worked, was to explore the mere: it knew how to cover his body-cave so that foe's grip might not harm his heart, or grasp of angry enemy his life. But the bright helmet guarded his head, one which was to stir up the lake-bottom, seek out the troubled water—made rich with gold, surrounded with splendid bands, as the weapon-smith had made it in far-off days, fashioned it wonderfully, set it about with boar-images so that thereafter no sword or battle-blade might bite into it. And of his strong supports that was not the least which Hrothgar's spokesman [7] lent to his need: Hrunting was the name of the hilted sword; it was one of the oldest of ancient treasures; its edge was iron, decorated with poison-stripes, hardened with battle-sweat. Never had it failed in war any man of those who grasped it in their hands, who dared enter on dangerous enterprises, onto the common meeting place of foes: this was not the first time that it should do work of courage. Surely the son of Ecglaf, great of strength, did not have in mind what, drunk with wine, he had spoken, when he lent that weapon to a better sword-fighter. He did not himself dare to risk his life under the warring waves, to engage his courage: there he lost his glory, his name for valor. It was not so with the other when he had armed himself for battle.

[BEOWULF ATTACKS GRENDEL'S MOTHER]

(XXII.) Beowulf spoke, the son of Ecgtheow: "Think now, renowned son of Healfdene, wise king, now that I am ready for the venture, gold-friend of warriors, of what we said before, that, if at your need I should go from life, you would always be in a father's place for me when I am gone: be guardian of my young retainers, my companions, if battle should take me. The treasure you gave me, beloved Hrothgar, send to Hygelac. The lord of the Geats may know from the gold, the son of Hrethel may see when he looks on that wealth, that I found a ring-giver good in his gifts, enjoyed him while I might. And let Unferth have the old heirloom, the wide-known man my splendid-waved sword, hard-edged: with Hrunting I shall get glory, or death will take me."

After these words the man of the Weather-Geats turned away boldly, would wait for no answer: the surging water took the warrior. Then was it a part of a day before he might see the

7. I.e., Unferth.

bottom's floor. Straightway that which had held the flood's tract a hundred half-years, ravenous for prey, grim and greedy, saw that some man from above was exploring the dwelling of monsters. Then she groped toward him, took the warrior in her awful grip. Yet not the more for that did she hurt his hale body within: his ring-armor shielded him about on the outside so that she could not pierce the war-dress, the linked body-mail, with hateful fingers. Then as she came to the bottom the sea-wolf bore the ring-prince to her house so that—no matter how brave he was —he might not wield weapons; but many monsters attacked him in the water, many a sea-beast tore at his mail-shirt with war-tusks, strange creatures afflicted him. Then the earl saw that he was in some hostile hall where no water harmed him at all, and the flood's onrush might not touch him because of the hall-roof. He saw firelight, a clear blaze shine bright.

Then the good man saw the accursed dweller in the deep, the mighty mere-woman. He gave a great thrust to his sword—his hand did not withhold the stroke—so that the etched blade sang at her head a fierce war-song. Then the stranger found that the battle-lightning would not bite, harm her life, but the edge failed the prince in his need: many a hand-battle had it endured before, often sheared helmet, war-coat of man fated to die: this was the first time for the rare treasure that its glory had failed.

But still he was resolute, not slow of his courage, mindful of fame, the kinsman of Hygelac. Then, angry warrior, he threw away the sword, wavy-patterned, bound with ornaments, so that it lay on the ground, hard and steel-edged: he trusted in his strength, his mighty hand-grip. So ought a man to do when he thinks to get long-lasting praise in battle: he cares not for his life. Then he seized by the hair Grendel's mother—the man of the War-Geats did not shrink from the fight. Battle-hardened, now swollen with rage, he pulled his deadly foe so that she fell to the floor. Quickly in her turn she repaid him his gift with her grim claws and clutched at him: then weary-hearted, the strongest of warriors, of foot-soldiers, stumbled so that he fell. Then she sat upon the hall-guest and drew her knife, broad and bright-edged. She would avenge her child, her only son. The woven breast-armor lay on his shoulder: that protected his life, withstood entry of point or of edge. Then the son of Ecgtheow would have fared amiss under the wide ground, the champion of the Geats, if the battle-shirt had not brought help, the hard war-net—and holy God brought about victory in war; the wise Lord, Ruler of the Heavens, decided it with right, easily, when Beowulf had stood up again.

(XXIII.) Then he saw among the armor a victory-blessed blade, an old sword made by the giants, strong of its edges, glory of warriors: it was the best of weapons, except that it was larger than any other man might bear to war-sport, good and adorned, the work of giants. He seized the linked hilt, he who fought for the Scyldings, savage and slaughter-bent, drew the patterned blade; desperate of life, he struck angrily so that it bit her hard on the neck, broke the bone-rings. The blade went through all the doomed body. She fell to the floor, the sword was sweating, the man rejoiced in his work.

The blaze brightened, light shone within, just as from the sky heaven's candle shines clear. He looked about the building; then he moved along the wall, raised his weapon hard by the hilt, Hygelac's thane, angry and resolute: the edge was not useless to the warrior, for he would quickly repay Grendel for the many attacks he had made on the West-Danes—many more than the one time when he slew in their sleep fifteen hearth-companions of Hrothgar, devoured men of the Danish people while they slept, and another such number bore away, a hateful prey. He had paid him his reward for that, the fierce champion, for there he saw Grendel, weary of war, lying at rest, lifeless with the wounds he had got in the fight at Heorot. The body bounded wide when it suffered the blow after death, the hard sword-swing; and thus he cut off his head.

At once the wise men who were watching the water with Hrothgar saw that the surging waves were troubled, the lake stained with blood. Gray-haired, old, they spoke together of the good warrior, that they did not again expect of the chief that he would come victorious to seek their great king; for many agreed on it, that the sea-wolf had destroyed him.

Then came the ninth hour of the day. The brave Scyldings left the hill. The gold-friend of warriors went back to his home. The strangers sat sick at heart and stared at the mere. They wished—and did not expect—that they would see their beloved lord himself.

Then the blade began to waste away from the battle-sweat, the war-sword into battle-icicles. That was a wondrous thing, that it should all melt, most like the ice when the Father loosens the frost's fetters, undoes the water-bonds—He Who has power over seasons and times: He is the true Ruler. Beowulf did not take from the dwelling, the man of the Weather-Geats, more treasures —though he saw many there—but only the head and the hilt, bright with jewels. The sword itself had already melted, its patterned blade burned away: the blood was too hot for it, the spirit that had died there too poisonous. Quickly he was swimming, he who had lived to see the fall of his foes; he plunged up through the water. The currents were all cleansed, the great tracts of the water, when the dire spirit left her life-days and this loaned world.

Then the protector of seafarers came toward the land, swimming stout-hearted; he had joy of his sea-booty, the great burden he had with him. They went to meet him, thanked God, the strong band of thanes, rejoiced in their chief that they might see him again sound. Then the helmet and war-shirt of the mighty one were quickly loosened. The lake drowsed, the water beneath the skies, stained with blood. They went forth on the foot-tracks, glad in their hearts, measured the path back, the known ways, men bold as kings. They bore the head from the mere's cliff, toilsomely for each of the great-hearted ones: four of them had trouble in carrying Grendel's head on spear-shafts to the gold-hall —until at last they came striding to the hall, fourteen bold warriors of the Geats; their lord, high-spirited, walked in their company over the fields to the mead-hall.

Then the chief of the thanes, man daring in deeds, enriched by new glory, warrior dear to battle, came in to greet Hrothgar. Then Grendel's head was dragged by the hair over the floor to where men drank, a terrible thing to the earls and the woman with them, an awful sight: the men looked upon it.

[FURTHER CELEBRATION AT HEOROT]

(XXIV.) Beowulf spoke, the son of Ecgtheow: "Yes, we have brought you this sea-booty, son of Healfdene, man of the Scyldings, gladly, as evidence of glory—what you look on here. Not easily did I come through it with my life, the war under water, not without trouble carried out the task. The fight would have been ended straightway if God had not guarded me. With Hrunting I might not do anything in the fight, though that is a good weapon. But the Wielder of Men granted me that I should see hanging on the wall a fair, ancient great-sword—most often He has guided the man without friends—that I should wield the weapon. Then in the fight when the time became right for me I hewed the house-guardians. Then that war-sword, wavy-patterned, burnt away as their blood sprang forth, hottest of battle-sweats. I have brought the hilt away from the foes. I have avenged the evil deeds, the slaughter of Danes, as it was right to do. I promise you that you may sleep in Heorot without care with your band of retainers, and that for none of the thanes of your people, old or young, need you have fear, prince of the Scyldings—for no life-injury to your men on that account, as you did before."

Then the golden hilt was given into the hand of the old man, the hoary war-chief—the ancient work of giants. There came into the possession of the prince of the Danes, after the fall of devils, the work of wonder-smiths. And when the hostile-hearted creature, God's enemy, guilty of murder, gave up this world, and his mother too, it passed into the control of the best of worldly kings between the seas, of those who gave treasure in the Northlands.

Hrothgar spoke—he looked on the hilt, the old heirloom, on which was written the origin of ancient strife, when the flood, rushing water, slew the race of giants—they suffered terribly: that was a people alien to the Everlasting Lord. The Ruler made them a last payment through water's welling. On the sword-guard of bright gold there was also rightly marked through rune-staves, set down and told, for whom that sword, best of irons, had first been made, its hilt twisted and ornamented with snakes. Then the wise man spoke, the son of Healfdene—all were silent: "Lo, this may one say who works truth and right for the folk, recalls all things far distant, an old guardian of the land: that this earl was born the better man. Glory is raised up over the far ways—your glory over every people, Beowulf my friend. All of it, all your strength, you govern steadily in the wisdom of your heart. I shall fulfill my friendship to you, just as we spoke before. You shall become a comfort, whole and long-lasting, to your people, a help to warriors.

"So was not Heremod to the sons of Ecgwela, the Honor-Scyldings. He grew great not for their joy, but for their slaughter, for the destruction of Danish people. With swollen heart he killed his table-companions, shoulder-comrades, until he turned away from the joys of men, alone, notorious king, although mighty God had raised him in power, in the joys of strength, had set him up over all men. Yet in his breast his heart's thought grew blood-thirsty: no rings did he give to the Danes for glory. He lived joyless to suffer the pain of that strife, the long-lasting harm of the people. Teach yourself by him, be mindful of munificence. Old of winters, I tell this tale for you.

"It is a wonder to say how in His great spirit mighty God gives wisdom to mankind, land and earlship—He possesses power over all things. At times He lets the thought of a man of high lineage move in delight, gives him joy of earth in his homeland, a stronghold of men to rule over, makes regions of the world so subject to him, wide kingdoms, that in his unwisdom he may not himself have mind of his end. He lives in plenty; illness and age in no way grieve him, neither does dread care darken his heart, nor does enmity bare sword-hate, for the whole world turns to his will—he knows nothing worse—(XXV.) until his portion of pride increases and flourishes within him; then the watcher sleeps, the soul's guardian; that sleep is too sound, bound in its own cares, and the slayer most near whose bow shoots treacherously. Then is he hit in the heart, beneath his armor, with the bitter arrow— he cannot protect himself—with the crooked dark commands of the accursed spirit. What he has long held seems to him too little, angry-hearted he covets, no plated rings does he give in men's honor, and then he forgets and regards not his destiny because of what God, Wielder of Heaven, has given him before, his portion of glories. In the end it happens in turn that the loaned body weakens, falls doomed; another takes the earl's ancient treasure, one who recklessly gives precious gifts, does not fearfully guard them.

"Keep yourself against that wickedness, beloved Beowulf, best of men, and choose better—eternal gains. Have no care for pride, great warrior. Now for a time there is glory in your might: yet soon it shall be that sickness or sword will diminish your strength, or fire's fangs, or flood's surge, or sword's swing, or spear's flight, or appalling age; brightness of eyes will fail and grow dark; then it shall be that death will overcome you, warrior.

"Thus I ruled the Ring-Danes for a hundred half-years under the skies, and protected them in war with spear and sword against many nations over middle-earth, so that I counted no one as my adversary underneath the sky's expanse. Well, disproof of that came to me in my own land, grief after my joys, when Grendel, ancient adversary, came to invade my home. Great sorrow of heart I have always suffered for his persecution. Thanks be to the Ruler, the Eternal Lord, that after old strife I have come to see in my lifetime, with my own eyes, his blood-stained head. Go now to your seat, have joy of the glad feast, made famous in battle. Many of our treasures will be shared when morning comes."

The Geat was glad at heart, went at once to seek his seat as the wise one bade. Then was a feast fairly served again, for a second time, just as before, for those famed for courage, sitting about the hall.

Night's cover lowered, dark over the warriors. The retainers all arose. The gray-haired one would seek his bed, the old Scylding. It pleased the Geat, the brave shield-warrior, immensely that he should have rest. Straightway a hall-thane led the way on for the weary one, come from far country, and showed every courtesy to the thane's need, such as in those days seafarers might expect as their due.

Then the great-hearted one rested; the hall stood high, vaulted and gold-adorned; the guest slept within until the black raven, blithe-hearted, announced heaven's joy. Then the bright light came passing over the shadows. The warriors hastened, the nobles were eager to set out again for their people. Bold of spirit, the visitor would seek his ship far thence.

Then the hardy one bade that Hrunting be brought to the son of Ecglaf,[8] that he take back his sword, precious iron. He spoke thanks for that loan, said that he accounted it a good war-friend, strong in battle; in his words he found no fault at all with the sword's edge: he was a thoughtful man. And then they were eager to depart, the warriors ready in their armor. The prince who had earned honor of the Danes went to the high seat where the other was: the man dear to war greeted Hrothgar.

[Beowulf Returns Home]

(XXVI.) Beowulf spoke, the son of Ecgtheow: "Now we sea-travelers come from afar wish to say that we desire to seek Hygelac. Here we have been entertained splendidly according to our desire: you have dealt well with us. If on earth I might in any way earn more of your heart's love, prince of warriors, than I have done before with warlike deeds, I should be ready at once. If beyond the sea's expanse I hear that men dwelling near threaten you with terrors, as those who hated you did before, I shall bring you a thousand thanes, warriors to your aid. I know of Hygelac, lord of the Geats, though he is young as a guardian of the people, that he will further me with words and works so that I may do you honor and bring spears to help you, strong support where you have need of men. If Hrethric, king's son, decides to come to the court of the Geats, he can find many friends there; far countries are well sought by him who is himself strong."

Hrothgar spoke to him in answer: "The All-Knowing Lord sent those words into your mind: I have not heard a man of so young age speak more wisely. You are great of strength, mature of mind, wise of words. I think it likely if the spear, sword-grim war, takes the son of Hrethel, sickness or weapon your prince, the people's ruler, and you have your life, that the Sea-Geats will not have a better to choose as their king, as guardian of their treasure, if you wish to hold the kingdom of your kinsmen. So well your heart's temper has long pleased me, beloved Beowulf. You have brought it about that peace shall be shared by the peoples, the folk of the Geats and the Spear-Danes, and enmity shall sleep, acts of malice which they practiced before; and there shall be, as long as I rule the wide kingdom, sharing of treasures, many a man shall greet his fellow with good gifts over the sea-bird's baths; the ring-prowed ship will bring gifts and tokens of friendship over the sea. I know your people, blameless in every respect, set firm after the old way both as to foe and to friend."

Then the protector of earls, the kinsman of Healfdene, gave

8. I.e., Unferth.

him there in the hall twelve precious things; he bade him with these gifts seek his own dear people in safety, quickly come back. Then the king noble of race, the prince of the Scyldings, kissed the best of thanes and took him by his neck: tears fell from the gray-haired one. He had two thoughts of the future, the old and wise man, one more strongly than the other—that they would not see each other again, bold men at council. The man was so dear to him that he might not restrain his breast's welling, for fixed in his heartstrings a deep-felt longing for the beloved man burned in his blood. Away from him Beowulf, warrior glorious with gold, walked over the grassy ground, proud of his treasure. The sea-goer awaited its owner, riding at anchor. Then on the journey the gift of Hrothgar was oft-praised: that was a king blameless in all things until age took from him the joys of his strength—old age that has often harmed many.

(XXVII.) There came to the flood the band of brave-hearted ones, of young men. They wore mail-coats, locked limb-shirts. The guard of the coast saw the coming of the earls, just as he had done before. He did not greet the guests with taunts from the cliff's top, but rode to meet them, said that the return of the warriors in bright armor in their ship would be welcome to the people of the Weather-Geats. There on the sand the broad sea-boat was loaded with armor, the ring-prowed ship with horses and rich things. The mast stood high over Hrothgar's hoard-gifts. He gave the boat-guard a sword wound with gold, so that thereafter on the mead-bench he was held the worthier for the treasure, the heirloom. The boat moved out to furrow the deep water, left the land of the Danes. Then on the mast a sea-cloth, a sail, was made fast by a rope. The boat's beams creaked: wind did not keep the sea-floater from its way over the waves. The sea-goer moved, foamy-necked floated forth over the swell, the ship with bound prow over the sea-currents until they might see the cliffs of the Geats, the well-known headlands. The ship pressed ahead, borne by the wind, stood still at the land. Quickly the harbor-guard was at the sea-side, he who had gazed for a long time far out over the currents, eager to see the beloved men. He [9] moored the deep ship in the sand, fast by its anchor ropes, lest the force of the waves should drive away the fair wooden vessel. Then he bade that the prince's wealth be borne ashore, armor and plated gold. It was not far for them to seek the giver of treasure, Hygelac son of Hrethel, where he dwelt at home near the sea-wall, himself with his retainers.

The building was splendid, its king most valiant, set high in the hall, Hygd [1] most youthful, wise and well-taught, though she

9. Beowulf.
1. Hygd is Hygelac's young queen. The suddenness of her introduction here is perhaps due to a faulty text.

had lived within the castle walls few winters, daughter of Hae-reth. For she was not niggardly, nor too sparing of gifts to the men of the Geats, of treasures. Modthryth,[2] good folk-queen, did dreadful deeds [in her youth]: no bold one among her retainers dared venture—except her great lord—to set his eyes on her in daylight, but [if he did] he should reckon deadly bonds pre-pared for him, arresting hands: that straightway after his seizure the sword awaited him, that the patterned blade must settle it, make known its death-evil. Such is no queenly custom for a woman to practice, though she is peerless—that one who weaves peace [3] should take away the life of a beloved man after pretended injury. However the kinsman of Hemming stopped that: [4] ale-drinkers gave another account, said that she did less harm to the people, fewer injuries, after she was given, gold-adorned, to the young warrior, the beloved noble, when by her father's teach-ing she sought Offa's hall in a voyage over the pale sea. There on the throne she was afterwards famous for generosity, while living made use of her life, held high love toward the lord of warriors, [who was] of all mankind the best, as I have heard, between the seas of the races of men. Since Offa was a man brave of wars and gifts, wide-honored, he held his native land in wisdom. From him sprang Eomer to the help of warriors, kinsman of Hemming, grandson of Garmund, strong in battle.[5]

(XXVIII.) Then the hardy one came walking with his troop over the sand on the sea-plain, the wide shores. The world-candle shone, the sun moved quickly from the south. They made their way, strode swiftly to where they heard that the protector of earls, the slayer of Ongentheow,[6] the good young war-king, was dispensing rings in the stronghold. The coming of Beowulf was straightway made known to Hygelac, that there in his home the defender of warriors, his comrade in battle, came walking alive to the court, sound from the battle-play. Quickly the way within was made clear for the foot-guests, as the mighty one bade.

2. A transitional passage introducing the contrast between Hygd's good be-havior and Modthryth's bad behavior as young women of royal blood seems to have been lost. Modthryth's practice of having those who looked into her face put to death may reflect the folk-motif of the princess whose unsuccessful suitors are executed, though the text does not say that Modthryth's victims were suitors. Modthryth's "great lord" was probably her father.

3. Daughters of kings were frequently given in marriage to the king of a hostile nation in order to bring about peace; hence Modthryth may be called "one who weaves peace."

4. Offa, a fourth-century continental Angle king, forebear of the famous English king, Offa of Mercia; who Hemming was—besides being a kin of Offa's—is unknown. *Ed.*

5. By praising Offa the Angle, his father, Garmund, and son, Eomer—heroes familiar to his audience—the poet reflects glory on the eighth-century English Offa. *Ed.*

6. Ongentheow was a Scylfing (Swedish) king, whose story is fully told below, sections XL and XLI. In fact Hygelac was not his slayer, but is called so because he led the attack on the Scylf-ings in which Ongentheow was killed.

Then he sat down with him, he who had come safe through the fight, kinsman with kinsman, after he had greeted his liege lord with formal speech, loyal, with vigorous words. Haereth's daughter moved through the hall-building with mead-cups, cared lovingly for the people, bore the cup of strong drink to the hands of the warriors. Hygelac began fairly to question his companion in the high hall, curiosity pressed him, what the adventures of the Sea-Geats had been. "How did you fare on your journey, beloved Beowulf, when you suddenly resolved to seek distant combat over the salt water, battle in Heorot? Did you at all help the wide-known woes of Hrothgar, the famous prince? Because of you I burned with seething sorrows, care of heart—had no trust in the venture of my beloved man. I entreated you long that you should in no way approach the murderous spirit, should let the South-Danes themselves settle the war with Grendel. I say thanks to God that I may see you sound."

Beowulf spoke, the son of Ecgtheow: "To many among men it is not hidden, lord Hygelac, the great encounter—what a fight we had, Grendel and I, in the place where he made many sorrows for the Victory-Scyldings, constant misery. All that I avenged, so that none of Grendel's kin over the earth need boast of that clash at night—whoever lives longest of the loathsome kind, wrapped in malice. There I went forth to the ring-hall to greet Hrothgar. At once the famous son of Healfdene, when he knew my purpose, gave me a seat with his own sons. The company was in joy: I have not seen in the time of my life under heaven's arch more mead-mirth of hall-sitters. At times the famous queen, peace-pledge of the people, went through all the hall, cheered the young men; often she would give a man a ring-band before she went to her seat. At times Hrothgar's daughter bore the ale-cup to the retainers, to the earls throughout the hall. I heard hall-sitters name her Freawaru when she offered the studded cup to warriors. Young and gold-adorned, she is promised to the fair son of Froda.[7] That has seemed good to the lord of the Scyldings, the guardian of the kingdom, and he believes of this plan that he may, with this woman, settle their portion of deadly feuds, of quarrels.[8] Yet most often after the fall of a prince in any nation the deadly spear rests but a little while, even though the bride is good.

"It may displease the lord of the Heatho-Bards and each thane of that people when he goes in the hall with the woman, [that while] the noble sons of the Danes, her retainers, [are] feasted,[9]

7. I.e., Ingeld, who succeeded his father as king of the Heatho-Bards.
8. I.e., the feud between the Danes and Heatho-Bards.
9. The text is faulty here.

the heirlooms of their ancestors will be shining on them[1]—the hard and wave-adorned treasure of the Heatho-Bards, [which was theirs] so long as they might wield those weapons, (**XXIX.**) until they led to the shield-play, to destruction, their dear companions and their own lives. Then at the beer he[2] who sees the treasure, an old ash-warrior who remembers it all, the spear-death of warriors—grim is his heart—begins, sad of mind, to tempt a young fighter in the thoughts of his spirit, to awaken war-evil, and speaks this word:

" 'Can you, my friend, recognize that sword, the rare iron-blade, that your father, beloved man, bore to battle his last time in armor, where the Danes slew him, the fierce Scyldings, got possession of the battle-field, when Withergeld[3] lay dead, after the fall of warriors? Now here some son of his murderers walks in the hall, proud of the weapon, boasts of the murder, and wears the treasure that you should rightly possess.' So he will provoke and remind at every chance with wounding words until that moment comes that the woman's thane,[4] forfeiting life, shall lie dead, blood-smeared from the sword-bite, for his father's deeds. The other escapes with his life, knows the land well. Then on both sides the oath of the earls will be broken; then deadly hate will well up in Ingeld, and his wife-love after the surging of sorrows will become cooler. Therefore I do not think the loyalty of the Heatho-Bards, their part in the alliance with the Danes, to be without deceit—do not think their friendship fast.

"I shall speak still more of Grendel, that you may readily know, giver of treasure, what the hand-fight of warriors came to in the end. After heaven's jewel had glided over the earth, the angry spirit came, awful in the evening, to visit us where, unharmed, we watched over the hall. There the fight was fatal to Hondscioh, deadly to one who was doomed. He was dead first of all, armed warrior. Grendel came to devour him, good young retainer, swallowed all the body of the beloved man. Yet not for this would the bloody-toothed slayer, bent on destruction, go from the gold-hall empty-handed; but, strong of might, he made trial of me, grasped me with eager hand. His glove[5] hung huge and wonderful, made fast with cunning clasps: it had been made all with craft, with devil's devices and dragon's skins. The fell doer of evils would

---

1. I.e., the weapons and armor which had once belonged to the Heatho-Bards and were captured by the Danes will be worn by the Danish attendants of Hrothgar's daughter Freawaru when she goes to the Heatho-Bards to marry king Ingeld.
2. I.e., some old Heatho-Bard warrior.

3. Apparently a leader of the Heatho-Bards in their unsuccessful war with the Danes.
4. I.e., the Danish attendant of Freawaru who is wearing the sword of his Heatho-Bard attacker's father.
5. Apparently a large glove that could be used as a pouch.

put me therein, guiltless, one of many. He might not do so after I had stood up in anger. It is too long to tell how I repaid the people's foe his due for every crime. My prince, there with my deeds I did honor to your people. He slipped away, for a little while had use of life's joy. Yet his right hand remained as his spoor in Heorot, and he went from there abject, mournful of heart sank to the mere's bottom.

"The lord of the Scyldings repaid me for that bloody combat with much plated gold, many treasures, after morning came and we sat down to the feast. There was song and mirth. The old Scylding, who has learned many things, spoke of times far-off. At times a brave one in battle touched the glad wood, the harp's joy; at times he told tales, true and sad; at times he related strange stories according to right custom; at times, again, the great-hearted king, bound with age, the old warrior, would begin to speak of his youth, his battle-strength. His heart welled within when, old and wise, he thought of his many winters. Thus we took pleasure there the livelong day until another night came to men.

"Then in her turn Grendel's mother swiftly made ready to take revenge for his injuries, made a sorrowful journey. Death had taken her son, war-hate of the Weather-Geats. The direful woman avenged her son, fiercely killed a warrior: there the life of Aeschere departed, a wise old counselor. And when morning came the folk of the Danes might not burn him, death-weary, in the fire, nor place him on the pyre, beloved man: she had borne his body away in fiend's embrace beneath the mountain stream. That was the bitterest of Hrothgar's sorrows, of those that had long come upon the people's prince. Then the king, sore-hearted, implored me by your life [6] that I should do a man's work in the tumult of the waters, venture my life, finish a glorious deed. He promised me reward. Then I found the guardian of the deep pool, the grim horror, as is now known wide. For a time there we were locked hand in hand. Then the flood boiled with blood, and in the war-hall I cut off the head of Grendel's mother with a mighty sword. Not without trouble I came from there with my life. I was not fated to die then, but the protector of earls again gave me many treasures, the son of Healfdene.

(XXXI.) "Thus the king of that people lived with good customs. I had lost none of the rewards, the meed of my might, but he gave me treasures, the son of Healfdene, at my own choice. I will bring these to you, great king, show my good will. On your kindnesses all still depends: I have few close kinsmen besides you, Hygelac."

Then he bade bring in the boar-banner—the head-sign—the

6. I.e., "in your name."

helmet towering in battle, the gray battle-shirt, the splendid sword —afterwards spoke words: "Hrothgar, wise king, gave me this armor; in his words he bade that I should first tell you about his gift: he said that king Heorogar,[7] lord of the Scyldings, had had it for a long time; not for that would he give it, the breast-armor, to his son, bold Heoroweard, though he was loyal to him. Use it all well!"

I have heard that four horses, swift and alike, followed that treasure, fallow as apples. He gave him the gift of both horses and treasure. So ought kinsmen do, not weave malice-nets for each other with secret craft, prepare death for comrades. To Hygelac his nephew was most true in hard fights, and each one mindful of helping the other. I have heard that he gave Hygd the neck-ring, the wonderfully wrought treasure, that Wealhtheow had given him—gave to the king's daughter as well three horses, supple and saddle-bright. After the gift of the necklace, her breast was adorned with it.

Thus Beowulf showed himself brave, a man known in battles, of good deeds, bore himself according to discretion. Drunk, he slew no hearth-companions. His heart was not savage, but he held the great gift that God had given him, the most strength of all mankind, like one brave in battle. He had long been despised,[8] so that the sons of the Geats did not reckon him brave, nor would the lord of the Weather-Geats do him much gift-honor on the mead-bench. They strongly suspected that he was slack, a young man unbold. Change came to the famous man for each of his troubles.

Then the protector of earls bade fetch in the heirloom of Hrethel,[9] king famed in battle, adorned with gold. There was not then among the Geats a better treasure in sword's kind. He laid that in Beowulf's lap, and gave him seven thousand [hides of land], a hall and a throne. To both of them alike land had been left in the nation, home and native soil: to the other more especially wide was the realm, to him who was higher in rank.

[Beowulf and the Dragon]

Afterwards it happened, in later days, in the crashes of battle, when Hygelac lay dead and war-swords came to slay Heardred [1] behind the shield-cover, when the Battle-Scylfings, hard fighters, sought him among his victorious nation, attacked bitterly the

---

7. Hrothgar's elder brother, whom Hrothgar succeeded as king.
8. Beowulf's poor reputation as a young man is mentioned only here.
9. Hygelac's father.
1. Hygelac's son Heardred, who suc-

ceeded Hygelac as king, was killed by the Swedes (Heatho-Scylfings) in his own land, as is explained more fully below, section XXXIII. His uncle Hereric was perhaps Hygd's brother.

nephew of Hereric—then the broad kingdom came into Beowulf's hand. He held it well fifty winters—he was a wise king, an old guardian of the land—until in the dark nights a certain one, a dragon, began to hold sway, which on the high heath kept watch over a hoard, a steep stone-barrow. Beneath lay a path unknown to men. By this there went inside a certain man [who made his way near to the heathen hoard; his hand took a cup, large, a shining treasure. The dragon did not afterwards conceal it though in his sleep he was tricked by the craft of the thief. That the people discovered, the neighboring folk—that he was swollen with rage].[2]

(XXXII.) Not of his own accord did he who had sorely harmed him [3] break into the worm's hoard, not by his own desire, but for hard constraint; the slave of some son of men fled hostile blows, lacking a shelter, and came there, a man guilty of wrong-doing. As soon as he saw him,[4] great horror arose in the stranger; [yet the wretched fugitive escaped the terrible worm . . . When the sudden shock came upon him, he carried off a precious cup.][5] There were many such ancient treasures in the earth-house, as in the old days some one of mankind had prudently hidden there the huge legacy of a noble race, rare treasures. Death had taken them all in earlier times, and the only one of the nation of people who still survived, who walked there longest, a guardian mourning his friends, supposed the same of himself as of them—that he might little while enjoy the long-got treasure. A barrow stood all ready on the shore near the sea-waves, newly placed on the headland, made fast by having its entrances skillfully hidden. The keeper of the rings carried in the part of his riches worthy of hoarding, plated gold; he spoke few words:

"Hold now, you earth, now that men may not, the possession of earls. What, from you good men got it first! War-death has taken each man of my people, evil dreadful and deadly, each of those who has given up this life, the hall-joys of men. I have none who wears sword or cleans the plated cup, rich drinking vessel. The company of retainers has gone elsewhere. The hard helmet must be stripped of its fair-wrought gold, of its plating. The polishers are asleep who should make the war-mask shine. And even so the coat of mail, which withstood the bite of swords after the crashing of the shields, decays like its warrior. Nor may the ring-mail travel wide on the war-chief beside his warriors. There is no harp-delight, no mirth of the singing wood, no

2. This part of the manuscript is badly damaged, and the text within brackets is highly conjectural.
3. The dragon.
4. The dragon.
5. Several lines of the text have been lost.

good hawk flies through the hall, no swift horse stamps in the castle court. Baleful death has sent away many races of men."

So, sad of mind, he spoke his sorrow, alone of them all, moved joyless through day and night until death's flood reached his heart. The ancient night-ravager found the hoard-joy standing open, he who burning seeks barrows, the smooth hateful dragon who flies at night wrapped in flame. Earth-dwellers much dread him. He it is who must seek a hoard in the earth where he will guard heathen gold, wise for his winters: he is none the better for it.

So for three hundred winters the harmer of folk held in the earth one of its treasure-houses, huge and mighty, until one man angered his heart. He bore to his master a plated cup, asked his lord for a compact of peace: thus was the hoard searched, the store of treasures diminished. His requests were granted the wretched man: the lord for the first time looked on the ancient work of men. Then the worm woke; cause of strife was renewed: for then he moved over the stones, hard-hearted beheld his foe's footprints—with secret stealth he had stepped forth too near the dragon's head. (So may an undoomed man who holds favor from the Ruler easily come through his woes and misery.) The hoard-guard sought him eagerly over the ground, would find the man who had done him injury while he slept. Hot and fierce-hearted, often he moved all about the outside of the barrow. No man at all was in the emptiness. Yet he took joy in the thought of war, in the work of fighting. At times he turned back into the barrow, sought his rich cup. Straightway he found that some man had tampered with his gold, his splendid treasure. The hoard-guard waited restless until evening came; then the barrow-keeper was in rage: he would requite that precious drinking cup with vengeful fire. Then the day was gone—to the joy of the worm. He would not wait long on the sea-wall, but set out with fire, ready with flame. The beginning was terrible to the folk on the land, as the ending was soon to be sore to their giver of treasure.

(XXXIII.) Then the evil spirit began to vomit flames, burn bright dwellings; blaze of fire rose, to the horror of men; there the deadly flying thing would leave nothing alive. The worm's warfare was wide-seen, his cruel malice, near and far—how the destroyer hated and hurt the people of the Geats. He winged back to the hoard, his hidden hall, before the time of day. He had circled the land-dwellers with flame, with fire and burning. He had trust in his barrow, in his war and his wall: his expectation deceived him.

Then the terror was made known to Beowulf, quickly in its truth, that his own home, best of buildings, had melted in surging flames, the throne-seat of the Geats. That was anguish of spirit to the good man, the greatest of heart-sorrows. The wise one supposed that he had bitterly offended the Ruler, the Eternal Lord, against old law. His breast within boiled with dark thoughts— as was not for him customary. The fiery dragon with his flames had destroyed the people's stronghold, the land along the sea, the heart of the country. Because of that the war-king, the lord of the Weather-Geats, devised punishment for him. The protector of fighting men, lord of earls, commanded that a wonderful battle-shield be made all of iron. Well he knew that the wood of the forest might not help him—linden against flame. The prince good from old times was to come to the end of the days that had been lent him, life in the world, and the worm with him, though he had long held the hoarded wealth. Then the ring-prince scorned to seek the far-flier with a troop, a large army. He had no fear for himself of the combat, nor did he think the worm's war-power anything great, his strength and his courage, because he himself had come through many battles before, dared perilous straits, clashes of war, after he had purged Hrothgar's hall, victorious warrior, and in combat crushed to death Grendel's kin, loathsome race.

Nor was that the least of his hand-combats where Hygelac was slain, when the king of the Geats, the noble lord of the people, the son of Hrethel, died of sword-strokes in the war-storm among the Frisians, laid low by the blade. From there Beowulf came away by means of his own strength, performed a feat of swimming; he had on his arm the armor of thirty earls when he turned back to the sea. There was no need for the Hetware[6] to exult in the foot-battle when they bore their shields against him: few came again from that warrior to seek their homes. Then the son of Ecgtheow swam over the water's expanse, forlorn and alone, back to his people. There Hygd offered him hoard and kingdom, rings and a prince's throne. She had no trust in her son, that he could hold his native throne against foreigners now that Hygelac was dead. By no means the sooner might the lordless ones get consent from the noble that he would become lord of Heardred or that he would accept royal power.[7] Yet he held him up among the people by friendly counsel, kindly with honor, until he became older,[8] ruled the Weather-Geats.

6. I.e., a tribe, with whom the Frisians were allied.
7. I.e., Beowulf refused to take the throne from the rightful heir Heardred.
8. I.e., Beowulf supported the young Heardred.

Outcasts from over the sea sought him, sons of Ohthere.[9] They had rebelled against the protector of the Scylfings, the best of the sea-kings of those who gave treasure in Sweden, a famous lord. For Heardred that became his life's limit: because of his hospitality there the son of Hygelac got his life's wound from the strokes of a sword. And the son of Ongentheow went back to seek his home after Heardred lay dead, let Beowulf hold the royal throne, rule the Geats: that was a good king.

(XXXIV.) In later days he was mindful of repaying the prince's fall, became the friend of the destitute Eadgils;[1] with folk he supported the son of Ohthere over the wide sea, with warriors and weapons. Afterwards he got vengeance by forays that brought with them cold care: he took the king's life.

Thus he had survived every combat, every dangerous battle, every deed of courage, the son of Ecgtheow, until that one day when he should fight with the worm. Then, one of twelve, the lord of the Geats, swollen with anger, went to look on the dragon. He had learned then from what the feud arose, the fierce malice to men: the glorious cup had come to his possession from the hand of the finder: he was the thirteenth of that company, the man who had brought on the beginning of the war, the sad-hearted slave—wretched, he must direct them to the place. Against his will he went to where he knew of an earth-hall, a barrow beneath the ground close to the sea-surge, to the struggling waves: within, it was full of ornaments and gold chains. The terrible guardian, ready for combat, held the gold treasure, old under the earth. It was no easy bargain for any man to obtain. Then the king, hardy in fight, sat down on the headland; there he saluted his hearth-companions, gold-friend of the Geats. His mind was mournful, restless and ripe for death: very close was the fate which should come to the old man, seek his soul's hoard, divide life from his body; not for long then was the life of the noble one wound in his flesh.

Beowulf spoke, the son of Ecgtheow: "In youth I lived through many battle-storms, times of war. I remember all that. I was seven winters old when the lord of treasure, the beloved king of the folk, received me from my father: King Hrethel had me and kept me, gave me treasure and feast, mindful of kinship. During his life I was no more hated by him as a man in his

9. Ohthere succeeded his father Ongentheow as king of the Scylfings (Swedes), but after his death his brother Onela seized the throne, driving out Ohthere's sons Eanmund and Eadgils. They were given refuge at the Geatish court by Heardred, whom Onela attacked for this act of hospitality. In the fight Eanmund and Heardred were killed, and Onela left the kingdom in Beowulf's charge. 1. The surviving son of Ohthere was befriended by Beowulf, who supported him in his successful attempt to gain the Swedish throne and who killed the usurper Onela.

castle than any of his own sons, Herebeald and Haethcyn, or
my own Hygelac. For the eldest a murder-bed was wrongfully
spread through the deed of a kinsman, when Haethcyn struck
him down with an arrow from his horned bow—his friend and
his lord—missed the mark and shot his kinsman dead, one brother
the other, with the bloody arrowhead. That was a fatal fight,
without hope of recompense, a deed wrongly done, baffling to
the heart; yet it had happened that a prince had to lose life
unavenged.

"So it is sad for an old man to endure that his son should ride
young on the gallows. Then he may speak a story, a sorrowful
song, when his son hangs for the joy of the raven, and, old
in years and knowing, he can find no help for him. Always with
every morning he is reminded of his son's journey elsewhere. He
cares not to wait for another heir in his hall, when the first through
death's force has come to the end of his deeds. Sorrowful he
sees in his son's dwelling the empty wine-hall, the windy resting
place without joy—the riders sleep, the warriors in the grave.
There is no sound of the harp, no joy in the dwelling, as there
was of old. (XXXV.) Then he goes to his couch, sings a song
of sorrow, one alone for one gone. To him all too wide has seemed
the land and the dwelling.

"So the protector of the Weather-Geats bore in his heart
swelling sorrow for Herebeald. In no way could he settle his
feud with the life-slayer; not the sooner could he wound the
warrior with deeds of hatred, though he was not dear to him.
Then for the sorrow that had too bitterly befallen him he gave up
the joys of men, chose God's light. To his sons he left—as a happy
man does—his land and his town when he went from life.

"Then there was battle and strife of Swedes and Geats, over
the wide water a quarrel shared, hatred between hardy ones, after
Hrethel died. And the sons of Ongentheow [2] were bold and active
in war, wanted to have no peace over the seas, but about Hreosnabeorh often devised awful slaughter. That my friends and kinsmen avenged, both the feud and the crime, as is well-known,
though one of them bought it with his life, a hard bargain: the
war was mortal to Haethcyn, lord of the Geats. [3] Then in the
morning, I have heard, one kinsman avenged the other on his
slayer with the sword's edge, when Ongentheow attacked Eofor:
the war-helm split, the old Scylfing fell mortally wounded: his

2. I.e., the Swedes Onela and Ohthere:
the reference is, of course, to a time
earlier than that referred to in section
XXXIII, note 9.
3. Haethcyn had succeeded his father
Hrethel as king of the Geats after his
accidental killing of his brother Herebeald. When Haethcyn was killed while
attacking the Swedes, he was succeeded
by Hygelac, who, as the next sentence
relates, avenged Haethcyn's death on
Ongentheow. The death of Ongentheow
is described below, sections XL and
XLI.

hand remembered feuds enough, did not withstand the life-blow.

"I repaid in war the treasures that he [4] gave me—with my bright sword, as was granted me by fate: he had given me land, a pleasant dwelling. There was not any need for him, any reason, that he should have to seek among the Gifthas or the Spear-Danes or in Sweden in order to buy with treasure a worse warrior. I would always go before him in the troop, alone in the front. And so all my life I shall wage battle while this sword endures that has served me early and late ever since I became Daeghrefn's slayer in the press—the warrior of the Hugas.[5] He could not bring armor to the king of the Frisians, breast ornament, but fell in the fight, keeper of the standard, a noble man. Nor was my sword's edge his slayer, but my warlike grip broke open his heart-streams, his bone-house. Now shall the sword's edge, the hand and hard blade, fight for the hoard."

[BEOWULF ATTACKS THE DRAGON]

Beowulf spoke, for the last time spoke words in boast: "In my youth I engaged in many wars. Old guardian of the people, I shall still seek battle, perform a deed of fame, if the evil-doer will come to me out of the earth-hall."

Then he saluted each of the warriors, the bold helmet-bearers, for the last time—his own dear companions. "I would not bear sword, weapon, to the worm, if I knew how else according to my boast I might grapple with the monster, as I did of old with Grendel. But I expect here hot battle-fire, steam and poison. Therefore I have on me shield and mail-shirt. I will not flee a foot-step from the barrow-ward, but it shall be with us at the wall as fate allots, the ruler of every man. I am confident in heart, so I forgo help against the war-flier. Wait on the barrow, safe in your mail-shirts, men in armor—which of us two may better bear wounds after our bloody meeting. This is not your venture, nor is it right for any man except me alone that he should spend his strength against the monster, do this man's deed. By my courage I shall get gold, or war will take your king, dire life-evil."

Then the brave warrior arose by his shield; hardy under helmet he went in his mail-shirt beneath the stone-cliffs, had trust in his strength—that of one man: such is not the way of the cowardly. Then he saw by the wall—he who had come through many wars, good in his great-heartedness, many clashes in battle when troops meet together—a stone arch standing, through it a stream bursting out of the barrow: there was welling of a current hot with killing fires, and he might not endure any while unburnt

4. Hygelac.   5. I.e., the Franks.

by the dragon's flame the hollow near the hoard. Then the man of the Weather-Geats, enraged as he was, let a word break from his breast. Stout-hearted he shouted; his voice went roaring, clear in battle, in under the gray stone. Hate was stirred up, the hoard's guard knew the voice of a man. No more time was there to ask for peace. First the monster's breath came out of the stone, the hot war-steam. The earth resounded. The man below the barrow, the lord of the Geats, swung his shield against the dreadful visitor. Then the heart of the coiled thing was aroused to seek combat. The good war-king had drawn his sword, the old heirloom, not blunt of edge. To each of them as they threatened destruction there was terror of the other. Firm-hearted he stood with his shield high, the lord of friends, while quickly the worm coiled itself; he waited in his armor. Then, coiling in flames, he came gliding on, hastening to his fate. The good shield protected the life and body of the famous prince, but for a shorter while than his wish was. There for the first time, the first day in his life, he might not prevail, since fate did not assign him such glory in battle. The lord of the Geats raised his hand, struck the shining horror so with his forged blade that the edge failed, bright on the bone, bit less surely than its folk-king had need, hard-pressed in perils. Then because of the battle-stroke the barrow-ward's heart was savage, he exhaled death-fire—the war-flames sprang wide. The gold-friend of the Geats boasted of no great victories: the war blade had failed, naked at need, as it ought not to have done, iron good from old times. That was no pleasant journey, not one on which the famous son of Ecgtheow would wish to leave his land; against his will he must take up a dwelling-place elsewhere—as every man must give up the days that are lent him.

It was not long until they came together again, dreadful foes. The hoard-guard took heart, once more his breast swelled with his breathing. Encircled with flames, he who before had ruled a folk felt harsh pain. Nor did his companions, sons of nobles, take up their stand in a troop about him with the courage of fighting men, but they crept to the wood, protected their lives. In only one of them the heart surged with sorrows: nothing can ever set aside kinship in him who means well.

(XXXVI.) He was called Wiglaf, son of Weohstan, a rare shield-warrior, a man of the Scylfings,[6] kinsman of Aelfhere.

6. Though in the next sentence Wiglaf is said to belong to the family of the Waegmundings, the Geatish family to which Beowulf belonged, he is here called a Scylfing (Swede), and immediately below his father Woehstan is represented as having fought for the Swede Onela in his attack on the Geats. But for a man to change his nation was not unusual, and Weohstan, who may have had both Swedish and Geatish blood, had evidently become a Geat long enough before to have brought up his son Wiglaf as one. The identity of Aelfhere is not known.

He saw his liege lord under his war-mask suffer the heat. Then he was mindful of the honors he had given him before, the rich dwelling-place of the Waegmundings, every folk-right such as his father possessed. He might not then hold back, his hand seized his shield, the yellow linden-wood; he drew his ancient sword. Among men it was the heirloom of Eanmund, the son of Ohthere: [7] Weohstan had become his slayer in battle with sword's edge—an exile without friends; and he bore off to his kin the bright-shining helmet, the ringed mail-armor, the old sword made by giants that Onela had given him,[8] his kinsman's war-armor, ready battle-gear: he did not speak of the feud, though he had killed his brother's son.[9] He [1] held the armor many half-years, the blade and the battle-dress, until his son might do manly deeds like his old father. Then he gave him among the Geats war-armor of every kind, numberless, when, old, he went forth on the way from life. For the young warrior this was the first time that he should enter the war-storm with his dear lord. His heart's courage did not slacken, nor did the heirloom of his kinsman fail in the battle. That the worm found when they had come together.

Wiglaf spoke, said many fit words to his companions—his mind was mournful: "I remember that time we drank mead, when we promised our lord in the beer-hall—him who gave us these rings—that we would repay him for the war-arms if a need like this befell him—the helmets and the hard swords. Of his own will he chose us among the host for this venture, thought us worthy of fame—and gave me these treasures—because he counted us good war-makers, brave helm-bearers, though our lord intended to do this work of courage alone, as keeper of the folk, because among men he had performed the greatest deeds of glory, daring actions. Now the day has come that our liege lord has need of the strength of good fighters. Let us go to him, help our war-chief while the grim terrible fire persists. God knows of me that I should rather that the flame enfold my body with my gold-giver. It does not seem right to me for us to bear our shields home again unless we can first fell the foe, defend the life of the prince of the Weather-Geats. I know well that it would be no recompense for past deeds that he alone of the company of

7. See above, section XXXIII, note 9. Not only did Weohstan support Onela's attack on the Geat king Heardred, but actually killed Eanmund whom Heardred was supporting, and it is Eanmund's sword that Wiglaf is now wielding.
8. The spoils of war belonged to the victorious king, who apportioned them among his fighters: thus Onela gave Weohstan the armor of Eanmund, whom Weohstan had killed.
9. This ironic remark points out that Onela did not claim *wergild* or seek vengeance from Weohstan, as in other circumstances he ought to have done inasmuch as Weohstan had killed Onela's close kinsman, his nephew Eanmund: but Onela was himself trying to kill Eanmund.
1. Weohstan.

the Geats should suffer pain, fall in the fight. For us both shall there be a part in the work of sword and helmet, of battle-shirt and war-clothing."

Then he waded through the deadly smoke, bore his war-helmet to the aid of his king, spoke in few words: "Beloved Beowulf, do all well, for, long since in your youth, you said that you would not let your glory fail while you lived. Now, great-spirited noble, brave of deeds, you must protect your life with all your might. I shall help you."

After these words, the worm came on, angry, the terrible malice-filled foe, shining with surging flames, to seek for the second time his enemies, hated men. Fire advanced in waves; shield burned to the boss; mail-shirt might give no help to the young spear-warrior; but the young man went quickly under his kinsman's shield when his own was consumed with flames. Then the war-king was again mindful of fame, struck with his war-sword with great strength so that it stuck in the head-bone, driven with force: Naegling broke, the sword of Beowulf failed in the fight, old and steel-gray. It was not ordained for him that iron edges might help in the combat. Too strong was the hand that I have heard strained every sword with its stroke, when he bore wound-hardened weapon to battle: he was none the better for it.

Then for the third time the folk-harmer, the fearful fire-dragon, was mindful of feuds, set upon the brave one when the chance came, hot and battle-grim seized all his neck with his sharp fangs: he was smeared with life-blood, gore welled out in waves.

(XXXVII.) Then, I have heard, at the need of the folk-king the earl at his side made his courage known, his might and his keenness—as was natural to him. He took no heed for that head,[2] but the hand of the brave man was burned as he helped his kinsman, as the man in armor struck the hateful foe a little lower down, so that the sword sank in, shining and engraved; and then the fire began to subside. The king himself then still controlled his senses, drew the battle-knife, biting and war-sharp, that he wore on his mail-shirt: the protector of the Weather-Geats cut the worm through the middle. They felled the foe, courage drove his life out, and they had destroyed him together, the two noble kinsmen. So ought a man be, a thane at need. To the prince that was the last moment of victory for his own deeds, of work in the world.

Then the wound that the earth-dragon had caused began to burn and to swell; at once he felt dire evil boil in his breast, poison within him. Then the prince, wise of thought, went to

---

2. I.e., the dragon's flame-breathing head.

where he might sit on a seat near the wall. He looked on the work of giants, how the timeless earth-hall held within it stone-arches fast on pillars. Then with his hands the thane, good without limit, washed him with water, blood-besmeared, the famous prince, his beloved lord, sated with battle; and he unfastened his helmet.

Beowulf spoke—despite his wounds spoke, his mortal hurts. He knew well he had lived out his days' time, joy on earth; all passed was the number of his days, death very near. "Now I would wish to give my son my war-clothing, if any heir after me, part of my flesh, were granted. I held this people fifty winters. There was no folk-king of those dwelling about who dared approach me with swords, threaten me with fears. In my land I awaited what fate brought me, held my own well, sought no treacherous quarrels, nor did I swear many oaths unrightfully. Sick with life-wounds, I may have joy of all this, for the Ruler of Men need not blame me for the slaughter of kinsmen when life goes from my body. Now quickly go to look at the hoard under the gray stone, beloved Wiglaf, now that the worm lies sleeping from sore wounds, bereft of his treasure. Be quick now, so that I may see the ancient wealth, the golden things, may clearly look on the bright curious gems, so that for that, because of the treasure's richness, I may the more easily leave life and nation I have long held."

(XXXVIII.) Then I have heard that the son of Weohstan straightway obeyed his lord, sick with battle-wounds, according to the words he had spoken, went wearing his ring-armor, woven battle-shirt, under the barrow's roof. Then he saw, as he went by the seat, the brave young retainer, triumphant in heart, many precious jewels, glittering gold lying on the ground, wonders on the wall, and the worm's lair, the old night-flier's—cups standing there, vessels of men of old, with none to polish them, stripped of their ornaments. There was many a helmet old and rusty, many an arm-ring skillfully twisted. (Easily may treasure, gold in the ground, betray each one of the race of men, hide it who will.) Also he saw a standard all gold hang high over the hoard, the greatest of hand-wonders, linked with fingers' skill. From it came a light so that he might see the ground, look on the works of craft. There was no trace of the worm, for the blade had taken him. Then I have heard that one man in the mound pillaged the hoard, the old work of giants, loaded in his bosom cups and plates at his own desire. He took also the standard, brightest of banners. The sword of the old lord—its edge was iron—had already wounded the one who for a long time had been guardian of the treasure, waged his fire-terror, hot for the hoard, rising up fiercely at midnight, till he died in the slaughter.

The messenger was in haste, eager to return, urged on by the treasures. Curiosity tormented him, whether eagerly seeking he should find the lord of the Weather-Geats, strength gone, alive in the place where he had left him before. Then with the treasures he found the great prince, his lord, bleeding, at the end of his life. Again he began to sprinkle him with water until this word's point broke through his breast-hoard—he spoke, the king, old man in sorrow, looked on the gold: "I speak with my words thanks to the Lord of All for these treasures, to the King of Glory, Eternal Prince, for what I gaze on here, that I might get such for my people before my death-day. Now that I have bought the hoard of treasures with my old life, you attend to the people's needs hereafter: I can be here no longer. Bid the battle-renowned make a mound, bright after the funeral fire, on the sea's cape. It shall stand high on Hronesness as a reminder to my people, so that sea-travelers later will call it Beowulf's barrow, when they drive their ships far over the darkness of the seas."

He took off his neck the golden necklace, bold-hearted prince, gave it to the thane, to the young spear-warrior—gold-gleaming helmet, ring, and mail-shirt, bade him use them well. "You are the last left of our race, of the Waegmundings. Fate has swept away all my kinsmen, earls in their strength, to destined death. I have to go after." That was the last word of the old man, of the thoughts of his heart, before he should taste the funeral pyre, hot hostile flames. The soul went from his breast to seek the doom of those fast in truth.

[*Beowulf's Funeral*]

(XXXIX.) Then sorrow came to the young man that he saw him whom he most loved on the earth, at the end of his life, suffering piteously. His slayer likewise lay dead, the awful earth-dragon bereft of life, overtaken by evil. No longer should the coiled worm rule the ring-hoard, for iron edges had taken him, hard and battle-sharp work of the hammers, so that the wide-flier, stilled by wounds, had fallen on the earth near the treasure-house. He did not go flying through the air at midnight, proud of his property, showing his aspect, but he fell to earth through the work of the chief's hands. Yet I have heard of no man of might on land, though he was bold of every deed, whom it should prosper to rush against the breath of the venomous foe or disturb with hands the ring-hall, if he found the guard awake who lived in the barrow. The share of the rich treasures became

Beowulf's, paid for by death: each of the two had journeyed to the end of life's loan.

Then it was not long before the battle-slack ones left the woods, ten weak troth-breakers together, who had not dared fight with their spears in their liege lord's great need. But they bore their shields, ashamed, their war-clothes, to where the old man lay, looked on Wiglaf. He sat wearied, the foot-soldier near the shoulders of his lord, would waken him with water: it gained him nothing. He might not, though he much wished it, hold life in his chieftain on earth nor change anything of the Ruler's: the judgment of God would control the deeds of every man, just as it still does now. Then it was easy to get from the young man a grim answer to him who before had lost courage. Wiglaf spoke, the son of Weohstan, a man sad at heart, looked on the unloved ones:

"Yes, he who will speak truth may say that the liege lord who gave you treasure, the war-gear that you stand in there, when he used often to hand out to hall-sitters on the ale-benches, a prince to his thanes, helmets and war-shirts such as he could find mightiest anywhere, both far and near—that he quite threw away the war-gear, to his distress when war came upon him. The folk-king had no need to boast of his war-comrades. Yet God, Ruler of Victories, granted him that he might avenge himself, alone with his sword, when there was need for his courage. I was able to give him little life-protection in the fight, and yet beyond my power I did begin to help my kinsman. The deadly foe was ever the weaker after I struck him with my sword, fire poured less strongly from his head. Too few defenders thronged about the prince when the hard time came upon him. Now there shall cease for your race the receiving of treasure and the giving of swords, all enjoyment of pleasant homes, comfort. Each man of your kindred must go deprived of his land-right when nobles from afar learn of your flight, your inglorious deed. Death is better for any earl than a life of blame."

(XL.) Then he bade that the battle-deed be announced in the city, up over the cliff-edge, where the band of warriors sat the whole morning of the day, sad-hearted, shield-bearers in doubt whether it was the beloved man's last day or whether he would come again. Little did he fail to speak of new tidings, he who rode up the hill, but spoke to them all truthfully: "Now the joy-giver of the people of the Weathers, the lord of the Geats, is fast on his death-bed, lies on his slaughter-couch through deeds of the worm. Beside him lies his life-enemy, struck down with dagger-wounds—with his sword he might not work wounds of any kind on the monster. Wiglaf son of Weohstan sits over

Beowulf, one earl by the lifeless other, in weariness of heart holds death-watch over the loved and the hated.

"Now may the people expect a time of war, when the king's fall becomes wide-known to the Franks and the Frisians. A harsh quarrel was begun with the Hugas when Hygelac came traveling with his sea-army to the land of the Frisians, where the Hetware assailed him in battle, quickly, with stronger forces, made the mailed warrior bow; he fell in the ranks: that chief gave no treasure to his retainers. Ever since then the good will of the Merewioing king has been denied us.

"Nor do I expect any peace or trust from the Swedish people, for it is wide-known that Ongentheow took the life of Haethcyn, Hrethel's son, near Ravenswood when in their over-pride the people of the Geats first went against the War-Scylfings. Straightway the wary father of Ohthere,[3] old and terrible, gave a blow in return, cut down the sea-king,[4] rescued his wife, old woman of times past, bereft of her gold, mother of Onela and Ohthere, and then he followed his life-foes until they escaped, lordless, painfully, to Ravenswood. Then with a great army he besieged those whom the sword had left, weary with wounds, often vowed woes to the wretched band the livelong night, said that in the morning he would cut them apart with sword-blades, [hang] some on gallows-trees as sport for birds. Relief came in turn to the sorry-hearted together with dawn when they heard Hygelac's horn and trumpet, his sound as the good man came on their track with a body of retainers. (XLI.) Wide-seen was the bloody track of Swedes and Geats, the slaughter-strife of men, how the peoples stirred up the feud between them. Then the good man went with his kinsmen, old and much-mourning, to seek his stronghold: the earl Ongentheow moved further away. He had heard of the warring of Hygelac, of the war-power of the proud one. He did not trust in resistance, that he might fight off the sea-men, defend his hoard against the war-sailors, his children and wife. Instead he drew back, the old man behind his earth-wall.

"Then pursuit was offered to the people of the Swedes, the standards of Hygelac overran the stronghold as Hrethel's people pressed forward to the citadel. There Ongentheow the gray-haired was brought to bay by sword-blades, and the people's king had to submit to the judgment of Eofor alone. Wulf [5] son of Wonred had struck him angrily with his weapon so that for the blow the

3. I.e., Ongentheow.
4. I.e., Haethcyn, king of the Geats. Haethcyn's brother Hygelac, who succeeded him, was not present at this battle, but arrived after the death of Haethcyn with reinforcements to relieve the survivors and to pursue Ongentheow in his retreat to his city.
5. The two sons of Wonred, Wulf and Eofor, attacked Ongentheow in turn. Wulf was struck down but not killed by the old Swedish king, who was then slain by Eofor.

blood sprang forth in streams beneath his hair. Yet not for that was he afraid, the old Scylfing, but he quickly repaid the assault with worse exchange, the folk-king, when he turned toward him. The strong son of Wonred could not give the old man a return blow, for Ongentheow had first cut through the helmet of his head so that he had to sink down, smeared with blood—fell on the earth: he was not yet doomed, for he recovered, though the wound hurt him. The hardy thane of Hygelac,⁶ when his brother lay low, let his broad sword, old blade made by giants, break the great helmet across the shield-wall; then the king bowed, the keeper of the folk was hit to the quick.

"Then there were many who bound up the brother, quickly raised him up after it was granted them to control the battle-field. Then one warrior stripped the other, took from Ongentheow his iron-mail, hard-hilted sword, and his helmet, too; he bore the arms of the hoary one to Hygelac. He accepted that treasure and fairly promised him rewards among the people, and he stood by it thus: the lord of the Geats, the son of Hrethel, when he came home, repaid Wulf and Eofor for their battle-assault with much treasure, gave each of them a hundred thousand [units] of land and linked rings: there was no need for any man on middle-earth to blame him for the rewards, since they had performed great deeds. And then he gave Eofor his only daughter as a pledge of friendship—a fair thing for his home.

"That is the feud and the enmity, the death-hatred of men, for which I expect that the people of the Swedes, bold shield-warriors after the fall of princes, will set upon us after they learn that our prince has gone from life, he who before held hoard and kingdom against our enemies, did good to the people, and further still, did what a man should. Now haste is best, that we look on the people's king there and bring him who gave us rings on his way to the funeral pyre. Nor shall only a small share melt with the great-hearted one, but there is a hoard of treasure, gold uncounted, grimly purchased, and rings bought at the last now with his own life. These shall the fire devour, flames enfold—no earl to wear ornament in remembrance, nor any bright maiden add to her beauty with neck-ring; but mournful-hearted, stripped of gold, they shall walk, often, not once, in strange countries—now that the army-leader has laid aside laughter, his game and his mirth. Therefore many a spear, cold in the morning, shall be grasped with fingers, raised by hands; no sound of harp shall waken the warriors, but the dark raven, low over the doomed, shall tell many tales, say to the eagle how he fared at the feast when with the wolf he spoiled the slain bodies."

6. I.e., Eofor.

Thus the bold man was a speaker of hateful news, nor did he much lie in his words or his prophecies. The company all arose. Without joy they went below Earnaness [7] to look on the wonder with welling tears. Then they found on the sand, soulless, keeping his bed of rest, him who in former times had given them rings. Then the last day of the good man had come, when the war-king, prince of the Weather-Geats, died a wonderful death. First they saw the stranger creature, the worm lying loathsome, opposite him in the place. The fire-dragon was grimly terrible with his many colors, burned by the flames; he was fifty feet long in the place where he lay. Once he had joy of the air at night, came back down to seek his den. Then he was made fast by death, had made use of the last of his earth-caves. Beside him stood cups and pitchers, plates and rich swords lay eaten through by rust, just as they had been there in the bosom of the earth for a thousand winters. Then that huge heritage, gold of men of old, was wound in a spell, so that no one of men must touch the ring-hall unless God himself, the True King of Victories—He is men's protection—should grant to whom He wished to open the hoard—whatever man seemed fit to Him.

(XLII.) Then it was seen that the act did not profit him who wrongly kept hidden the handiworks under the wall. The keeper had first slain a man like few others, then the feud had been fiercely avenged. It is a wonder where an earl famed for courage may reach the end of his allotted life—then may dwell no longer in the mead-hall, man with his kin. So it was with Beowulf when he sought quarrels, the barrow's ward: he himself did not then know in what way his parting with the world should come. The great princes who had put it [8] there had laid on it so deep a curse until doomsday that the man who should plunder the place should be guilty of sins, imprisoned in idol-shrines, fixed with hell-bonds, punished with evils—unless the Possessor's favor were first shown the more clearly to him who desired the gold.

Wiglaf spoke, the son of Weohstan: "Often many a man must suffer distress for the will of one man, as has happened to us. We might by no counsel persuade our dear prince, keeper of the kingdom, not to approach the gold-guardian, let him lie where he long was, live in his dwelling to the world's end. He held to his high destiny. The hoard has been made visible, grimly got. What drove the folk-king thither was too powerfully fated. I have been therein and looked at it all, the rare things of the chamber, when it was granted me—not at all friendly was the journey that I was permitted beneath the earth-wall. In haste I seized with

7. The headland near where Beowulf   8. The treasure.
had fought the dragon.

my hands a huge burden of hoard-treasures, of great size, bore
it out here to my king. He was then still alive, sound-minded and
aware. He spoke many things, old man in sorrow, and bade greet
you, commanded that for your lord's deeds you make a high
barrow in the place of his pyre, large and conspicuous, since
he was of men the worthiest warrior through the wide earth,
while he might enjoy wealth in his castle.

"Let us now hasten to see and visit for the second time the
heap of precious jewels, the wonder under the walls. I shall
direct you so that you may look on enough of them from near
at hand—rings and broad gold. Let the bier be made ready,
speedily prepared, when we come out, and then let us carry our
prince, beloved man, where he shall long dwell in the Ruler's
protection."

Then the son of Weohstan, man brave in battle, bade command
many warriors, men who owned houses, leaders of the people,
that they carry wood from afar for the pyre for the good man.
"Now shall flame eat the chief of warriors—the fire shall grow
dark—who often survived the iron-shower when the storm of
arrows driven from bow-strings passed over the shield-wall—
the shaft did its task, made eager by feather-gear served the
arrowhead."

And then the wise son of Weohstan summoned from the host
thanes of the king, seven together, the best; one of eight warriors,
he went beneath the evil roof. One who walked before bore a
torch in his hands. Then there was no lot to decide who should
plunder that hoard, since the men could see that every part of
it rested in the hall without guardian, lay wasting. Little did any
man mourn that hastily they should bear out the rare treasure.
Also they pushed the dragon, the worm, over the cliff-wall, let
the wave take him, the flood enfold the keeper of the treasure.
Then twisted gold was loaded on a wagon, an uncounted number
of things, and the prince, hoary warrior, borne to Hronesness.

(XLIII.) Then the people of the Geats made ready for him a
funeral pyre on the earth, no small one, hung with helmets,
battle-shields, bright mail-shirts, just as he had asked. Then in the
midst they laid the great prince, lamenting their hero, their
beloved lord. Then warriors began to awaken on the barrow the
greatest of funeral-fires; the wood-smoke climbed, black over the
fire; the roaring flame mixed with weeping—the wind-surge died
down—until it had broken the bone-house, hot at its heart. Sad
in spirit they lamented their heart-care, the death of their liege
lord. And the Geatish woman, wavy-haired, sang a sorrowful song
about Beowulf, said[9] again and again that she sorely feared for herself

9. The manuscript is badly damaged and the interpretation conjectural.

invasions of armies, many slaughters, terror of troops, humiliation, and captivity. Heaven swallowed the smoke.

Then the people of the Weather-Geats built a mound on the promontory, one that was high and broad, wide-seen by seafarers, and in ten days completed a monument for the bold in battle, surrounded the remains of the fire with a wall, the most splendid that men most skilled might devise. In the barrow they placed rings and jewels, all such ornaments as troubled men had earlier taken from the hoard. They let the earth hold the wealth of earls, gold in the ground, where now it still dwells, as useless to men as it was before. Then the brave in battle rode round the mound, children of nobles, twelve in all, would bewail their sorrow and mourn their king, recite dirges and speak of the man. They praised his great deeds and his acts of courage, judged well of his prowess. So it is fitting that man honor his liege lord with words, love him in heart when he must be led forth from the body. Thus the people of the Geats, his hearth-companions, lamented the death of their lord. They said that he was of world-kings the mildest of men and the gentlest, kindest to his people, and most eager for fame.

Backgrounds and Sources

ROBERT C. HUGHES

The Origins of Old English to 800 A.D.†[1]

Pre-history of England and the Celtic Settlements

By the best available estimates, the land we now call England had been inhabited for 50 to 250 thousand years before the recorded history of the English-speaking peoples. Paleolithic man roamed the area when the North Sea was only a minor river and when no channel separated England from the Continent. Neolithic man from the Mediterranean with his polished and ground stone implements, his agrarian interests, his domesticated animals, and his rituals of burial lived in these lands from ca. 5000 B.C. The Stone Age lasted in this region until ca. 2000 B.C., and the Bronze Age settlements continued probably to ca. 500 B.C. The early Celts made their way to this land in the last centuries of the Bronze Age and remained the chief population through the early centuries of the Iron Age in England.

By the time of Christ, Celtic peoples lived not only in England, but also had migrated throughout many other parts of western Europe. Although, as far as we know, the Celts had no single name for England, early Latin writers referred to these western lands as "Britannia" ("island of the Bretons"). The Celts lived in small groups or tribes of kinsmen without the larger political unity necessary for a nation or empire. The language of the Celts in England, near kinsmen of the Celts in Gaul, was probably first Gaelic and then later Britannic, from which Welsh, Breton, and Cornish derived.

Roman Occupation of England

In 55 B.C. and again in 54 B.C., Julius Caesar invaded the Celtic lands in England, not necessarily to conquer the islands, but perhaps to retaliate for the British fellowship with the Gallic Celts who had

† Copyright © 1975 by Robert C. Hughes and printed with his permission. This essay appears here in print for the first time.

1. This brief review of the Old English language and peoples is extensively indebted to Albert C. Baugh, *A History of the English Language*, 2nd ed. (New York: Appleton, 1957). For additional material on the internal and external history of Old English, see Henry Alexander, *The Story of Our Language* (1940; rpt. New York: Anchor, 1969); Otto Jespersen, *Growth and Structure of the English Language*, 9th ed. (New York: Anchor, 1955); Samuel Moore and Thomas A. Knott, *The Elements of Old English*, 10th ed. (Ann Arbor: Wahr, 1965); John Nist, *A Structural History of English*, (New York: St. Martin's, 1966); Thomas Pyles, *The Origins and Development of the English Language*, 2nd ed. (New York: Harcourt, 1971); and Stuart Robertson and Frederic G. Cassidy, *The Development of Modern English*, 2nd ed. (Englewood Cliffs, N.J.: Prentice-Hall, 1954).

fought him on the Continent. Neither invasion was successful even though Caesar established his forces for a time in the southeast and demanded tribute which the Britannic Celts never paid. Not until 43 A.D. did the Romans under Emperor Claudius seriously attempt to occupy Britannia. Between 78 and 85 A.D., the Roman governor of Britain, Agricola, completed the conquest of the southern and midland Celtic populace; however, the Roman forces never entirely overcame the Celts in the northern mountains and in the far western land of Wales, where many Celts had retreated in the face of Roman advances. The Roman occupation was challenged from time to time from the North and from the West; for instance, in the second century the Celts from the North revolted and pushed the Romans south of the Humber River. In reaction, after the northern Celts were driven back, the Emperor Hadrian came to England and constructed "Hadrian's Wall" (73 miles long) from Wallsend on the Tyne River to the head of the Solway Firth, ca. 121–27 A.D., a line of fortifications which helped the Romans defend themselves later against the Picts.

By the end of the fourth century, the Roman rulers had begun to recall their military forces from the frontiers of the Empire to help defend the homeland from the increasing hostility of the Germanic tribes on the move, kinsmen of the Teutons who would settle in England from the second half of the fifth century. The Angles, Saxons, and Jutes (L. *Iuti*) shared a common Germanic history and culture with other migratory peoples who challenged Roman sovereignty in western Europe, with tribes such as the Goths, Vandals, Franks, and Danes.[2]

By ca. 410, the last of the Roman legions were recalled from Britannia and left the British Celts without protection from their own kinsmen in the North and West. With the end of the Roman sovereignty in England and with the British Celts weakened militarily after over three centuries of Roman occupation, the Gaelic Scots (Irishmen) from the West and the Britannic Picts from the North began to encroach upon the Celtic dominance south of the Humber. For a narrative account of what then happened in Britain, we have Venerable Bede (673?–735) to thank for his history of these times in his *Ecclesiastical History of the English People*.

Germanic Invasions

In his Latin work written in 731, Bede relates that the Celtic chieftain Vortigern offered the Germanic Jutes the island of Thanet in exchange for military support against the Picts and the Scots.

2. Note how stories and figures from all these related Germanic cultures are interwoven in *Beowulf*. Ed.

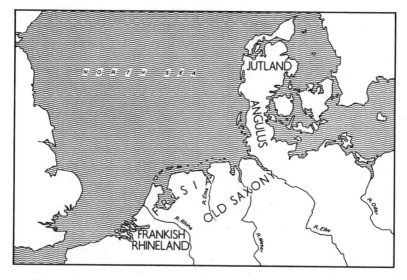

The continental homelands of the Germanic invaders
(From Ralph Arnold, *A Social History of England*)

The Jutes, led by the brothers Hengest[3] and Horsa, came in force and fulfilled their obligation to the Celts, but they decided to stay and settled in Kent and on the Isle of Wight. This first Germanic tribe to occupy part of England seems to have come from the Frankish Rhineland and was closely related to the Frisians, many of whom had joined with the Jutes in their military adventures.

Within a generation, the Saxons came to England in great numbers and settled in Sussex by 477 and in Wessex by 495. The mythic King Arthur from Wales supposedly helped fight off the Saxon advance to the West; in the fifth century, many Celts were driven into Wales and Cornwall and over to Brittany by the Saxons. These Saxons, sea-raiders of the English coasts from the fourth century, migrated from the area between the Rhine and Elbe Rivers.

Within another generation after the Saxon invasions, the Angles from South Denmark had invaded East Anglia and the midland between the Humber and the Thames. By 547 the Angles had set up yet another area of dominance in Northumbria. The tribal divisions of England and the European homes of the Germanic tribes are matters of scholarly opinion and should be understood as probable rather than historical locations. For instance, by the end of the

3. He may be the same Hengest referred to in the Finn Episode in *Beowulf*
(see pp. 19–21) and in the *Fight at
Finnsburg. Ed.*

fifth century both Saxons and Angles inhabited the midland regions
in England. By the seventh century, the Anglo-Saxon heptarchy
constituted the main political divisions of the land later named
after the Angles: Northumbria, Mercia, and East Anglia populated
by the Angles; Kent settled by the Jutes; and Essex, Wessex, and
Sussex controlled by the Saxons. In the seventh century, Northumbria dominated politically; in the eighth century, Mercia; and in
the ninth century, Wessex, first under Egbert (802–39), and then

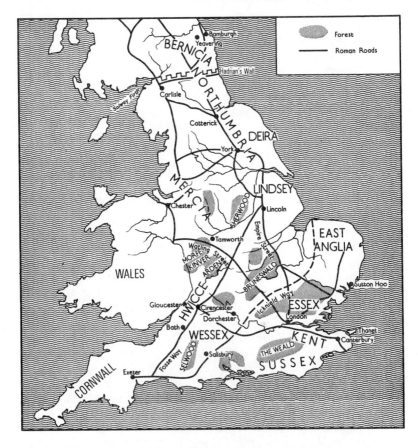

The English kingdoms at the beginning of the seventh century A.D.
(From Ralph Arnold, *A Social History of England*)

under King Alfred, who ruled the West Saxons and hence the heptarchy from 871 to 899.

The name "Anglo-Saxon" originally referred to Saxons in England as distinct from those on the Continent, but by the sixteenth century the term was used in reference to both the peoples and the language of England after the Germanic migration. In 601, Pope Gregory I referred to Ethelbert, the Jutish king, as "Rex Anglorum" ("King of the Angles"), and a century later Bede entitled his work *Historia Ecclesiastica Gentis Anglorum.* By the year 1000, the English people were often called "Angul-cynn" ("race of the Angles"). The word "Englisc" actually predates the term "Englalond" which came into use about 1000.[4]

Christianity in England

The Celts had their first contact with Christianity through the Roman occupation of the third century, before the Germanic invasions. Some of the Celts in the North and West remained Christian even after the Teutons settled in England in the fifth century. Irish missionaries from Iona in the Hebrides, a mission established in the sixth century by St. Columba to convert the Scots, helped to introduce the Northumbrians to Christianity through the work of St. Aidan and his missionaries from 635 to 655.

In 597, Pope Gregory I appointed St. Augustine, a Roman Benedictine monk, to convert the central and southern regions of England to Christianity. With some forty monks, Augustine first arrived in Kent at the reluctant invitation of King Ethelbert, who had married Bertha, a Christian Frankish princess. At the end of the sixth century, King Ethelbert was the strongest overlord in the lands south of the Humber. After Ethelbert granted Augustine some lands in Canterbury, Augustine began his work for which he was later called the "Apostle of the English"; within three months, the king himself became one of Augustine's first English converts to Christianity. By the end of the seventh century, almost all of the English had been converted by missionaries through the efforts of Aidan in the North and of Augustine's monks in the South. For centuries thereafter, the Germanic myths and pagan rituals survived barely beneath the surface of Christian philosophy and theology, with *Wyrd* ("fate, doom") and Providence often scarcely distinguishable.

The "Englisc" Language

The language that the Germanic tribes spoke at the time of their invasions of England sprang from a common language used by the early Teutonic peoples in prehistoric times. By the fifth century, the Angles, Saxons, and Jutes spoke dialects of the same language understandable in large measure by each of the tribes. Old English (OE), as the shared language is called, belongs to the low West Teutonic (Germanic) branch of the Indo-European family of languages. OE is related to the North Teutonic languages (Icelandic and the Scandinavian tongues, Danish, Norwegian, and Swedish), to the East Teutonic (Gothic, now extinct), and to other West Teutonic languages such as Frisian and Franconian. OE, like Latin and Greek, was a highly inflected, synthetic language in which person, number, and tense in verbs, and case, number, and gender in nouns, adjectives, and pronouns were established by adding special endings to words or by making internal changes in words. As is the case with modern German, the major method of word formation in OE was the compounding of base forms with one another or with affixes.

With the exception of place names, the British Celts contributed only a small number of words to OE, the language of their conquerors. The Latin influence upon the Germanic dialects when these tribes were on the Continent amounted to several hundred words. Although Latin contributed over six hundred words to the British Celts, very few of these words found their way from Celtic to OE. The greatest influence of Latin upon OE before the Norman invasion came about coincident with English conversion to Christianity, and with the subsequent introduction of philosophical, theological, liturgical, and administrative vocabulary used by the Roman Church in England. To the tenth century, OE dialects (Northumbrian, Mercian, and West Saxon) only reluctantly and sparingly borrowed from other languages, and even then usually only in vocabulary, with a few important exceptions from the Scandinavian languages.

Literature and Learning

Since the West Saxon dialect became the literary standard of OE in the eighth and ninth centuries, it is the dialect in which the vernacular literature is preserved. When they invaded England, the Germanic tribes apparently did not keep written records, but relied on a strong oral tradition for the transmission of their depository of literary and historical matters to later generations. Not until the conversion of the Anglo-Saxons to Christianity with its use of the Roman alphabet and with its commitment to the preservation of written historical records do we have extant examples of OE vernacular. The earliest OE work extant is a code of laws promulgated by King Ethelbert, the first Christian King of the Jutes, ca.

600. Since nearly all OE works are preserved in copies compiled years after their composition, it is very difficult to ascertain a definite chronology for them and to testify to their authorship with certainty. The earliest and most important Germanic epic, *Beowulf*, was probably composed in the oral tradition at a time roughly contemporaneous with Bede's *Ecclesiastical History* in the first half of the eighth century.

From the end of the seventh century to the close of the eighth, York and Canterbury were the main centers of learning in England. Both Alcuin (735?–804), who established a school in the court of Charlemagne ca. 781, and Venerable Bede, who did his work in Northumbria, were from the school at York. The scholars at Canterbury spent much of their efforts in teaching Latin and Greek. Cædmon, who is our first known English poet, flourished ca. 670 at the Abbey of Whitby. Bede quotes a Latin version of Cædmon's "Hymn" in his *Ecclesiastical History*. *Widsith* also belongs to this early period of OE literature, ca. 650–700; in this poem of less than 150 lines, the scop, who is the "far traveller," describes his visits to famous Germanic kings and praises their generosity in the gifts they gave him in return for his works. The chieftains looked to the poets in the oral tradition for the recording of their heroic deeds, thereby to attain immortality through succeeding generations who would marvel over the exploits of their ancestors.

From these works emerges a portrait of the Germanic tribes not very different from Tacitus' description of the continental Teutons in his *Germania*, written in 98 A.D. The Germanic traditions in the legal payments for offenses (such as the *wergild*, or "man-price," paid by a murderer to the bereaved family), in the composition of the society as a *comitatus*, or brotherhood of men who owed allegiance to a chieftain and expected his benevolence in return, and in the heroic ideal of excellence in kingly behavior form some of the basic tenets of the Old English society from the fifth to the eighth century. Even with this heroic ethic established, however, the atmosphere remains dark and ominous as heroic man struggles against the natural and supernatural forces that are perhaps malevolent or, what is worse, indifferent to his survival, honor, and nobility. Heroic literature, typified by *Beowulf*, at least held out the possibility of the dignity that comes alone from demonstrated skill and courage in struggles engaged in for the manly values of the community.

STANLEY B. GREENFIELD

Nature and Quality of Old English Poetry†

* * *

Almost all of the surviving Old English poetry has been pre-served in four manuscripts, known familiarly as the *Beowulf* MS (Cotton Vitellius A.xv), the Exeter Book, the Junius MS, and the Vercelli MS.[1] The first three reside in England, in the British Museum, the Chapter Library of Exeter Cathedral, and the Bodleian Library at Oxford respectively; the fourth somehow crossed the Alps during the Middle Ages, where it remains to this day in the Cathedral Library at Vercelli * * *. All four manuscripts date from around the year 1000; their dialect is mainly late West Saxon, the language of Ælfric, with an admixture of Anglian and North-umbrian forms that undoubtedly survived as part of the common poetic vocabulary from the earlier centuries. The dates of composi-tion of the poems in these manuscripts, whether of oral or written provenience, cannot be determined with precision; but critics generally agree upon an early period, ranging from the late seventh to the early ninth century, which includes the composition of *Beowulf* and the Cædmonian poems; the period of Cynewulf, ninth century; and a ninth-tenth-century period, which saw the making of *Genesis B, Judith,* and the late battle poems, among others. * * *

The four main manuscript collections of Old English poems, and others containing one to several pieces, offer a variety of poetic genres, from lyric through epic and allegory, from riddles to didactic verses. Some of the poems are exclusively secular in their thought and content, others are devotionally or doctrinally oriented. Some have their roots in Germanic pagan antiquity, some in Christian Latinity. * * *

† Reprinted by permission of New York University Press from Stanley B. Green-field, *A Critical History of Old English Literature,* pp. 78–79. Copyright © 1966 by New York University.

1. Facsimiles have been made of all four * * *. The complete poetic corpus has been edited by G. P. Krapp and E. V. K. Dobbie in *The Anglo-Saxon Poetic Records* (New York, 1931–53) * * *.

E. TALBOT DONALDSON

[Old English Prosody and Cædmon's *Hymn*] †

All the poetry of Old English is in the same verse form. The verse unit is the single line, since rhyme was not used to link one line to another, except very occasionally in late Old English. The organizing device of the line is alliteration, the beginning of several words with the same sound ("Foemen fled"). The Old English alliterative line contains four principal stresses, and is divided into two half-lines of two stresses each by a strong medial caesura, or pause. These two half-lines are linked to each other by the alliteration: at least one of the two stressed words in the first half-line, and usually both of them, begin with the same sound as the first stressed word of the second half-line (the second stressed word is generally non-alliterative). The fourth line of *Beowulf* is an example:

> Oft Scyld Scefing   sceaþena þreatum.

[As can be seen in lines 4, 5, and 8 of Cædmon's *Hymn*, any vowel alliterates with any other vowel.] In addition to the alliteration, the length of the unstressed syllables and their number and pattern are governed by a highly complex set of rules. When sung or intoned— as it was—to the rhythmic strumming of a harp, Old English poetry must have been wonderfully impressive in the dignified, highly formalized way which aptly fits both its subject matter and tone.

Cædmon's *Hymn* is one of the oldest of preserved English poems, having been written between 658 and 680. Bede, the great cleric of Old English times, tells the story of its composition in his *Ecclesiastical History of the English People* (completed in 731). Cædmon, a Northumbrian layman, had all his life felt himself incompetent in the art of verse, and when, according to the custom that was used at feasts, the harp was passed around the table so that each guest might entertain the others with a song, Cædmon always found a pretext to take himself from the table before the harp reached him. One night when he had thus avoided singing, he fell asleep in the stable where he had gone to tend the animals. He dreamed that someone came to him and said: "Cædmon, sing me something," and when Cædmon excused himself, the other

† Adapted from *The Norton Anthology of English Literature*, M. H. Abrams and others, eds., 3rd ed. (New York: W. W. Norton & Co., Inc., 1974), I, 18, 21–22. Copyright © 1974, 1968, 1962 by W. W. Norton & Co., Inc. Reprinted by permission of the publisher. For a more detailed discussion of Old English prosody see J. R. R. Tolkien's classic Prefatory Remarks to *Beowulf and the Finnesburg Fragment*, John R. Clark Hall, trans., ed. with notes and an introduction by C. L. Wrenn (London: Allen & Unwin, 1950).

insisted that he sing, directing him to celebrate the beginning of created things. Cædmon at once sang the *Hymn*. On waking, he remembered his verses; and thereafter, Bede tells us, he was able to express any given sacred topic in excellent poetry after only a few hours of work. He became a monk and devoted his life to the composition of Christian verse, but none of the religious poetry in Old English that has been preserved may surely be ascribed to him except his first short work.

[Cædmon's *Hymn* is an early example of the revolutionary transformation that took place as Germanic verse form and vocabulary were turned to Christian usage after the conversion of the Anglo-Saxons. Cædmon seems to have been the first to use this form for Christian subjects, and to use words like *Weard* ("Guardian"), *Driht* ("Lord"), and *Frea* ("Ruler") in a Christian rather than earthly connotation. These and words like them also appear frequently in the Christian sense in *Beowulf*, most likely as a result of the influence of Cædmon and his poetic followers. Perhaps the *Beowulf*-poet had Cædmon's *Hymn* in mind when he made the

Cædmon's *Hymn*

Nu sculon herigean heofonrices Weard,
Now we must praise *heaven-kingdom's Guardian,*

Meotodes meahte and his modgeþanc,
the Creator's might *and his mind-plans,*

weorc Wuldor-Fæder, swa he wundra gehwæs,
the work of the Glory-Father, *when he of wonders of every one,*

ece Drihten, or onstealde.
eternal Lord, *the beginning established.*[1]

He ærest sceop ielda[2] bearnum
He first created *for men's sons*

heofon to hrofe, halig Scyppend;
heaven as a roof, *holy Creator;*

ða middangeard, moncynnes Weard,
then middle-earth, *mankind's Guardian,*

ece Drihten, æfter teode
eternal Lord, *afterwards made—*

firum foldan Frea ælmihtig.
for men earth, *Master almighty.*

1. I.e., "established the beginning of every one of wonders."
2. The later manuscript copies read *eorþan*, "earth," for *ælda* (West Saxon *ielda*), "men's."

scop at Hrothgar's court sing of the creation of the world (ll.
90–98). *Ed.*]

The poem is given here in a West Saxon form with a literal
interlinear translation. In Old English spelling, *æ* (as in Cædmon's
name and line 3) is a vowel symbol that has not survived; it represented both a short *a* sound and a long open *e* sound. *þ* (line 2)
and *ð* both represented the sound *th*. The large space in the middle
of the line indicates the caesura.

E. G. STANLEY

[Manuscript—Sources—Audience] †

* * *

The evidence of the Anglo-Saxons' own interest in the poem lies
chiefly in the manuscript itself. It is of the late tenth or early
eleventh century, a long time after the composition of the poem,
which is usually thought to have taken place no later than the
eighth century. Several copyings (probably made in different parts
of England where different dialects of Old English were spoken)
lie between the only extant manuscript and the author's original.
Of course, we cannot be sure what in each case made them copy
the poem; as far as the extant manuscript is concerned, however, it
seems that a finer sense of its value as poetry was less to the fore
than its associations with monsters. The manuscript contains also
some prose texts. One of them is a life of a dog-headed St.
Christopher, in the course of which we learn that the saint was
twelve fathoms tall—twelve cubits, or roughly eighteen feet, in
the Latin source—and he is treated and behaves accordingly.
Another text in the manuscript is about *The Wonders of the East*;
the monsters there are so numerous and so varied that strangely
tall men are among the lesser marvels, for: 'There are dragons born
which are a hundred and fifty feet long. They are as big as great
stone pillars. On account of the size of those dragons no man can
easily travel into that land'.[1] A third text in the manuscript, *Letter
of Alexander the Great to Aristotle*, has its monsters too; though
it is disappointing to find that where the Old English text has a
great battle between men and water monsters, *nicras*, the Latin
source reads something like *hippopotami* for the Old English
nicras.

† From *Continuations and Beginnings:
Studies in Old English Literature*, Eric
Gerald Stanley, ed. (London: Thomas
Nelson & Sons, Ltd., 1966), pp. 105–7,
134–36, 139–40. Reprinted by permission
of the publishers.

1. * * * EETS os 161, 59. [The OE is
omitted; Stanley's translation has been
moved from this note into the body of
the essay.]

Now a dragon and water monsters belong to the Beowulf story, and in England Beowulf's king, Hygelac of the Geats, was renowned because he was exceptionally tall. In a book, probably roughly contemporary with *Beowulf*, called *Liber Monstrorum*; or, *De Monstris et de Belluis* ('Book of Monsters; or, Of Monsters and Wild Beasts') the following passage occurs: 'And there are monsters of wonderful size; such as King Higlacus who ruled the Getæ and was killed by the Franks, whom from his twelfth year no horse could carry. His bones are preserved on an island in the Rhine, where it flows forth into the ocean, and are shown to those who come from afar as a miracle.'[2] It has been shown that the *Liber Monstrorum* is English in origin. It preserves a reasonably good form of Hygelac's name and a form of the name of his people, the Geats, not remembered otherwise (as far as our evidence goes) on the Continent at that time. It is not an unreasonable speculation to think it possible that the centre which produced the *Liber Monstrorum* would have been interested in the subject-matter of *Beowulf*; the direction of that interest runs parallel with that shown by those who put together * * * the material in our *Beowulf* Manuscript. A dragon, monsters, strangely tall men, these excited the Anglo-Saxons and seem to have done so over a long period. Nothing more literary than that is needed to explain the preservation of the poem.

* * *

We know, merely through the poet's choice of subject, that he resembles the ideal minstrel whom he presents to us on two occasions in this, that he too delights in the exercise of a well-stored memory deeply imbued with traditions, enshrined also in some of the genealogies of the Anglo-Saxons by which their kings appear as descendants of Scyld. The genealogies contain some of the Danish names in the poem: Beow,[3] Scyld, Sceaf, and Heremod. It seems likely that before these names, all appearing as ancestors of Woden,[4] were incorporated in the genealogies. Woden must have been euhemerised (as he is explicitly in the *Chronicle* of Æthelweard, almost certainly a member of the West Saxon royal house living in the tenth century). This act of euhemerisation is clear evidence that members of the royal families took these genealogies seriously, even in Christian times. The extension of the genealogies beyond Woden, though presumably quite unhistorical, shows that they wished to associate these figures, of whom they knew (*Beowulf*

2. Quoted from Dorothy Whitelock, *The Audience of Beowulf*, p. 46. Professor Whitelock's discussion of the relationship between the *Liber Monstrorum* and *Beowulf* is of fundamental importance in this connection.

3. For the view that the name *Beowulf* at lines 18 and 53 is probably an error for *Beow* see A. J. Bliss, *The Metre of Beowulf*, 1958, p. 58, as well as the editions.

4. God of death and battle, called Wodan in Germanic and Odin in Norse mythology. *Ed.*

is witness to that), with their own royal dynasties. *Beowulf* could well have been written late enough for at least some of the Danes mentioned in the poem to have been regarded by the poet and his audience as ancestors of Anglo-Saxon kings in England.[5]

It is likely that the rulers who knew of their ancient descent were stirred by the memory of glorious deeds of those men from whom they were descended. The use to which the *Anglo-Saxon Chronicle* puts Offa's genealogy in the annal for the year of his accession (in 757) seems to indicate a deliberate exploitation of the lists of kings going back to Woden as contributing to the glorification of Offa. If, as is natural, Anglo-Saxon rulers delighted in the ancient nobility of their dynasty, their retainers must have been aware of these traditions also. The beginning of the poem with its piece of Danish history is relevant to England, to English kings and therefore to their retainers, as much as the Trojan origins of the British dynasty relevantly introduce poems, like *Sir Gawain and the Green Knight*, on British themes.

There is evidence that there was in Anglo-Saxon England a considerable knowledge of the legends of the Germanic heroic age. Interest in these legends is not likely to have been swiftly reduced when Christianity came, and the poet of *Beowulf* was able to rely on his audience's familiarity with the ancient traditions to such an extent that he introduced allusive references and not fully coherent accounts of feuds, apparently without needing to fear that he would not be understood. The Finn Episode (lines 1063–1159) could not be understood by an audience not already familiar with the facts; perhaps the original audience was familiar with these events because (if the Hengest of the Episode was identified with the Hengest of the Anglo-Saxon Settlement) the feud was held to belong to proto-Kentish history. The wars between the Geats and the Swedes are not told by the poet in chronological sequence, but allusively and selectively. In lines 2177–89, praise of Beowulf and a reference to his ignominious youth encloses an allusion to Heremod, who had been trusted in his youth: change came to both of them. The allusion is missed by anyone who fails to seize on Heremod as one pattern of evil in a king.

As the poet's ideal minstrel relates Beowulf's merit, gained from present exploits in Denmark, to the merit of past figures, Sigemund and Heremod, so the poet analyses a Christian ideal, appropriate to the English audience for whom he is writing, in terms of an ideal figure of the past: Beowulf. The language which he uses, the traditional poetic vocabulary of the Anglo-Saxons, with many formulas expected by the audience to whom no other language seemed fit

5. For a comprehensive and fundamental account of the genealogies, see K. Sisam, *PBA*, 39 (1953), 287–348.

for poetry, has led the poet to seek his material outside Christian story in the Germanic traditions to which his language had had its first, its most direct application. His habit of mind which finds expression in an annexive syntax, such as goes well with the alliterative metre, is associative. He does not always make explicit how his associations are linked to his main theme, no more than the minstrel does in Heorot who fails to make explicit why in singing the praise of Beowulf he should recall what he heard tell of Sigemund's exploits and the tyranny of Heremod.

* * *

We have no means of telling who the poet's first audience was: perhaps in some royal hall, where the lord and his men still delighted in the ancient nobility of the dynasty; or perhaps in some monastery to which a king retired, as we know King Sigeberht of East Anglia did when he gave up his throne in the second quarter of the seventh century, and as King Ethelred of Mercia did in 704, and Ceolwulf of Northumbria in 737, and Eadberht of Northumbria in 758. Kings like these proved by their abdication that they thought the pagan glory of pledging in the hall, of victory in the field, of treasure-giving and of loyalty to an earthly throne, a vain ideal. A poet may have written a poem like *Beowulf* for one of many courts, to teach a king wisdom, or for some monastery whose refectory contained a man descended from a line of Spear-Danes and not contemptuous of that ancestry. It is only a guess; but that is the kind of original audience that would have heard *Beowulf* with understanding.

DOROTHY WHITELOCK

[Time and Milieu of *Beowulf*'s Composition]†

* * *

A little before the year 700 all England had been won, nominally, to Christianity, but it is to the eighth century that one must assign much of the steady, unspectacular advance which brought a deeper knowledge of the faith to the ordinary layfolk all over the land, by the gradual establishment of parish churches and the provision of a permanent income for the Church. Missionary zeal in the eighth century was free to turn abroad, and the upper classes, at any rate, over all England followed the work of the missionaries on the Continent with great interest. The people of Northumbria appear

† From *The Audience of Beowulf* (1951), pp. 99–105, by permission of the Clarendon Press, Oxford.

to have felt a particular responsibility for the mission to the
Frisians, which had been begun in the late seventh century by the
Northumbrian Willibrord, and later for that to the Old Saxons. It
was to York that young Frisians came to be educated in the mid-
eighth century, and there also a bishop for the Old Saxons, called
Aluberht, was consecrated in 767; a Northumbrian synod, under
King Alhred, was responsible for sending Willehad, the later
missionary to the Old Saxons, to Frisia between 766 and 774. Even
in political concerns, the picture of unrelieved gloom in Northumbria in the eighth century can be overdrawn. It was, in fact, to
the reign of Eadberht Eating (737–58) that later Northumbrian
writers looked back as a golden age;[1] and even later, although civil
wars between rival claimants to the throne were frequent, and
deeds of treachery and violence no rarity, there were reigns in
which kings ruled well, paying due attention to spiritual concerns.
A ninth-century Latin poem, which tells the history of a Northumbrian monastery, by no means looks back on the eighth century
as solely a period of strife and disorder; on the contrary, it speaks
of the prosperity of this house and of the great gifts it received from
Northumbrian noblemen.[2] As regards scholarship, Northumbria
continued to be regarded as one of the leading centres in Europe.
It has not hitherto been noted that it was in touch with the
Frankish court as early as the reign of Eadberht Eating, to whom
King Pippin sent letters and gifts;[3] and the bond with the Frankish
kingdom was naturally much strengthened after the Northumbrian
scholar, Alcuin, went on Charles the Great's invitation to take
charge of his palace school and direct his educational reforms.

It is not surprising, therefore, that Carolingian influence should
become visible in Northumbrian art, eventually culminating in the
great works such as the Easby and Rothbury crosses. Art historians
are inclined to date these works at about the extreme limit of the
period I would allow for *Beowulf*, but Dr. Kendrick admits that the
period which saw, in his words, 'nothing less than a re-awakening
of the classically conceived sculptural art' is only 'somewhat vaguely
centered upon the year 800.'[4] At least we can see that the Northumbrians of the end of the eighth century were not so sunk in
political disturbances as to be totally uninterested in other matters,
but were alive to artistic influences, and quick to respond to an
impetus from outside. Nor was art dead in the intervening period,
which separates the greatest work of the Hiberno-Saxon style, as

1. See Alcuin, *Carmen de Sanctis Ebora-*
censis Ecclesiae, ll. 1247–86; *Historia*
Dunelmensis Ecclesiae, ed. T. Arnold,
Symeonis Monachi Opera [*Omnia*, R.S.
(1882)], i. 47–49.
2. *Carmen Æðelwulfi*, ed. T. Arnold,

op. cit., i. 267–94, especially chaps. 15,
20.
3. *Historia Dunelmensis Ecclesiae*, loc.
cit..
4. T. D. Kendrick, *Anglo-Saxon Art to*
A.D. 900 (London, 1938), pp. 152, 158.

at Bewcastle and Ruthwell, from the masterpieces in the new manner; impressive work of the traditional school was still being produced. Acca's cross, if it is Acca's cross, must be dated about 740, and illuminated manuscripts like the Durham Cassiodorus and the Echternach Gospels are usually assigned to the middle of this century. Moreover, Northumbria maintained its contacts with the Celtic lands; intercourse with Ireland was facilitated by the continuance of an Anglo-Saxon see at Inishboffin off the coast of Mayo, and links with Iona were not permanently disrupted by the decision of the Synod of Whitby on the Easter question in 663. One learns incidentally of the visit of an abbot of Iona to Ripon in the middle of the eighth century.[5] I doubt whether, for the purpose of dating *Beowulf*, one can build securely on Professor Girvan's claim that 680–700 'was the period when Northumbria was at the height of its greatness politically and artistically; it was also the period when it was on the edge of decline.'[6] The decline was not so marked and so continuous as to make the later production of a great poem impossible, or even unlikely.

There is, however, no good reason for assigning the poem to Northumbria, and perhaps, if we had as much evidence relating to the great age of Mercia as we have for the great age of Northumbria, 'the age of Bede' would lose some of its appeal for *Beowulf* scholars. But there is no Mercian chronicle, there is no biographer of Æthelbald or of Offa, and the laws of the latter king, known to King Alfred and perhaps alluded to by Alcuin when he speaks of 'the good, moderate and chaste customs which Offa of blessed memory established,'[7] have perished. Yet, in spite of the unsatisfactory nature of the evidence, enough can be learnt from charters and the correspondence with the missionaries to show that Mercia had religious houses that were centres of learning, and that its people were interested in the spread of the Christian faith on the Continent. The missionary Lul asks for a rare book from a bishop of Worcester;[8] Alcuin sends a scholar to King Offa at his request,[9] and corresponds with Mercian noblemen and ladies. Politically, as we have seen, Mercia was the leading kingdom in the eighth century, and in direct contact with the court of Charles the Great. Its achievements included not only the lost laws of Offa, but also that impressive monument, Offa's Dyke.

The evidence for the condition of the other English kingdoms is not very full, but it can be seen that all shared in the interest in

5. A note in the Chartres manuscript of the *Historia Brittonum*. See F. Lot, *Nennius et l'Historia Brittonum* (Bibliothèque de l'École des Hautes Études, fasc. 263, 1934), p. 29.
6. *Beowulf and the Seventh Century* [London: Methuen, 1935], p. 25.

7. *Alcuini Epistolae* [ed. Dümmler (Mon. Germ. Hist., Epistolae Karolini Aevi, ii)], p. 180.
8. *S. Bonifatii et Lullii Epistolae* [ed. M. Tangl (Mon. Germ. Hist., Epistolae Selectae, i)], p. 245.
9. *Alcuini Epistolae*, p. 107.

foreign missions and the increased contact with the Continent which these occasioned. Kent, containing the metropolitan see, was on this account and by its position on the shortest cross-Channel route much exposed to influence from abroad. It possessed, at Canterbury, a school with a long tradition behind it, and to this centre is attributed a style of manuscript illumination at about the middle of the eighth century, of which the Golden Gospels of Stockholm and the Vespasian Psalter are the best known examples. It is a style which combines classical feeling and some Merovingian motifs with the interlace and trumpet-patterns typical of the Hiberno-Saxon art of the North, thus illustrating in the sphere of art that political barriers did not prevent intercourse between the various kingdoms of the Heptarchy. We know from the references in letters to and from Boniface and Lul that book-production went on in the eighth century in the other southern kingdoms; their products are probably indistinguishable from those of Canterbury. Wessex was able to supply a number of well-educated men and women to the German missions in the early and mid-eighth century, and between 755 and 766, Bishop Cyneheard of Winchester asked his kinsman, the missionary Lul, to send him from the Continent any books he came across which Winchester had not already got, including books of secular knowledge, especially those on medical matters.[1] As for East Anglia, we know at least that Cuthwine, bishop of Dunwich from 716 to 731, was a collector of illuminated manuscripts,[2] and that King Ælfwald, who died in 749, commissioned Felix to write the Latin *Life of St. Guthlac*. In short, it would be unsafe to argue that any part of England was in the eighth century insufficiently advanced in intellectual attainments for a sophisticated poem like *Beowulf* to have been composed there and appreciated.

KEMP MALONE

[The Old English *Scop* and *Widsith*] †

* * *

At an early date Germanic kings began to keep professional poets, with functions not wholly unlike those of the poet laureate or official poet of later times. Among the English a court poet was

1. *S. Bonifatii et Lullii Epistolae*, pp. 246 f.
2. W. Levison, *England and the Continent in the Eighth Century* [London: Oxford University Press, 1946], p. 133.
† From Kemp Malone, "The Old Tradition: Courtly Poetry," in Albert C. Baugh, ed., *A Literary History of England*, 2nd ed., pp. 45–47, © 1967. Reprinted by permission of Prentice-Hall, Inc., Englewood Cliffs, N. J., and Routledge & Kegan Paul, Ltd.

called a *scop* or *gleeman*.[1] We are lucky enough to have in *Widsith* an early English poem on the scop.[2] From this poem (named after its hero) we learn something of the career and the repertory of an ideal gleeman, creature of a seventh-century poet's fancy.[3] The poem consists of a prologue (9 lines), a speech by Widsith (125 lines), and an epilogue (9 lines). The speech is built up round three old thulas[4] and a thula-fragment (47 lines in all * * *), which the author puts in his hero's mouth; to these are added 78 lines of the author's own composition. Structurally, the speech falls into five parts: an introduction, three fits or main divisions, and a conclusion. Each fit comprises (1) a thula and (2) passages added by the author.[5] The thulas were put in Widsith's mouth to bring out his knowledge of history, ethnology, and heroic story. Several of the added passages serve the same purpose. Other passages bring out the hero's professional experience and first-hand information (as do the second and third thulas); more particularly, they emphasize his success in his chosen calling. Thus, we are told of his professional performances: "When Scilling and I, with sure voice, as one,/ made music, sang before our mighty lord,/ the sound of harp and song rang out;/ then many a man, mindful of splendor,/ those who well could know, with words spoke and said/ that they never heard a nobler song" (lines 103–8). Even the critics thought highly of Widsith's art! From this passage we learn, incidentally, that the scop sang his poems to the accompaniment of the harp. Whether Scilling was Widsith's harpist or a fellow scop (in which case the performance was a duet) we cannot tell; it has even been conjectured, indeed, that Scilling was the name of Widsith's harp.[6]

1. ["Scop," from OE *scieppan*, "to create, form, shape," hence a "poet"; "gleeman," from OE *gleo-man*, "joyman, gleeman, musician, minstrel." Most contemporary scholars seem to prefer the term "scop," which includes both the ideas of poet and performer.] See L. F. Anderson, *The Anglo-Saxon Scop* (Toronto, 1903).

2. Recent edition: K. Malone, *Widsith* (1936) [and more recently *Anglistica*, 13 (Copenhagen, 1963)]. See also Lascelles Abercrombie, "*Widsith* as Art," *Sewanee Rev.*, 46 (1938), 124–28. The edition of R. W. Chambers (*Widsith*, Cambridge, 1912) will always remain the best presentation of nineteenth-century continental Widsithian scholarship. This scholarship is now largely out of date, because of the great advances made during the present century in our understanding of the poem; for crucial particulars see K. Malone, *JEGP*, 38 (1939), 226–28; 43 (1944), 451; and 45 (1946), 147–52. But Chambers' book still has more than historical interest.

3. For recent speculations about the author of *Widsith*, see especially W. H. French, *PMLA*, 60 (1945), 623–30.

4. Thula: a metrical list of names. Perhaps the earliest remaining poem in any modern language, *Widsith* names many of the tribes and kings of *Beowulf*. Mentioned are Eormenric the Goth, the Franks, Breca the Bronding, Finn the Frisian, Hnaef the Hocing, the Wylfings, Ongentheow the Swede, the Hetware, Offa the Angle (who is especially praised), Hama, the Geats, the South-Danes, and Heorot itself. It also tells us that Hrothgar and his nephew Hrothulf defeated Ingeld and the Heatho-Bards at Heorot, which strife Beowulf predicts in general terms on pp. 35–36 of our text. *Ed.*

5. For a fuller analysis, see K. Malone, *ELH*, 5 (1938), 49–66.

6. W. J. Sedgefield, *MLR*, 26 (1931), 75. In humbler circles the performer played his own accompaniment, as we learn from Bede's story of Cædmon.

The author makes it clear that his hero was composer as well as performer (though he would hardly have understood the distinction we make between these offices). Widsith sings in mead-hall about his own experiences (lines 54–56), and he composes and sings a poem in praise of his patroness, Queen Ealhhild (lines 99–102). We may safely presume that an actual scop would do as much for the kings who made him welcome at their courts and gave him gifts. The relationship between a scop and his royal patron comes out in the epilogue of our poem:[7] "As gleemen go, guided by fortune,/ as they pass from place to place among men,/ their wants they tell, speak the word of thanks,/ south or north find someone always/ full of song-lore, free in giving,/ who is fain to heighten his favor with the worthy,/ do noble deeds, till his day is ended,/ life and light together; below he wins praise,/ he leaves under heaven a lasting fame" (lines 135–43). The word of thanks is to be taken as a poem in honor of the prince, whose fame could hardly have been expected to last unless celebrated in song; poetry was then the only historical record. We conclude that the scop had the important function of immortalizing his patron by singing his praises. These poems of praise, handed down by word of mouth, and making part of the repertory of many a gleeman, were meant to keep the prince's name and deeds alive in the minds of men forever.

But the scop had another function, older and even more important: that of entertainer. In *Beowulf* we get descriptions of the entertainment. From these we gather that a gleeman's performance was short, and made part of a celebration which included amusements of other kinds. Thus, the royal scop sang one morning out of doors, in an interval between horse-races (864–918); the day before, he had sung at a feast in the hall (489–98). A given song might deal with contemporaries (witness the gleeman who celebrated, the morning after the deed, Beowulf's triumph over Grendel), or it might deal with figures of the past. But always, so far as we know, its theme was high and its tone earnest. The entertainment which the scop had to offer made demands on the audience; it could not be enjoyed without keen participation in thought and feeling; there was little about it restful or relaxing. The scop held his hearers because he and they were at one: schooled and bound in the traditions of a poetry that gave voice to their deepest loyalties and highest resolves. The theme that moved them most was the theme of sacrifice, dominant in the old poems and

7. The metrical translations of *Widsith* 103–8 and 135–43 are taken, by permission, from K. Malone, *Ten Old English* *Poems* (Baltimore: Johns Hopkins Press) [copyright © 1941 by The Johns Hopkins University Press].

strong in the life which these poems reflected and glorified. King and dright[8] made a company of warriors held together by the bond of sacrificial friendship. The king shared his goods with the dright and took them into his very household; the dright shielded him with their bodies on the field of battle, and if he fell they fought on, to victory or to death, deeming it base to give ground or flee when their lord lay slain. The famous speech of Byrhtwold in *Maldon* tells us more than pages of exposition could:[9] "Thought shall be the harder, heart the keener,/ mood shall be the more, as our might lessens./ Here lies our earl, all hewn to earth,/ the good one, on the ground. He will regret it always,/ the one who thinks to turn from this war-play now./ My life has been long. Leave I will not,/ but beside my lord I will sink to earth,/ I am minded to die by the man so dear" (lines 312–19). But the theme of sacrifice need not take the form which it takes in *Maldon*. And other themes might be used, as we have seen. Whatever the theme, the old poems had strength in them to stir the heart and steel the mood. The scop sang of heroes and called his hearers to the heroic life. He held out no false hopes: heroism leads to hardship, wounds, and death. But though all must go down in defeat at last, the fight is worth making: the hero may hope for a good name among men. The value set upon the esteem of others, and in particular upon fame, marks this philosophy social and secular (heathen is hardly the word). The gleemen who taught it in song were upholding the traditional morality of the English people, a way of life known to us from the pages of Tacitus. The entertainment that the scops gave was *ei blot for lyst*.[1] The old poems, and the new ones composed in the same spirit, kept alive for hundreds of years after the conversion to Christianity the old customs, conventions, and ideals of conduct. In so doing they did not stand alone, of course; many other things in English life made for conservatism. But they had a great and worthy part to play in the preservation of the nobler features of our Germanic heritage. It must not be thought, however, that the scops were conservators and nothing more. It was they who made the important stylistic shift from pre-classical to classical; the clerics who produced most of the classical poetry extant simply carried on and elaborated a style the basic features of which had already been set by the scops.

* * *

---

8. Comitatus, body of retainers.
9. From K. Malone, *Ten Old English Poems* (Baltimore: Johns Hopkins Press) [copyright © 1941 by The Johns Hopkins University Press], by permission.
1. "Not merely for pleasure," the old motto of the Royal Theatre in Copenhagen.

FR. KLAEBER

Genesis of the Poem†

* * *

In discussing this highly problematic subject we confine ourselves in the main to outlining what seems the most probable course in the development of the story-material in our epic poem.

1. That the themes of the main story, i.e., the contest with the Grendel race and the fight with the dragon, are of direct Scandinavian provenience, may be regarded as practically certain. The same origin is to be assigned to the distinctly historical episodes of the Swedish-Geatish wars of which no other traces can be found in England.

2. Of the episodic matter introduced into the first part, the allusions to the Germanic legends of *Eormenric* and *Hama*[1] as well as of *Weland*[2] are drawn from the ancient heroic lore brought over by the Anglo-Saxons from their continental home. The *Finn* legend of Ingvaeonic [early Norse] associations reached England through the same channels of popular transmission. Whether old Frisian lays were used as the immediate source of the Beowulfian episode is somewhat doubtful on account of the markedly Danish point of view which distinguishes the Episode even more than the Fragment.[3] That tales of *Breca*, chief of the *Brondingas*, were included in the repertory of the Anglo-Saxon *scop*, is possibly to be inferred from the allusion, *Wids[ið]* 25 (cp. l. 63: *mid Heaþo-Reamum*), but the brilliant elaboration of the story and its connection with the life of the great epic hero must be attributed to the author himself.[4] Ancient North German tradition was brought into relation with Danish matters in the story of *Scyld Scefing*.[5] Danish legends form the direct basis of the *Heremod* episodes[6] and possibly even the *Sigemund* allusion.[7] That the tragedy of the Heaðo-Bard feud and the glory of Hroðgar, Hroðulf, and the fair hall Heorot were celebrated themes of Anglo-Saxon song, may be concluded from the references in *Widsið*, but the form in which the dynastic element is introduced so as to serve as historical setting * * * make[s] it appear probable that ancient popular tradition was reinforced by versions emanating directly from Denmark.

† Reprinted by permission of the publisher, from Fr. Klaeber, *Beowulf*, 3rd ed. (Lexington, Mass.: D. C. Heath & Co., 1950), pp. cxiii–cxviii.
1. Ll. 1197–1201. *Ed.*
2. L. 455. *Ed.*
3. Cf. Introd. to *The Fight at Finnsburg*
[Klaeber, pp. 231–38; see also Stanley B. Greenfield ("The Finn Episode and Its Parallel") in our text].
4. Ll. 499 ff. *Ed.*
5. Ll. 4–52. *Ed.*
6. Ll. 901–15. *Ed.*
7. Ll. 875–900. *Ed.*

A specific Frisian source has been urged for the story of Hyge-lac's disastrous Viking expedition of which Scandinavian sources betray no definite knowledge.[8] A genuine Anglo-Saxon, or rather Angle, legend is contained in the episode of Offa and his strong-minded queen.[9]

3. There is no evidence to show that 'a Beowulf legend,' i.e., a legend centering in Beowulf and embodying the substance of the epic account, had gradually grown up out of popular stories that had been brought over to England by the migrating Angles. Cer-tainly, we cannot, as in the case of the *Nibelungenlied,* trace definite earlier stages and follow up step by step the unfolding of the literary product. * * *

* * *

4. Evidently, we cannot entertain the notion that there was in existence even an approximately complete Scandinavian original ready to be put into Anglo-Saxon verse. If nothing else, the style and tone of *Beowulf* would disprove it, since they are utterly unlike anything to be expected in early Scandinavian poetry. But a number of lays * * * dealing with a variety of subjects became known in England, and, with the comparatively slight differences between the two languages in those times, could be easily mastered and turned to account by an Anglo-Saxon poet. We may well imagine, e.g., that the Englishman knew such a lay or two on the slaying of Grendel and his mother, another one on the dragon adventure, besides, at any rate, two Danish (originally Geatish) poems on the warlike encounters between Geats and Swedes leading up to the fall of Ongenþeow and Onela respectively.

Whether the picture of the life of the times discloses any traces of Scandinavian originals is a fascinating query that can be answered only in very general and tentative terms. An enthusiastic archæol-ogist[1] set up the claim that a good deal of the original cultural background had been retained in the Old English poem, as shown, e.g., by the helmets and swords described in *Beowulf* which appear to match exactly those used in the Northern countries in the period between A.D. 550 and 650. Again, it would not be surprising if Norse accounts of heathen obsequies had inspired the brilliant funeral scene at the close of the poem, ll. 3137 ff. * * * But, on the whole, it is well to bear in mind that Anglo-Saxon and Scandinavian conditions of life were too much alike to admit of drawing a clear line of division in our study of Beowulfian antiquities. Certain features, however, can be mentioned that are plainly indicative of English civilization, such as the institution

8. See Sarrazin Käd. 90 ff. [Klaeber, p. cxxxvii, 16, (3)] * * *.

9. Ll. 1931–62. *Ed.*

1. Stjerna, L 9.39 [Klaeber, p. clxxix].

of the *witan*,[2] the use of the harp, the vaulted stone chamber [of the dragon's barrow, formed in a similar way to early English and Irish stone graves] * * * (2717 ff.), the paved street [in the Roman fashion, trod by Beowulf and his men on the way to Heorot] (320, cp. 725), and, above all, of course, the high degree of gentleness, courtesy, and spiritual refinement.

* * *

5. The author's part in the production of the poem was vastly more than that of an adapter or editor. It was he who combined the Grendel stories with the dragon narrative and added, as a connecting link, the account of Beowulf's return [to Hygelac's Geatish court], in short, conceived the plan of an extensive epic poem with a great and noble hero as the central figure. Various modifications of the original legends were thus naturally introduced.[3] * * * Leisurely elaboration and expansion by means of miscellaneous episodic matter became important factors in the retelling of the original stories.[4] Hand in hand with such fashioning of the legends into a poem of epic proportions went a spiritualizing and Christianizing process.[5] A strong element of moralization was mingled with the narrative. The characters became more refined, the sentiment softened, the ethics ennobled. Beowulf rose to the rank of a truly ideal hero, and his contests were viewed in the light of a struggle between the powers of good and evil,[6] thus assuming a new weight and dignity which made them appear a fit subject for the main narrative theme.

That the idea of creating an epic poem on a comparatively large scale was suggested to the author, directly or indirectly, by classic models is more than an idle guess, though incontrovertible proof is difficult to obtain. In any event, it is clear that a biblical poem like the Old English *Genesis* paraphrase, consisting of a loose series of separate stories, could not possibly have served as a pattern. Whether there was any real epic among the lost poems of the Anglo-Saxon period we have no means of ascertaining.[7]

The question of the influence of the *Æneid* has received a good

2. I.e., a king's council; Finn listens to his in making peace with Hengest, *Beowulf*, p. 20. *Ed.*
3. The names of Hygd and Unferð were perhaps coined by the poet himself.
4. See Adrien Bonjour, *The Digressions in Beowulf* (Oxford: Blackwell, 1965). *Ed.*
5. See F. A. Blackburn, "The Christian Coloring in the *Beowulf*," *PMLA*, 12 (1897), 205–25; rpt. in *An Anthology of Beowulf Criticism* (hereafter *ABC*),

ed. Lewis E. Nicholson (Notre Dame, Ind.: University of Notre Dame Press, 1963), pp. 1–21; see also Fr. Klaeber, "The Christian Coloring," in our text. *Ed.*
6. See M. B. McNamee, "*Beowulf*—An Alegory of Salvation?" *JEGP*, 59 (April 1960), 190–207 (rpt. in *ABC*, pp. 331–52), and the Kaske, Goldsmith, and Lee selections in our text. *Ed.*
7. The *Waldere* fragments, of course, show epic proportions.

deal of attention from scholars.[8] There is assuredly no lack of parallels calling for examination. * * * In fact, surprisingly large lists of analogies have been drawn up, and it is to be granted that certain verbal agreements look like instances of imitation on the part of the Anglo-Saxon poet.

The great popularity of the *Æneid* in Ireland should be noted in this connection. The even larger claim that the author derived some of his subject-matter from Vergil is, of course, much more difficult to establish. The most important influence to be recognized is, after all, the new conception of a true epic poem which the Anglo-Saxon, very likely, learned from the Roman classic.

* * *

R. W. CHAMBERS

[A Scandinavian Parallel—The *Grettis Saga*] †

The *Grettis Saga* tells the adventures of the most famous of all Icelandic outlaws, Grettir the strong. As to the historic existence of Grettir there is no doubt: we can even date the main events of his life, in spite of chronological inconsistencies, with some precision. But between the year 1031, when he was killed, and the latter half of the thirteenth century, when his saga took form, many fictitious episodes, derived from folk-lore, had woven themselves around his name. Of these, one bears a great, if possibly accidental, likeness to the Grendel story: the second is emphatically and unmistakably the same story as that of Grendel and his mother. In the first, Grettir stops at a farm house which is haunted by Glam, a ghost of monstrous stature. Grettir awaits his attack alone, but, like Beowulf, lying down. Glam's entry and onset resemble those of Grendel: when Grettir closes with him he tries to get out. They wrestle the length of the hall, and break all before them. Grettir supports himself against anything that will give him foothold, but for all his efforts he is dragged as far as the door. There he suddenly changes his tactics, and throws his whole weight upon his adversary. The

8. See W. W. Lawrence, *Beowulf and Epic Tradition* (Cambridge, Mass.: Harvard University Press, 1928), and Tom Burns Haber, *A Comparative Study of the Beowulf and the Aeneid* (Princeton: Princeton University Press, 1931); for a contrasting view, see Larry D. Benson, "The Originality of *Beowulf*," *Harvard English Studies*, I (1970), 1–43. *Ed.*
† Reprinted from *Beowulf: An Intro-* duction, by R. W. Chambers, 3rd ed. with Supplement by C. L. Wrenn (Cambridge, 1963), pp. 48–53, by permission of Cambridge University Press. For the Bothvar Bjarki parallel and other folk elements, see pp. 54–68, 142–46, 163–82, and Wrenn, 291–304. For modern English versions, see S. N. Garmonsway and Jacqueline Simpson, trans., *Beowulf and Its Analogues* (London: J. M. Dent & Sons, Ltd., 1968).

monster falls, undermost, so that Grettir is able to draw, and strike off his head; though not till Glam has laid upon Grettir a curse which drags him to his doom.

The second story—the adventure of Grettir at Sandhaugar (Sand-heaps)—begins in much the same way as that of Grettir and Glam. Grettir is staying in a haunted farm, from which first the farmer himself and then a house-carl have, on two successive Yuletides, been spirited away. As before, a light burns in the room all night, and Grettir awaits the attack alone, lying down, without having put off his clothes. As before, Grettir and his assailant wrestle down the room, breaking all in their way. But this time Grettir is pulled out of the hall, and dragged to the brink of the neighbouring gorge. Here, by a final effort, he wrenches a hand free, draws, and hews off the arm of the ogress, who falls into the torrent below.

Grettir conjectures that the two missing men must have been pulled by the ogress into the gulf. This, after his experience, is surely a reasonable inference: but Stein, the priest, is unconvinced. So they go together to the river, and find the side of the ravine a sheer precipice: it is ten fathom[s] down to the water below the fall. Grettir lets down a rope: the priest is to watch it. Then Grettir dives in: "the priest saw the soles of his feet, and then knew no more what had become of him." Grettir swims under the fall and gets into the cave, where he sees a giant sitting by a fire: the giant aims a blow at him with a weapon with a wooden handle ("such a weapon men then called a *hefti-sax*"). Grettir hews it asunder. The giant then grasps at another sword hanging on the wall of the cave, but before he can use it Grettir wounds him. Stein, the priest, seeing the water stained with blood from this wound, concludes that Grettir is dead, and departs home, lamenting the loss of such a man. "But Grettir let little space come between his blows till the giant lay dead." Grettir finds the bones of the two dead men in the cave, and bears them away with him to convince the priest: but when he reaches the rope and shakes it, there is no reply, and he has to climb up, unaided. He leaves the bones in the church porch, for the confusion of the priest, who has to admit that he has failed to do his part faithfully.

Now if we compare this with *Beowulf*, we see that in the Icelandic story much is different: for example, in the *Grettis saga* it is the female monster who raids the habitation of men, the male who stays at home in his den. In this the *Grettis saga* probably represents a corrupt tradition: for, that the female should remain at home whilst the male searches for his prey, is a rule which holds good for devils as well as for men. The change was presumably made in order to avoid the difficulty—which the *Beowulf* poet seems also to have realized—that after the male has been slain, the rout of the female is felt to be a deed of less note—something of an anti-climax.[1]

The sword on the wall, also, which in the *Beowulf*-story is used by the hero, is, in the *Grettir*-story, used by the giant in his attack on the hero.

But that the two stories are somehow connected cannot be disputed. Apart from the general likeness, we have details such as the escape of the monster after the loss of an arm, the fire burning in the cave, the *hefti-sax*, a word which, like its Old English equivalent (*hæft-mēce, Beowulf*, 1457), is found in this story only, and the strange reasoning of the watchers that the blood-stained water must necessarily be due to the hero's death.[2]

Now obviously such a series of resemblances cannot be the result of an accident. Either the *Grettir*-story is derived directly or indirectly from the *Beowulf* epic, more or less as we have it, or both stories are derived from one common earlier source. The scholars who first discovered the resemblance believed that both stories were independently derived from one original. This view has generally been endorsed by later investigators, but not universally. And this is one of the questions which the student cannot leave open, because our view of the origin of the *Grendel*-story will have to depend largely upon the view we take as to its connection with the episode in the *Grettis saga*.

If this episode be derived from *Beowulf*, then we have an interesting literary curiosity, but nothing further. But if it is independently derived from a common source, then the episode in the *saga*, although so much later, may nevertheless contain features which have been obliterated or confused or forgotten in the *Beowulf* version. In that case the story, as given in the *Grettis saga*, would be of great weight in any attempt to reconstruct the presumed original form of the *Grendel*-story.

The evidence seems to me to support strongly the view of the majority of scholars—that the *Grettir*-episode is not derived from *Beowulf* in the form in which that poem has come down to us, but that both come from one common source.

It is certain that the story of the monster invading a dwelling of men and rendering it uninhabitable, till the adventurous deliverer arrives, did not originate with Hrothgar and Heorot. It is an ancient and widespread type of story, of which one version is localized at the Danish court. When therefore we find it existing, independently

1. Cf. *Beowulf*, ll. 1282–87.
2. There are other coincidences which *may* be the result of mere chance. In each case, before the adventure with the giants, the hero proves his strength by a feat of endurance in the ice-cold water.

And, at the end of the story, the hero in each case produces, as evidence of his victory, a trophy with a runic inscription: in *Beowulf* an engraved sword hilt; in the *Grettis saga* bones and a "rune-staff."

of its Danish setting, the presumption is in favour of this being a survival of the old independent story. Of course it is *conceivable* that the Hrothgar-Heorot setting might have been first added, and subsequently stripped off again so clean that no trace of it remains. But it seems going out of our way to assume this, unless we are forced to do so.

Again, it is certain that these stories—like all the subject matter of the Old English epic—did not originate in England, but were brought across the North Sea from the old home. And that old home was in the closest connection, so far as the passage to and fro of story went, with Scandinavian lands. Nothing could be intrinsically more probable than that a story, current in ancient Angel and carried thence to England, should also have been current in Scandinavia, and thence have been carried to Iceland.

Other stories which were current in England in the eighth century were also current in Scandinavia in the thirteenth. Yet this does not mean that the tales of Hroar and Rolf, or of Athils and Ali, were borrowed from English epic accounts of Hrothgar and Hrothulf, or Eadgils and Onela. They were part of the common inheritance—as much so as the strong verbs or the alliterative line. Why then, contrary to all analogy, should we assume a literary borrowing in the case of the *Beowulf-Grettir*-story? The compiler of the *Grettis saga* could not possibly have drawn his material from a MS of *Beowulf*:[3] he could not have made sense of a single passage. He conceivably *might* have drawn from traditions *derived* from the Old English epic. But it is difficult to see how. Long before his time these traditions had for the most part been forgotten in England itself. One of the longest lived of all, that of Offa, is heard of for the last time in England at the beginning of the thirteenth century. That a Scandinavian sagaman at the end of the century could have been in touch, in any way, with Anglo-Saxon epic tradition seems on the whole unlikely. The Scandinavian tradition of Offa,[4] scholars are now agreed, was not borrowed from England, and there is no reason why we should assume such borrowing in the case of Grettir.

The probability is, then, considerable, that the *Beowulf*-story and the *Grettir*-story are independently derived from one common original.

And this probability would be confirmed to a certainty if we should find that features which have been confused and half obliterated in the OE story become clear when we turn to the Icelandic. This argument has lately been brought forward by Dr.

---

3. Even assuming that a MS of *Beowulf* had found its way to Iceland, it would have been unintelligible. This is shown by the absurd blunders made when Icelanders borrowed names from OE genealogies.

4. Famous fourth-century continental Angle king mentioned in *Beowulf*, p. 34. *Ed.*

Lawrence in his essay on "The Haunted Mere in *Beowulf*."[5] Impressive as the account of this mere is, it does not convey any very clear picture. Grendel's home seems sometimes to be in the sea: and again it seems to be amid marshes, moors and fens, and again it is "where the mountain torrent goes down under the darkness of the cliffs—the water below the ground (i.e. beneath overhanging rocks)."[6]

This last account agrees admirably with the landscape depicted in the *Grettis saga*, and the gorge many fathoms deep through which the stream rushes, after it has fallen over the precipice; not so the other accounts. These descriptions are best harmonized if we imagine an original version in which the monsters live, as in the *Grettis saga*, in a hole under the waterfall. This story, natural enough in a Scandinavian country, would be less intelligible as it travelled South. The Angles and Saxons, both in their old home on the Continent and their new one in England, were accustomed to a somewhat flat country, and would be more inclined to place the dwelling of outcast spirits in moor and fen than under waterfalls, of which they probably had only an elementary conception. "The giant must dwell in the fen, alone in the land."[7]

Now it is in the highest degree improbable that, after the landscape had been blurred as it is in *Beowulf*, it could have been brought out again with the distinctness it has in the *Grettis saga*. To preserve the features so clearly the *Grettir*-story can hardly be derived from *Beowulf*: it must have come down independently.

But if so, it becomes at once of prime importance. For by a comparison of *Beowulf* and *Grettir* we must form an idea of what the original story was, from which both were derived.

STANLEY B. GREENFIELD

[The Finn Episode and Its Parallel] †

* * *

The Finn Episode (ll. 1068–1159), a sample of the entertainment provided by the scop in Heorot after the defeat of Grendel, is an excellent tragedy in itself, focusing as it does on the conflicting claims imposed upon Hengest: to revenge his dead leader Hnæf

5. William Witherle Lawrence, *PMLA*, 27 (1912), 208–45. *Ed.*
6. See *Beowulf*, p. 24. For an allegorical view of Grendel's mere, see D. W. Robertson, Jr., "The Doctrine of Charity in Medieval Gardens: A Topical Approach Through Symbolism and Allegory," *Speculum*, 26 (1951), 24–49 (rpt.

in *ABC*, pp. 165–88). *Ed.*
7. *Cotton, Gnomic Verses*, ll. 42–43.
† Reprinted by permission of New York University Press from Stanley B. Greenfield's *A Critical History of Old English Literature*, pp. 90–92. Copyright © 1966 by New York University.

on the one hand, and to keep the peace pact he has been forced to make with Hnæf's slayer, King Finn of Frisia, on the other. The final resolution, with Hengest and the Danes slaughtering Finn and his retainers in their hall, and thus exacting revenge, is presented by Hrothgar's scop as a Danish victory, and on this level alone would find its *raison d'être* in the context of *Beowulf*. But the Episode operates on more subtle lines in the over-all unity of the poem. For though the scop has concentrated on Hengest, the *Beowulf* poet himself gives another perspective through Hildeburh's wretchedness: her loss of brother (Hnæf), son, and finally of husband (Finn), so that the heroic-elegiac pattern of the whole poem is reflected in miniature in this story. On another level, the theme of treachery is emphasized at the beginning, in the litotical comment that Hildeburh, Finn's wife, had "little reason to speak well of the loyalty of the Jutes," and the theme of treachery runs throughout the piece, to be picked up after the scop finishes his song when the *Beowulf* poet alludes to the future treachery in Heorot itself. In another way, the Episode reveals the failure of human attempts to achieve peaceful compromise, a theme echoing throughout the *Beowulf*. * * *

The Finn Episode in *Beowulf* presents a part of what must have been a series of stories about the Danish-Frisian conflict. Another segment is preserved in the fragmentary *Fight at Finnsburg* * * *.[1] Only some forty-seven lines of this probably early oral poem remain, recounting an earlier stage in the hostilities, when the Frisians began the attack on Hnæf. From what can be pieced together from the Fragment and the Episode, Hnæf and his band of sixty Danes evidently had been paying a visit to Hnæf's sister Queen Hildeburh and her husband King Finn, when through the treachery of the Eotens (Jutes?) in the service of Finn, Hnæf's party was attacked in their quarters by the Frisians. The Fragment's beginning is missing, but clearly a sentinel for the Danes spots the moonlight (or torchlight) glittering on swords as the treacherous attack is about to be launched. The Danes, after taking up positions at the two doors of the Germanic hall, hold out against the besiegers for five days without losing a man. As the Fragment ends, a Dane—some critics say a Frisian—is wounded severely and is queried by Hnæf—or Finn?—as to how the warriors are surviving their wounds. From the Episode, we know that in the continuation of the fighting Hnæf died, and was succeeded by Hengest, who ultimately made a truce with Finn when both forces were decimated. The Episode's concentration, as we have seen, was on the tragedy of Hengest and Hildeburh, and the final revenge on Finn.

1. The text is edited in most editions of *Beowulf*; for bibliography, see Klaber's edition, pp. 239–43.

The emphasis and the style of the Fragment are quite different from those of the Episode, and from the epic *Beowulf*. The *Fight at Finnsburg* is no curtailed epic, but a bona fide *lay*, a brief narrative with compressed description and rapid conversation. The poem must have opened with the sentry's questions about the meaning of the light he sees, for Hnæf replies: "This is no daylight dawning from the east, nor dragon flying, nor gables of this hall on fire; but here they bring forth (arms), the birds (of prey) sing, the gray-coated one [i.e., the wolf] shrieks, the battle wood resounds, shield answers shaft." The narrative progresses in a series of *then* announcements: "Then arose many a gold-adorned thane, girded on his sword"; "Then yet Guthhere tried to restrain Garulf"; "Then was the noise of battle in the hall"; "Then a wounded warrior departed"; "Then the guardian of the people straightway asked him." The movement jerks along powerfully, as the poet commends the small band for their courage and devotion in repaying their leader for the "white mead" (meed?) he had dealt out in more prosperous days. Although the *Fight* is mainly valued for the light it throws on the whole complex of the Finnsburg story, and particularly on the *Beowulf*ian Episode, it is in its own right a moving account of stark, unvarnished heroic action in the best spirit of ancient Germanic poetry, such a lay as might well have delighted the audience in a Germanic chieftain's hall.

* * *

FR. KLAEBER

[The Danish–Heaðo-Bard Feud]†

* * *

* * * we may give the following brief, connected account of the outstanding events of Danish history as underlying the allusions of the poem.[1] Froda, king of the Bards, slays Healfdene[2] (about A.D. 498); (Heorogar), Hroðgar, and Halga make a war of revenge,[2] Froda falls in battle (A.D. 499). After an interval of nearly twenty years, when Froda's son, Ingeld (born A.D. 498), has grown up, Hroðgar, the renowned and venerable king, desirous of forestalling a fresh outbreak of the feud, marries his daughter Freawaru to the young Heaðo-Bard king (A.D. 518). Yet before long, the flame

† Reprinted by permission of the publisher, from Fr. Klaeber, *Beowulf*, 3rd ed. (Lexington, Mass.: D. C. Heath & Co., 1950), p. xxxvi. Bracketed material in the text is by Klaeber.

1. On the meaning of the dates given, see Klaeber, p. xxxi. *Ed.*
2. There is no mention of this in *Beowulf*. * * *

of revenge is kindled again, the Bards invade the Danish dominions and burn Heorot, but are completely routed, A.D. 520. The foreign enemy having been overcome, new trouble awaits the Danes at home. Upon Hroðgar's death (A.D. 525), his nephew Hroðulf forcibly seizes the kingship, pushing aside and slaying his cousin Hreðric, the heir presumptive. [Of the subsequent attack of Heoroweard, who had a still older claim to the throne, and the fall of Hroðulf (A.D. 545) no mention is made in the *Beowulf*.]

* * *

C. L. WRENN

[The Historicity of Beowulf] †

The historicity of Beowulf himself must be, at best, but very shadowy. It is true that the mere attribution to him of supernatural feats of strength need not in itself imply that he had in fact no existence. For, as Ritchie Girvan has well argued in the third lecture of his *Beowulf and the Seventh Century*,[1] such a view would also make King Richard I a mere figment of the mediæval romantic imagination because of the miraculous deeds attributed in romance to Richard Cœur-de-Lion. But from the beginning the poet seems to assume that Beowulf is capable of more than human actions while at the same time remaining a very human hero; and the fact that no clear allusions to this hero have so far been found outside the poem, and that the name Beowulf is only once found in OE in ordinary use (in the *Book of Life* of the Lindisfarne monks of the early ninth century) and in two not very secure early place-names, tells against historical reality. True, we should expect the audience to look for a hero from the known or traditional Germanic past: but Beowulf may well have been known to them as a great hero from a kind of 'historicized folk-mythology' much as was Weland (*cf.* l. 455), the Germanic hero, artificer in metals, and magician. True, again, the one fully authenticated historical fact repeatedly mentioned in *Beowulf* is the closing event of the life of the Geat king Hygelac, Beowulf's uncle—and there are reasons for believing that the accounts of Geatish happenings in the poem are more accurate than those concerned with Hrothgar the Dane. Yet there is no mention of this greatest of poetic heroes known to England before the Normans in *Widsith*, which contains so much of

† From *Beowulf with the Finnesburg Fragment* (Boston: D. C. Heath & Co., 1953), p. 45. Reprinted by permission of the publishers of the 3rd ed. rev. W. F. Bolton (New York and London, 1973), St. Martin's Press, Inc., and George G. Harrap & Co., Ltd.
1. (London: Methuen, 1935). *Ed.*

remembered names from Germanic history. On the other hand, *Widsith* does not know of the undoubtedly historical Hygelac the Geat, though it knows both Hrothgar the Danish king and his nephew and successor Hrothulf. The historicity of Beowulf himself, then, must remain for the present as 'not proven,' but by no means impossible.

RALPH ARNOLD

[Royal Halls—The Sutton Hoo Ship Burial]†

* * *

The poem *Beowulf* * * * is the best guide as to what a royal hall in one of the pagan English kingdoms was like, for though the setting of this famous epic is south Sweden, the Germanic peoples it depicts were first cousins to the English and lived the same kind of lives.

King Hrothgar, the poem relates, having collected an unrivalled band of 'companions', determined to build the greatest hall ever known. When it had been put up—tall, wide-gabled, and towering —he called it 'Heorot'. It seems to have been a large wooden rectangular barn-like structure surrounded by smaller wooden buildings some of which served as separate sleeping quarters or 'bowers' for the king and for especially favoured guests. The walls of the hall were made of timber posts clamped together with iron. Inside, there were fixed benches ranged round the walls to serve by day as seats at the trestle tables that were set up only at mealtimes and by night as beds for the senior members of the household. The floor of the hall was paved in a 'variegated' pattern; and its entrance door was wide enough and high enough to admit a man on horseback. 'Heorot', the poem says, was 'plated with gold' and tapestries woven with golden thread covered its walls.

A royal hall really came into its own on the occasions of feasts. 'When we sat down to feast', Beowulf is made to say, 'the King of the Danes rewarded me generously . . . with treasures and beaten gold. Songs and entertainment followed, and the patriarch Hrothgar,

† From *A Social History of England: 55 B.C. to A.D. 1215* (London: Constable Young Books, Ltd., 1967, and Barnes & Noble Books, New York), pp. 125–29. Copyright © 1967 by R. C. M. Arnold. Reprinted by permission of Harper & Row, Publishers, Inc., Penguin Books, Ltd., and Winant Towers, Ltd., for the Arnold Estate. See also R. L. S.

Bruce-Mitford, *The Sutton Hoo Ship Burial, A Handbook*, 2nd ed. (London: British Museum, 1972); and Rosemary Cramp, "*Beowulf* and Archaeology," *Medieval Archaeology*, I (1957), 57–77, rpt. in *The Beowulf Poet* (hereafter *BP*), Donald K. Fry, ed. (Englewood Cliffs, N.J.: Prentice-Hall, 1968), pp. 114–40.

who knew many stories by heart, told anecdotes about past times and every now and then played a melody on the harp. Sometimes a true and unhappy ballad was recited; and occasionally the King would relate a curious legend. . . .' Arguments at feast about who was the 'best' champion present sometimes led to fights; but in 'Heorot' proceedings seem to have been orderly enough, the queen customarily bringing the entertainment to an end by carrying a jewelled 'loving-cup' round the hall before leading the king off to his sleeping-quarters.

Gold—Beowulf's own helmet was 'inlaid with gold, hooped with lordly bands, and decorated with effigies of boars'—is a thread that runs through the poem just as it is a thread that runs through the heroic way of life led by the pagan English rulers. Lust for gold as a symbol of royal wealth and for gold to give away probably accounted for much of the warfare in which the early English kings indulged.

The only archaeological evidence of what Heroic Age royal halls in England were like comes from Yeavering in Glendale in present-day Northumberland, where the site of one of the royal townships of the English kings of Northumbria has been identified and investigated. The wooden buildings, of which only the post-holes have survived, probably belonged to the seventh * * * century * * *. The township appears to have comprised a scatter of substantial timber buildings, a fort, and a meeting-place for the king's council.

The largest of the timber buildings has been identified as the king's hall. Its walls were built of squared timber posts set upright in a foundation trench, and its roof was partly supported by external buttresses. Within, the hall appears to have been divided by two rows of posts or timber pillars into a 'nave' with two flanking 'aisles', and there was a shut-off space at one end that may have served as a sleeping apartment for the king. The detached wooden buildings probably housed senior nobles. Among these buildings was a pagan temple that was later converted to Christian use.

The fort, a strongly fenced enclosure, provided a refuge in the event of hostile raids. The most interesting feature of the township is the suggestion of a bank of tiered wooden seats resembling a segment of a Roman theatre. This, it is thought, was the 'grand-stand' from which the king could address full-dress assemblies of the members of his council.

If nothing is known about the ceremony by which an Heroic Age English king was made, *Beowulf* provides an explicit account of how an Heroic Age pagan king, Scyld, King of the Danes, was buried. The translation of this passage is by Michael Alexander.

> A boat with a ringed neck rode in the haven,
> icy, out-eager, the atheling's vessel,
> and there they laid out their lord and master,
> dealer of wound gold, in the waist of the ship,
> in majesty by the mast. A mound of treasures
> from far countries was fetched aboard her,
> and it is said that no boat was ever more bravely fitted out
> with the weapons of a warrior, war accoutrement,
> swords and body-armour; on his breast were set
> treasures and trappings to travel with him
> on his far faring into the flood's sway. . . .
> High over head they hoisted and fixed
> a gold *signum*; gave him to the flood,
> let the seas take him, with sour hearts
> and mourning mood. Men under heaven's
> shifting skies, though skilled in counsel,
> cannot say surely who unshipped that cargo.[1]

Confirmation of what might otherwise have been dismissed as a flight of poetic fancy came in the year 1939 when a ship loaded with the gear and treasure of an Heroic Age English king was found buried in a trench under a large mound of earth on the heathy upland that forms the eastern escarpment of the estuary of the River Deben in Suffolk. The parish in which the ship was found is called Sutton Hoo. The ship's timbers had perished, but the lines of the hull of a 90-foot clinker-built mastless rowing-boat could be traced.

It is believed that the gear and treasure that were found belonged to one of the English kings of East Anglia who had probably died around the year 650. His treasure was every bit as fine as Scyld's treasure in the poem and the manner of his funeral similar, except that Scyld's funeral ship was launched off on to the bosom of the ocean whereas the Sutton Hoo ship was buried on dry land— burial, according to archaeologists, being in fact a more usual practice than random launching.

The hero's war-gear found in the Sutton Hoo ship consisted of a helmet-cum-mask with ribs of gold and with garnets set above the eye-holes, a coat of mail that had been reduced to a lump of rusted metal, a magnificent sword and the harness belonging to it complete with a great gold belt-buckle, shoulder-clasps, and a purse lid, and an elaborately mounted shield that measured almost a yard across.[2] There was an iron pole, more than 6 feet high and surmounted by the effigy of a stag that may have been a royal

---

1. From *Beowulf* translated by Michael Alexander (Penguin Classics, 1973), p. 52. Copyright © 1973 by Michael Alexander. Reprinted by permission of Penguin Books, Ltd. You might wish to compare Donaldson, pp. 1–2. *Ed.*

2. For black-and-white illustrations of many of these objects, see Arnold, pp. 128, 130. The color illustration to scale of the gold belt buckle facing his title page is especially beautiful. *Ed.*

standard (a grisly alternative suggestion is that it was a rack for the display of scalps), and an elaborately mounted whetstone that may have been a primitive royal sceptre.

The reason that there was no body aboard the Sutton Hoo ship may have been because the king whose body should have been there had been lost at sea. Or again if the king in question had been a convert to Christianity, it is possible that he had been given a Christian burial elsewhere which had failed to satisfy his still pagan subjects.

There were gold coins in the treasure that had been minted in Gaul; and the king's material needs in an after-life had been further catered for by the provision of bronze cauldrons complete with the iron chains by which they were suspended, and by iron-bound buckets. A stack of silver bowls and a ladle had been provided so that he would be able to eat in suitable style; he had been given no fewer than seven silver-mounted drinking-horns, two of them fashioned from aurochs' horns and holding six pints apiece; and there were a silver platter, bronze bowls, three hanging-bowls, the dismembered pieces of a small six-stringed harp in a sealskin bag,[3] and two silver spoons, one inscribed *Saulos* in Greek characters and the other *Paulos*.

The spoons were Byzantine and so, probably, were the silver bowls. The sword and the magnificently decorated helmet and the shield may have come from Sweden. The gold sword-belt buckle with its surface decorated with interlaced snakes was the work of Anglo-Saxon artist-craftsmen, as were the garnet and glass inlays on the gold frame and the flap of the purse and on the two exquisite jewelled shoulder clips with garnets and pieces of glass set in cells formed from thin gold wire. It is thought that some of the English-made jewellery may actually have been heirlooms made in the sixth century. The three hanging bowls, with their enamelled bosses, were almost certainly made by British [Celtish], not English, craftsmen and had probably been imported from Wales, Scotland, or Ireland.

The identity of the East Anglian king for whom this cenotaph had been provided is comparatively unimportant in this context. What matters is that there was a ruler in one of the smaller of the English kingdoms at this time rich enough to have owned such sumptuous possessions. It is also significant that English craftsmen in the sixth and seventh centuries were capable of producing work

3. Illustrated in Arnold, p. 130. The harp has been reconstructed and J. B. Bessinger uses a replica to accompany his reading in the original OE of *Beowulf, Cædmon's Hymn, and Other Old English Poems* (New York: Caedmon TC 1161, 1962). See also Jess B. Bessinger, Jr., "The Sutton Hoo Harp Replica and Old English Musical Verse," in *Old English Poetry* (hereafter *OEP*), Robert P. Creed, ed. (Providence, R.I.: Brown University Press, 1967), pp. 3–26. *Ed.*

that would excite astonished admiration if it was displayed today alongside the work of the finest contemporary goldsmiths and jewellers in Bond Street or Fifth Avenue or the Rue de la Paix.

* * *

Criticism

E. TALBOT DONALDSON

[Overview of] The Poem†

Beowulf, the oldest of the great long poems written in English, was probably composed more than twelve hundred years ago, in the first half of the eighth century. Its author may have been a native of what was then West Mercia, the West Midlands of England today, though the late tenth-century manuscript, which alone preserves the poem, originated in the south in the kingdom of the West Saxons. In 1731, before any modern transcription of the text had been made, the manuscript was seriously damaged in the fire that destroyed the building in London which housed the extraordinary collection of medieval English manuscripts made by Sir Robert Bruce Cotton (1571–1631). As a result of the fire and of subsequent deterioration of the manuscript, a number of lines and words have been lost from the poem, but even if the manuscript had not been damaged, the poem would still have been difficult, because the poetic Old English (or Anglo-Saxon) in which it was written is itself hard, the style is allusive, the ideas often seem remote and strange to modern perceptions, and because the text was inevitably corrupted during the many transcriptions which must have intervened in the two and a half centuries between the poem's composition and the copying of the extant manuscript. Yet despite its difficulty, the sombre grandeur of *Beowulf* is still capable of stirring the hearts of readers, and because of its excellence as well as its antiquity, the poem merits the high position that it is generally assigned in the study of English poetry.

While the poem itself is English in language and origin, it deals not with native Englishmen, but with their Germanic forbears, especially with two south Scandinavian tribes, the Danes and the Geats, who lived on the Danish island of Zealand and in southern Sweden, respectively. Thus, the historical period it concerns—insofar as it may be said to refer to history at all—is some two centuries before the poem was written; that is, it concerns a time following the initial invasion of England by Germanic tribes in 449, but before the Anglo-Saxon migration was completed, and perhaps before the arrival of the ancestors of the audience to whom the poem was sung: this audience may have considered itself to be of the same Geatish stock as the hero, Beowulf. The one datable fact of history mentioned in the poem is a raid on the

† From *Beowulf,* a new prose translation by E. Talbot Donaldson, pp. vii–xii. Copyright © 1966 by W. W. Norton & Co., Inc. Reprinted by permission of the publisher.

Franks made by Hygelac, the king of the Geats at the time Beowulf was a young man, and this raid occurred in the year 520. Yet despite their antiquity, the poet's materials must have been very much alive to his audience, for the elliptical way in which he alludes to events not directly concerned with his plot demands of the listener a wide knowledge of traditional Germanic history. This knowledge was probably kept alive by other heroic poetry, of which little has been preserved in English, though much must once have existed. As it stands, *Beowulf* is not only unique as an example of the Old English epic, but is also the greatest of the surviving epics composed by the Germanic peoples.

It is generally agreed that the poet who put the old materials into their present form was a Christian, and that his poem reflects a Christian tradition: the conversion of the Germanic settlers in England had largely been completed during the century preceding the one in which the poet wrote. But there is little general agreement as to how clearly *Beowulf* reflects a Christian tradition or, conversely, the actual nature of the Christian tradition that it is held to reflect. Many specifically Christian references occur, especially to the Old Testament: God is said to be the Creator of all things and His will seems recognized (sporadically if not systematically) as being identical with Fate (*wyrd*); Grendel is described as a descendant of Cain, and the sword that Beowulf finds in Grendel's mother's lair has engraved on it the story of the race of giants and their destruction by flood; the dead await God's judgment, and Hell and the Devil are ready to receive the souls of Grendel and his mother, while believers will find the Father's embrace; Hrothgar's speech of advice to Beowulf (section XXV) seems to reflect patristic doctrine in its emphasis on conscience and the Devil's lying in wait for the unwary. Yet there is no reference to the New Testament—to Christ and His Sacrifice which are the real bases of Christianity in any intelligible sense of the term. Furthermore, readers may well feel that the poem achieves rather little of its emotional power through invocation of Christian values or of values that are consonant with Christian doctrine as we know it. Perhaps the sense of tragic waste which pervades the Finnsburg episode (section XVI) springs from a Christian perception of the insane futility of the primitive Germanic thirst for vengeance; and the facts that Beowulf's chief adversaries are not men but monsters and that before his death he is able to boast that as king of the Geats he did not seek wars with neighboring tribes may reflect a Christian's appreciation for peace among men. But while admitting such values, the poet also invokes many others of a very different order, values that seem to belong to an ancient, pagan, warrior society of the kind described by the Roman historian Tacitus at the end of the first century. It should be noted that even Hrothgar's speech about conscience is directed more toward making Beowulf a good Germanic leader of men than a good Christian. One must, indeed, draw the conclusion from the poem itself that while Christian is a correct term for the religion of the poet and of his audience, it was a Christianity that had not yet by any means succeeded in obliterating an older pagan tradition, which still called forth powerful responses from men's hearts, despite the fact that many aspects of this tradition must be abhorrent to a sophisticated Christian. In this connection it is well to recall that the missionaries from Rome who initiated the conversion of the English proceeded in a conciliatory manner, not so much uprooting paganism in order to plant Christianity as planting Christianity in the faith that it would ultimately choke out the weeds of paganism. And the English clung long to some of their ancient traditions: for instance, the legal principle of the payment of *wergild* (defined below) remained in force until the Norman Conquest, four centuries after the conversion of the English.

In the warrior society whose values the poem constantly invokes, the most important of human relationships was that which existed between the warrior—the thane—and his lord, a relationship based less on subordination of one man's will to another's than on mutual trust and respect. When a warrior vowed loyalty to his lord, he became not so much his servant as his voluntary companion, one who would take pride in defending him and fighting in his wars. In return, the lord was expected to take affectionate care of his thanes and to reward them richly for their valor: a good king, one like Hrothgar or Beowulf, is referred to by such poetic epithets as "protector of warriors" and "dispenser of treasure" or "ring-giver," and the failure of bad kings is ascribed to their ill-temper and avarice, both of which alienate them from their retainers. The material benefit of this arrangement between lord and thane is obvious, yet under a good king the relationship seems to have had a significance more spiritual than material. Thus the treasure that an ideal Germanic king seizes from his enemies and rewards his retainers with is regarded as something more than mere wealth that will serve the well-being of its possessor; rather, it is a kind of visible proof that all parties are realizing themselves to the full in a spiritual sense—that the men of this band are congenially and successfully united with one another. The symbolic importance of treasure is illustrated by the poet's remark that the gift Beowulf gave the Danish coast-guard brought the latter honor among his companions, and even more by the fact that although Beowulf dies while obtaining a great treasure for his people, such objects as are removed from the dragon's hoard are actually buried with him as a fitting sign of his ultimate achievement.

The relationship between kinsmen was also of deep significance to this society and provides another emotional value for Old English heroic poetry. If one of his kinsmen had been slain, a man had the special duty of either killing the slayer or exacting from him the payment of *wergild* ("man-price"): each rank of society was evaluated at a definite price, which had to be paid to the dead man's kinsmen by the killer who wished to avoid their vengeance—even if the killing had been accidental. Again, the money itself had less significance as wealth than as a proof that the kinsmen had done what was right. Relatives who failed either to exact *wergild* or to take vengeance could never be happy, having found no practical way of satisfying their grief for their kinsmen's death. "It is better for a man to avenge his friend than much mourn," Beowulf says to the old Hrothgar, who is bewailing Aeschere's killing by Grendel's mother. And one of the most poignant passages in the poem describes the sorrow of King Hrethel after one of his sons had accidentally killed another: by the code of kinship Hrethel was forbidden to kill or to exact compensation from a kinsman, yet by the same code he was required to do one or the other in order to avenge the dead. Caught in this curious dilemma, Hrethel became so disconsolate that he could no longer face life.

It is evident that the need to take vengeance would create never-ending feuds, which the practice of marrying royal princesses to the kings or princes of hostile tribes did little to mitigate, though the purpose of such marriages was to replace hostility by alliance. Hrothgar wishes to make peace with the Heatho-Bards by marrying his daughter to their king, Ingeld, whose father was killed by the Danes; but as Beowulf predicts, sooner or later the Heatho-Bards' desire for vengeance on the Danes will erupt, and there will be more bloodshed. And the Danish princess Hildeburh, married to Finn of the Jutes, will see her son and her brother both killed while fighting on opposite sides in a battle at her own home, and ultimately will see her husband killed by the Danes in revenge for her brother's death. Beowulf himself is, for a Germanic hero, curiously free of involvement in feuds of this sort, though he does boast that he avenged the death of his king, Heardred, on his slayer Onela. Yet the potentiality—or inevitability—of sudden attack, sudden change, swift death is omnipresent in *Beowulf*: men seem to be caught in a vast web of reprisals and counterreprisals from which there is little hope of escape. This is the aspect of the poem which is apt to make the most powerful impression on the reader—its strong sense of doom.

Beowulf himself is chiefly concerned not with tribal feuds but with fatal evil both less and more complex. Grendel and the dragon are threats to the security of the lands they infest just as human enemies would be, but they are not part of the social order and presumably have no one to avenge their deaths (that Grendel's mother appeared as an avenger seems to have been a surprise both to Beowulf and to the Danes). On the other hand, because they are outside the normal order of things, they require of their conqueror something greater than normal warfare requires. In each case, it is the clear duty of the king and his companions to put down the evil. But the Danish Hrothgar is old and his companions unenterprising, and excellent though Hrothgar has been in the kingship, he nevertheless lacks the quality that later impels the old Beowulf to fight the dragon that threatens his people. The poem makes no criticism of Hrothgar for this lack; he merely seems not to be the kind of man—one might almost say he was not fated—to develop his human potential to the fullest extent that Fate would permit: that is Beowulf's role. In undertaking to slay Grendel, and later Grendel's mother, Beowulf is testing his relationship with unknowable destiny. At any time, as he is fully aware, his luck may abandon him and he may be killed, as, indeed, he is in the otherwise successful encounter with the dragon. But whether he lives or dies, he will have done all that any man could do to develop his character heroically. It is this consciousness of testing Fate that probably explains the boasting that modern readers of heroic poetry often find offensive. When he boasts, Beowulf is not only demonstrating that he has chosen the heroic way of life, but is also choosing it, for when he invokes his former courage as pledge of his future courage, his boast becomes a vow; the hero has put himself in a position from which he cannot withdraw.

Courage is the instrument by which the hero realizes himself. "Fate often saves an undoomed man when his courage is good," says Beowulf in his account of his swimming match: that is, if Fate has not entirely doomed a man in advance, courage is the quality that can perhaps influence Fate against its natural tendency to doom him now. It is this complex statement (in which it is hard to read the will of God for Fate) that Beowulf's life explores: he will use his great strength in the most courageous way by going alone, even unarmed, against monsters. Doom, of course, ultimately claims him, but not until he has fulfilled to its limits the pagan ideal of a heroic life. And despite the desire he often shows to Christianize pagan virtues, the Christian poet remains true to the older tradition when, at the end of his poem, he leaves us with the impression that Beowulf's chief reward is pagan immortality: the memory in the minds of later men of a hero's heroic actions. The poem itself is, indeed, a noble expression of that immortality.

FR. KLAEBER

The Christian Coloring†

The presentation of the story-material in Beowulf has been influenced, to a considerable extent, by ideas derived from Christianity.

The poem abounds, to be sure, in supernatural elements of pre-Christian associations. Heathen practices are mentioned in several places, such as the vowing of sacrifices at idol fanes (175 ff), the observing of omens (204), the burning of the dead (3137 ff., 1107 ff., 2124 ff.), which was frowned upon by the Church. The frequent allusions to the power of fate * * *, the motive of blood revenge * * *, the praise of worldly glory * * * bear testimony to an ancient background of pagan conceptions and ideals. On the other hand, we hear nothing of angels, saints, relics, of Christ and the cross, of divine worship, church observances, or any particular dogmatic points. Still, the general impression we obtain from the reading of the poem is certainly the opposite of pagan barbarism. We almost seem to move in normal Christian surroundings. God's governance of the world and of every human being, the evil of sin, the doings of the devil, the last judgment, heaven and hell are ever and anon referred to as familiar topics. * * * Though mostly short, these allusions show by their remarkable frequency how thoroughly the whole life was felt to be dominated by Christian ideas. The author is clearly familiar with the traditional Christian terminology in question and evinces some knowledge of the Bible, liturgy, and ecclesiastical literature. Of specific motives derived from the Old Testament (and occurring in Genesis A also) we note the story of Cain, the giants, and the deluge (107 ff., 1261 ff., 1689 ff.), and the song of Creation (92 ff.).

† Reprinted by permission of the publisher, from Fr. Klaeber, Beowulf, 3rd ed. (Lexington, Mass.: D. C. Heath & Co., 1950), pp. xlviii–li. Bracketed modern English versions of the OE are from Donaldson. In the latter part of this essay, Klaeber opposes the popular early critical view that Beowulf was essentially a pagan poem to which were added Christian coloring and interpolations. For a modern approach, see Larry D. Benson, "The Pagan Coloring of Beowulf," OEP, pp. 193–213.

Furthermore, the transformation of old heathen elements in accordance with Christian thought may be readily observed. The pagan and heroic cremation finds a counterpart in the peaceful burial of the dead, which the Church enforced (1007 f., 2457 f.; cp. 445 f., 3107 ff.). The curse placed on the fateful treasure is clothed in a Christian formula (3071 ff.) and is declared to be void before the higher will of God (3054 ff.). By the side of the heathen fate is seen the almighty God. *Gæð a wyrd swa hio scel* ["Fate always goes as it must"], exclaims Beowulf in expectation of the Grendel fight, 455, but again, in the same speech, he avows: *ðær gelyfan sceal/ Dryhtnes dome se þe hine deað nimeð* ["The one whom death takes can trust the Lord's judgment"], 440. The functions of fate[1] and God seem quite parallel: *wyrd oft nereð unfægne eorl* ["Fate often saves an undoomed man"] . . . 572; *swa mæg unfæge eaðe gedigan/ wean ond wræcsið se ðe Waldendes/ hyldo gehealdeþ* ["So may an undoomed man who holds favor from the Ruler easily come through his woes and misery"], 2291 * * *. Yet God is said to control fate: *nefne him witig God wyrd forstode/ ond ðæs mannes mod* ["if wise God and the man's courage had not forestalled that fate"], 1056. Moreover, the fundamental contrast between the good God and the blind and hostile fate is shown by the fact that God invariably grants victory (even in the tragic dragon fight, 2874), whereas it is a mysterious, hidden spell that brings about Beowulf's death, 3067 ff.

Predominantly Christian are the general tone of the poem and its ethical viewpoint. We are no longer in a genuine pagan atmosphere. The sentiment has been softened and purified. The virtues of moderation, unselfishness, consideration for others are practised and appreciated. The manifest readiness to express gratitude to God on all imaginable occasions (625 ff., 1397 f., 928 f., * * *), and the poet's sympathy with weak and unfortunate beings like Scyld the foundling (7, 46) and even Grendel (e.g., 105, 721, 973, 975, 1351) and his mother (1546 f.), are typical of the new note. Particularly striking is the moral refinement of the two principal characters, Beowulf and Hroðgar. Those readers who, impressed by Beowulf's martial appearance at the beginning of the action, expect to find an aggressive warrior hero of the Achilles or Sigfrit type, will be disposed at times to think him somewhat tame, sentimental, and fond of talking. Indeed, the final estimate of the hero's character by his own faithful thanes lamenting his death is chiefly a praise of Beowulf's gentleness and kindness: *cwædon þæt he wære wyruldcyning[a]/ manna mildust ond monðwærust,/ leodum liðost ɔnd lofgeornost* ["They said that

---

1. Still, *wyrd* is not felt to be a personal being; the term is often used in a colorless way * * *.

he was of world-kings the mildest of men and the gentlest, kindest to his people, and most eager for fame"], 3180.

The Christian elements are almost without exception so deeply ingrained in the very fabric of the poem that they cannot be explained away as the work of a reviser or later interpolator. In addition, it is instructive to note that whilst the episodes are all but free from those modern influences,[2] the main story has been thoroughly imbued with the spirit of Christianity. It is true, the action itself is not modified or visibly influenced by Christianization. But the quality of the plot is changed. The author has fairly exalted the fights with fabled monsters into a conflict between the powers of good and of evil. The figure of Grendel, at any rate, while originally an ordinary Scandinavian troll, and passing in the poem as a sort of man-monster,[3] is at the same time conceived of as an impersonation of evil and darkness, even an incarnation of the Christian devil. Many of his appellations are unquestionable epithets of Satan (e.g., *feond mancynnes* ["enemy of mankind"], *Godes andsaca* ["God's enemy"], *feond on helle* ["the devil in hell"], *helle hæfta* ["the hell-slave"] * * *), he belongs to the wicked progeny of Cain, the first murderer, his actions are represented in a manner suggesting the conduct of the evil one * * *, and he dwells with his demon mother in a place which calls up visions of hell [see 1357 ff.]. Even the antagonist of the third adventure, though less personally conceived than the Grendel pair, is not free from the suspicion of similar influences, especially as the dragon was in ecclesiastical tradition the recognized symbol of the archfiend. * * *

That the victorious champion, who overcomes this group of monsters, is a decidedly unusual figure of very uncertain historical associations, has been pointed out before. The poet has raised him to the rank of a singularly spotless hero, a 'defending, protecting, redeeming being,'[4] a truly ideal character. We might even feel inclined to recognize features of the Christian Savior in the destroyer of hellish fiends, the warrior brave and gentle, blameless in thought and deed, the king that dies for his people. Though delicately kept in the background, such a Christian interpretation of the main story on the part of the Anglo-Saxon author could not but give added strength and tone to the entire poem. It helps to explain one of the great puzzles of our epic. It would indeed be hard to understand why the poet contented himself with a plot of

2. The Christian turn given the Heremod motive (901 ff., 1709 ff.) and some allusions in the Scyld prologue are the chief exceptions. * * *
3. See, e.g., 105, 1352, also 1379.
4. (See [John M.] Kemble [, ed., *The Anglo-Saxon Poems of Beowulf, The Traveller's Song, and the Battle of* *Finnesburh*, 2nd ed. (London, 1837)], ii, p. x.) In his role as a deliverer from the ravages of monsters he might well be likened to ancient heroes like Hercules and Theseus.—With all the heroic attributes the poet has conferred on him, the dominant trait of the hero is his wonderful eagerness to help others. * * *

mere fabulous adventures so much inferior to the splendid heroic setting, unless the narrative derived a superior dignity from suggesting the most exalted hero-life known to Christians.

J. R. R. TOLKIEN

Beowulf: The Monsters and the Critics†

* * *

Nearly all the censure, and most of the praise, that has been bestowed on *The Beowulf* has been due either to the belief that it was something that it was *not*—for example, primitive, pagan, Teutonic, an allegory (political or mythical), or most often, an epic; or to disappointment at the discovery that it was itself and not something that the scholar would have liked better—for example, a heathen heroic lay, a history of Sweden, a manual of Germanic antiquities, or a Nordic *Summa Theologica*.

I would express the whole industry in yet another allegory. A man inherited a field in which was an accumulation of old stone, part of an older hall. Of the old stone some had already been used in building the house in which he actually lived, not far from the old house of his fathers. Of the rest he took some and built a tower. But his friends coming perceived at once (without troubling to climb the steps) that these stones had formerly belonged to a more ancient building. So they pushed the tower over, with no little labour, in order to look for hidden carvings and inscriptions, or to discover whence the man's distant forefathers had obtained their building material. Some suspecting a deposit of coal under the soil began to dig for it, and forgot even the stones. They all said: "This tower is most interesting." But they also said (after pushing it over): "What a muddle it is in!" And even the man's own descendants, who might have been expected to consider what he had been about, were heard to murmur: "He is such an odd fellow! Imagine his using these old stones just to build a nonsensical tower! Why did not he restore the old house? He had no sense of proportion." But from the top of that tower the man had been able to look out upon the sea.

I hope I shall show that that allegory is just—even when we consider the more recent and more perceptive critics (whose concern is in intention with literature). To reach these we must pass in

† From *"Beowulf*: The Monsters and the Critics," by J. R. R. Tolkien, *PBA*, 22 (1936), 245–95, published by Oxford University Press. Copyright © 1936 by the Oxford University Press. Reprinted by permission of the British Academy. The entire essay has also been reprinted and is readily available in *ABC*, pp. 51–103, and *BP*, 8–56.

rapid flight over the heads of many decades of critics. As we do so a
conflicting babel mounts up to us, which I can report as something
after this fashion.[1] "*Beowulf* is a half-baked native epic the development of which was killed by Latin learning; it was inspired by
emulation of Virgil, and is a product of the education that came in
with Christianity; it is feeble and incompetent as a narrative; the
rules of narrative are cleverly observed in the manner of the learned
epic; it is the confused product of a committee of muddle-headed
and probably beer-bemused Anglo-Saxons (this is a Gallic voice);
it is a string of pagan lays edited by monks; it is the work of a
learned but inaccurate Christian antiquarian; it is a work of genius,
rare and surprising in the period, though the genius seems to have
been shown principally in doing something much better left undone
(this is a very recent voice); it is a wild folk-tale (general chorus);
it is a poem of an aristocratic and courtly tradition (same voices);
it is a hotchpotch; it is a sociological, anthropological, archaeological document; it is a mythical allegory (very old voices these and
generally shouted down, but not so far out as some of the newer
cries); it is rude and rough; it is a masterpiece of metrical art; it
has no shape at all; it is singularly weak in construction; it is a
clever allegory of contemporary politics (old John Earle with some
slight support from Mr. Girvan, only they look to different periods);
its architecture is solid; it is thin and cheap (a solemn voice); it is
undeniably weighty (the same voice); it is a national epic; it is a
translation from the Danish; it was imported by Frisian traders;
it is a burden to English syllabuses; and (final universal chorus of
all voices) it is worth studying."

It is not surprising that it should now be felt that a view, a
decision, a conviction are imperatively needed. But it is plainly
only in the consideration of *Beowulf* as a poem, with an inherent
poetic significance, that any view or conviction can be reached or
steadily held.

* * *

In *Beowulf* we have * * * an historical poem about the pagan
past, or an attempt at one—literal historical fidelity founded on
modern research was, of course, not attempted. It is a poem by a
learned man writing of old times, who looking back on the heroism
and sorrow feels in them something permanent and something symbolical. So far from being a confused semi-pagan—historically unlikely for a man of this sort in the period—he brought probably
first to his task a knowledge of Christian poetry, especially that of
the Cædmon school, and especially *Genesis*. He makes his minstrel

1. I include nothing that has not some-
where been said by someone, if not in
my exact words; but I do not, of course,
attempt to represent all the *dicta*, wise
or otherwise, that have been uttered.

sing in Heorot of the Creation of the earth and the lights of Heaven. So excellent is this choice as the theme of the harp that maddened Grendel lurking joyless in the dark without that it matters little whether this is anachronistic or not. *Secondly,* to his task the poet brought a considerable learning in native lays and traditions: only by learning and training could such things be acquired; they were no more born naturally into an Englishman of the seventh or eighth centuries, by simple virtue of being an "Anglo-Saxon," than ready-made knowledge of poetry and history is inherited at birth by modern children.

It would seem that, in his attempt to depict ancient pre-Christian days, intending to emphasize their nobility, and the desire of the good for truth, he turned naturally when delineating the great King of Heorot to the Old Testament. In the *folces hyrde* [people's keeper: king] of the Danes we have much of the shepherd patriarchs and kings of Israel, servants of the one God, who attribute to His mercy all the good things that come to them in this life. We have in fact a Christian English conception of the noble chief before Christianity, who could lapse (as could Israel) in times of temptation into idolatry. On the other hand, the traditional matter in English, not to mention the living survival of the heroic code and temper among the noble households of ancient England, enabled him to draw differently, and in some respects much closer to the actual heathen *hæleð* [hero], the character of Beowulf, especially as a young knight, who used his great gift of *mægen* [strength] to earn *dom* [glory] and *lof* [renown] among men and posterity.

Beowulf is not an actual picture of historic Denmark or Geatland or Sweden about A.D. 500. But it is (if with certain minor defects) on a general view a self-consistent picture, a construction bearing clearly the marks of design and thought. The whole must have succeeded admirably in creating in the minds of the poet's contemporaries the illusion of surveying a past, pagan but noble and fraught with a deep significance—a past that itself had depth and reached backward into a dark antiquity of sorrow. This impression of depth is an effect and a justification of the use of episodes and allusions to old tales, mostly darker, more pagan, and desperate than the foreground.

To a similar antiquarian temper, and a similar use of vernacular learning, is probably due the similar effect of antiquity (and melancholy) in the *Aeneid*—especially felt as soon as Aeneas reaches Italy and the *Saturni gentem . . . sponte sua veterisque dei se more tenentem. Ic þa leode wat ge wið feond ge wið freond fæste worhte, æghwæs untæle ealde wisan* [I know the people firmly disposed toward friend and foe both, entirely blameless in the old way]. Alas for the lost lore, the annals and old poets that Virgil knew, and only used in the making of a new thing! The criticism that the important matters are put on the outer edges misses this point of artistry, and indeed fails to see why the old things have in *Beowulf* such an appeal: it is the poet himself who made antiquity so appealing. His poem has more value in consequence, and is a greater contribution to early mediaeval thought than the harsh and intolerant view that consigned all the heroes to the devil. We may be thankful that the product of so noble a temper has been preserved by chance (if such it be) from the dragon of destruction.

The general structure of the poem, so viewed, is not really difficult to perceive, if we look to the main points, the strategy, and neglect the many points of minor tactics. We must dismiss, of course, from mind the notion that *Beowulf* is a "narrative poem," that it tells a tale or intends to tell a tale sequentially. The poem "lacks steady advance": so Klaeber heads a critical section in his edition.[2] But the poem was not meant to advance, steadily or unsteadily. It is essentially a balance, an opposition of ends and beginnings. In its simplest terms it is a contrasted description of two moments in a great life, rising and setting; an elaboration of the ancient and intensely moving contrast between youth and age, first achievement and final death. It is divided in consequence into two opposed portions, different in matter, manner, and length: A from 1 to 2199 (including an exordium of 52 lines); B from 2200 to 3182 (the end). There is no reason to cavil at this proportion; in any case, for the purpose and the production of the required effect, it proves in practice to be right.

This simple and *static* structure, solid and strong, is in each part much diversified, and capable of enduring this treatment. In the conduct of the presentation of Beowulf's rise to fame on the one hand, and of his kingship and death on the other, criticism can find things to question, especially if it is captious, but also much to praise, if it is attentive. But the only serious weakness, or apparent weakness, is the long recapitulation: the report of Beowulf to Hygelac. This recapitulation is well done. Without serious discrepancy it retells rapidly the events in Heorot, and retouches the account; and it serves to illustrate, since he himself describes his own deeds, yet more vividly the character of a young man, singled out by destiny, as he steps suddenly forth in his full powers. Yet this is perhaps not quite sufficient to justify the repetition. The explanation, if not complete justification, is probably to be sought in different directions.

For one thing, the old tale was not first told or invented by this poet. So much is clear from investigation of the folk-tale analogues.

2. Though only explicitly referred to here and in disagreement, this edition is, of course, of great authority, and all who have used it have learned much from it.

Even the legendary association of the Scylding court with a marauding monster, and with the arrival from abroad of a champion and deliverer was probably already old. The plot was not the poet's; and though he has infused feeling and significance into its crude material, that plot was not a perfect vehicle of the theme or themes that came to hidden life in the poet's mind as he worked upon it. Not an unusual event in literature. For the contrast—youth and death—it would probably have been better, if we had no journeying. If the single nation of the *Geatas* had been the scene, we should have felt the stage not narrower, but symbolically wider. More plainly should we have perceived in one people and their hero all mankind and its heroes. This at any rate I have always myself felt in reading *Beowulf*; but I have also felt that this defect is rectified by the bringing of the tale of Grendel to Geatland. As Beowulf stands in Hygelac's hall and tells his story, he sets his feet firm again in the land of his own people, and is no longer in danger of appearing a mere *wrecca*, an errant adventurer and slayer of bogies that do not concern him.

There is in fact a double division in the poem: the fundamental one already referred to, and a secondary but important division at line 1887. After that the essentials of the previous part are taken up and compacted, so that all the tragedy of Beowulf is contained between 1888 and the end.[3] But, of course, without the first half we should miss much incidental illustration; we should miss also the dark background of the court of Heorot that loomed as large in glory and doom in ancient northern imagination as the court of Arthur: no vision of the past was complete without it. And (most important) we should lose the direct contrast of youth and age in the persons of Beowulf and Hrothgar which is one of the chief purposes of this section: it ends with the pregnant words *oþ þæt hine yldo benam mægenes wynnum, se þe oft manegum scod* [until age took from him the joys of his strength—old age that has often harmed many].

In any case we must not view this poem as in intention an exciting narrative or a romantic tale. The very nature of Old English metre is often misjudged. In it there is no single rhythmic pattern progressing from the beginning of a line to the end, and repeated with variation in other lines. The lines do not go according to a tune. They are founded on a balance; an opposition between two halves of roughly equivalent[4] phonetic weight, and significant content, which are more often rhythmically contrasted

3. The least satisfactory arrangement possible is thus to read only lines 1–1887 and not the remainder. This procedure has none the less been, from time to time, directed or encouraged by

more than one "English syllabus."
4. Equivalent, but not necessarily *equal*, certainly not as such things may be measured by machines.

than similar. They are more like masonry than music. In this
fundamental fact of poetic expression I think there is a parallel
to the total structure of *Beowulf*. *Beowulf* is indeed the most successful Old English poem because in it the elements, language,
metre, theme, structure, are all most nearly in harmony. Judgement
of the verse has often gone astray through listening for an accentual
rhythm and pattern: and it seems to halt and stumble. Judgement
of the theme goes astray through considering it as the narrative
handling of a plot: and it seems to halt and stumble. Language and
verse, of course, differ from stone or wood or paint, and can be only
heard or read in a time-sequence; so that in any poem that deals at
all with characters and events some narrative element must be
present. We have none the less in *Beowulf* a method and structure
that within the limits of the verse-kind approaches rather to sculpture or painting. It is a composition not a tune.

This is clear in the second half. In the struggle with Grendel one
can as a reader dismiss the certainty of literary experience that the
hero will not in fact perish, and allow oneself to share the hopes
and fears of the Geats upon the shore. In the second part the author
has no desire whatever that the issue should remain open, even
according to literary convention. There is no need to hasten like
the messenger, who rode to bear the lamentable news to the waiting
people (2892 ff.). They may have hoped, but we are not supposed
to. By now we are supposed to have grasped the plan. Disaster is
foreboded. Defeat is the theme. Triumph over the foes of man's
precarious fortress is over, and we approach slowly and reluctantly
the inevitable victory of death.[5]

"In structure," it was said of *Beowulf*, "it is curiously weak, in
a sense preposterous," though great merits of detail were allowed.
In structure actually it is curiously strong, in a sense inevitable,
though there are defects of detail. The general design of the poet
is not only defensible, it is, I think, admirable. There may have
previously existed stirring verse dealing in straightforward manner
and even in natural sequence with the Beowulf's deeds, or with the
fall of Hygelac; or again with the fluctuations of the feud between
the houses of Hrethel the Geat and Ongentheow the Swede; or
with the tragedy of the Heathobards, and the treason that destroyed
the Scylding dynasty. Indeed this must be admitted to be
practically certain: it was the existence of such connected legends—
connected in the mind, not necessarily dealt with in chronicle

5. That the particular bearer of enmity, the Dragon, also dies is important chiefly to Beowulf himself. He
was a great man. Not many even in
dying can achieve the death of a single
worm, or the temporary salvation of
their kindred. Within the limits of human
life Beowulf neither lived nor died in
vain—brave men might say. But there is
no hint, indeed there are many to the
contrary, that it was a war to end war,
or a dragon-fight to end dragons. It is
the end of Beowulf, and of the hope of
his people.

fashion or in long semi-historical poems—that permitted the peculiar use of them in *Beowulf*. This poem cannot be criticized or
comprehended, if its original audience is imagined in like case to
ourselves, possessing only *Beowulf* in splendid isolation. For *Beowulf* was not designed to tell the tale of Hygelac's fall, or for that
matter to give the whole biography of Beowulf, still less to write
the history of the Geatish kingdom and its downfall. But it used
knowledge of these things for its own purpose—to give that sense of
perspective, of antiquity with a greater and yet darker antiquity
behind. These things are mainly on the outer edges or in the background because they belong there, if they are to function in this
way. But in the centre we have an heroic figure of enlarged
proportions.

Beowulf is not an "epic," not even a magnified "lay." No terms
borrowed from Greek or other literatures exactly fit: there is no
reason why they should. Though if we must have a term, we should
choose rather "elegy." It is an heroic-elegiac poem; and in a sense
all its first 3136 lines are the prelude to a dirge: *him þa gegiredan
Geata leode ad ofer eorðan unwaclicne* [Then the Geatish people
made ready no mean pyre on the earth]: one of the most moving
ever written. But for the universal significance which is given to
the fortunes of its hero it is an enhancement and not a detraction,
in fact it is necessary, that his final foe should be not some Swedish
prince, or treacherous friend, but a dragon: a thing made by
imagination for just such a purpose. Nowhere does a dragon come
in so precisely where he should. But if the hero falls before a
dragon, then certainly he should achieve his early glory by van-
quishing a foe of similar order.

There is, I think, no criticism more beside the mark than that
which some have made, complaining that it is monsters in both
halves that is so disgusting; one they could have stomached more
easily. That is nonsense. I can see the point of asking for *no* monsters. I can also see the point of the situation in *Beowulf*. But no
point at all in mere reduction of numbers. It would really have
been preposterous, if the poet had recounted Beowulf's rise to fame
in a "typical" or "commonplace" war in Frisia, and then ended
him with a dragon. Or if he had told of his cleansing of Heorot,
and then brought him to defeat and death in a "wild" or "trivial"
Swedish invasion! If the dragon is the right end for Beowulf, and I
agree with the author that it is, then Grendel is an eminently suitable beginning. They are creatures, *feond mancynnes* [enemies of
mankind], of a similar order and kindred significance. Triumph
over the lesser and more nearly human is cancelled by defeat before
the older and more elemental. And the conquest of the ogres comes
at the right moment: not in earliest youth, though the nicors are

referred to in Beowulf's *geogoðfeore* [period of youth] as a presage of the kind of hero we have to deal with; and not during the later period of recognized ability and prowess; but in that first moment, which often comes in great lives, when men look up in surprise and see that a hero has unawares leaped forth. The placing of the dragon is inevitable: a man can but die upon his death-day.

I will conclude by drawing an imaginary contrast. Let us suppose that our poet had chosen a theme more consonant with "our modern judgement"; the life and death of St. Oswald. He might then have made a poem, and told first of Heavenfield, when Oswald as a young prince against all hope won a great victory with a remnant of brave men; and then have passed at once to the lamentable defeat of Oswestry, which seemed to destroy the hope of Christian Northumbria; while all the rest of Oswald's life, and the traditions of the royal house and its feud with that of Deira might be introduced allusively or omitted. To any one but an historian in search of facts and chronology this would have been a fine thing, an heroic-elegiac poem greater than history. It would be much better than a plain narrative, in verse or prose, however steadily advancing. This mere arrangement would at once give it more significance than a straightforward account of one king's life: the contrast of rising and setting, achievement and death. But even so it would fall far short of *Beowulf*. Poetically it would be greatly enhanced if the poet had taken violent liberties with history and much enlarged the reign of Oswald, making him old and full of years of care and glory when he went forth heavy with foreboding to face the heathen Penda: the contrast of youth and age would add enormously to the original theme, and give it a more universal meaning. But even so it would still fall short of *Beowulf*. To match his theme with the rise and fall of poor "folk-tale" Beowulf the poet would have been obliged to turn Cadwallon and Penda into giants and demons. It is just because the main foes in *Beowulf* are inhuman that the story is larger and more significant than this imaginary poem of a great king's fall. It glimpses the cosmic and moves with the thought of all men concerning the fate of human life and efforts; it stands amid but above the petty wars of princes, and surpasses the dates and limits of historical periods, however important. At the beginning, and during its process, and most of all at the end, we look down as if from a visionary height upon the house of man in the valley of the world. A light starts—*lixte se leoma ofer landa fela* [that light shined over many lands]—and there is a sound of music; but the outer darkness and its hostile offspring lie ever in wait for the torches to fail and the voices to cease. Grendel is maddened by the sound of harps.

And one last point, which those will feel who to-day preserve the ancient *pietas* towards the past: *Beowulf* is not a "primitive" poem; it is a late one, using the materials (then still plentiful) preserved from a day already changing and passing, a time that has now forever vanished, swallowed in oblivion; using them for a new purpose, with a wider sweep of imagination, if with a less bitter and concentrated force. When new *Beowulf* was already antiquarian, in a good sense, and it now produces a singular effect. For it is now to us itself ancient; and yet its maker was telling of things already old and weighted with regret, and he expended his art in making keen that touch upon the heart which sorrows have that are both poignant and remote. If the funeral of Beowulf moved once like the echo of an ancient dirge, far-off and hopeless, it is to us as a memory brought over the hills, an echo of an echo. There is not much poetry in the world like this; and though *Beowulf* may not be among the very greatest poems of our western world and its tradition, it has its own individual character, and peculiar solemnity; it would still have power had it been written in some time or place unknown and without posterity, if it contained no name that could now be recognized or identified by research. Yet it is in fact written in a language that after many centuries has still essential kinship with our own, it was made in this land, and moves in our northern world beneath our northern sky, and for those who are native to that tongue and land, it must ever call with a profound appeal—until the dragon comes.

* * *

KENNETH SISAM

The Structure of *Beowulf*†

* * *

In 1936 Professor Tolkien delivered his lecture on *Beowulf; the Monsters and the Critics,*[1] which brought fresh ideas and has influenced all later writers on the poem. Knowing well the detailed problems that occupy critics, he has withdrawn from them to give a general view of *Beowulf* as poetry, with a fineness of perception and elegance of expression that are rare in this field. The lecture, with its subsidiary notes, requires very careful reading. It does not lend itself to summary or dissection. As an account of what the poem means to Professor Tolkien, or of the way in which he, as a story-

† From *The Structure of Beowulf*, pp. 20–28. Copyright © 1965 Oxford University Press. Reprinted by permission of The Clarendon Press, Oxford. 1. *PBA*, 22 (1936), 245–95. References are to the separate print.

teller, would treat the plot, I have no criticism of it; and on many issues on which he differs from other critics I agree. But I dissent on two matters which especially concern the structure of the poem. The one is his explanation of the architecture of *Beowulf* as an artistic balance between the first two-thirds (1–2199) and the last part (2200–3182), analogous to the balance between the two halves of an Anglo-Saxon alliterative line; the other, his view that the central theme is the battle, hopeless in this world, of man against evil.

The idea that the structure of the poem is parallel with that of its long line has been criticized as fanciful.[2] On the metrical side the conception of balance is an elastic one, as may be seen from the variety of half-lines that are coupled together. But some objective tests can be applied: for example, a half-line of three syllables or one having no alliteration would seem unbalanced to most ears. No such test can be applied to the balance between the last part of *Beowulf* and the rest. Still the parallel throws light on the way in which 'balance' is used. 'The lines . . . are founded on a balance, an opposition between two halves of roughly equivalent phonetic weight, and significant content, which are more often rhythmically contrasted than similar.[3] In the first place 'balance' comes nearest to a primary sense 'equipoise'. Then we have the sense 'opposition', 'contrast', which does not imply equivalent weight. And yet a third, more elusive sense is involved in the discussion, i.e. 'harmony' of design. That its keyword should have such a range of meaning is a weakness of the interpretation.

The nature of the balance in the poem is stated: 'It is essentially a balance, an opposition of ends and beginnings. In its simplest terms it is a contrasted description of two moments in a great life, rising and setting; an elaboration of the ancient and intensely moving contrast between youth and age, first achievement and final death.'[4] Professor Tolkien avowedly favours the mythological school, and follows the method of interpretation by pairs of opposites, which tend to be vague. It is not clear what beginnings in the earlier part and what ends in the last part are opposed, or why Beowulf's rise to the throne should come in the last part. But time will be saved by concentrating on one of the pairs—youth and age.

In the earlier part of the story a distinction between the ages of Beowulf and Hrothgar is necessary: Hrothgar's greatness could not be maintained if he were fit to fight Grendel. 'Hampered by age, he lamented the loss of his youth, of his strength in battle' (2111 ff., cf. 1885 ff.). Beowulf was confident in his strength (669 ff.).

2. E.g. in a wide-ranging article by van Meurs, 'Beowulf and Literary Criticism', *Neophil*, 39 (1955), 114–30.

3. [Tolkien,] *Beowulf* &c., p. 31.
4. Op. cit., p. 29.

Really the contrast lies in this. Hrothgar's age is emphasized, not Beowulf's youth. 'Young' is applied to him only once, when Hrothgar says he has never heard one so young speak more wisely (1843). In over two thousand lines this and Wealhtheow's use of *hyse* (1217) are the express signs that Beowulf is a very young man. Nor is he represented as untried before he fights Grendel. On the contrary, the poet introduces him as the strongest man alive (196 f.). Hrothgar has heard from across the seas that he had the strength of thirty men (377 ff.). Unferth knew of his swimming match against Breca, a prodigious feat even in his version. At the beginning of his first speech in Heorot Beowulf claims: 'I have undertaken many great enterprises in my youth' (408 f.), and goes on to say that the wisest of the Geats had advised him to make the expedition because they had experience of his powers—how he had punished the race of giants and killed sea-monsters in the dark. When he first appears in the story he is a confident and proved hero.

Within the last part there is a contrast between Beowulf's age and Wiglaf's youth, but the emphasis and purpose are different. For Wiglaf, 'young' is the stock epithet.[5] The poet shows that when first achievement is in his mind he can express it: 'That was the first time the young warrior had to fight beside his lord' (2625 ff.). And, after the fight, Wiglaf says that it was 'beyond his powers' (2879). Beowulf is often described as old (*frod, gamol, har, eald, ealdhlaford*), but without elaboration. The one express contrast between his age and his youth is not striking.[6] There is no suggestion that age was a disadvantage in his fight with the Dragon —that he would have done better had he been younger. He still trusts to his own unaided strength (2540 ff.). The demonstration that no sword could bear the force of his stroke is reserved for this last fight (2684 ff.). The contest is beyond the power of any other man (2532 ff.).

To put my argument shortly—if the two parts of the poem are to be solidly bound together by the opposition of youth and age, it is not enough that the hero should be young in the one part and old in the other. The change in his age must be shown to change his ability to fight monsters, since these fights make the main plot. Instead, Beowulf is represented from beginning to end as the scourge of monsters, always seeking them out and destroying them by the shortest way.

Professor Tolkien's general interpretation—that the monsters symbolize Evil, and that the unifying theme is 'man at war with the

5. At lines 2626, 2674, 2675, 2811, 2860; cf. *unfrod* 2821.
6. 'I have undertaken many warlike adventures in my youth. Now that I am an old king, I will still seek battle and win fame' (2511 ff.). The first sentence echoes the beginning of his speech when he entered Heorot as a young man: hæbbe ic mærða fela/ongunnen on geogoðe (408 f.).

hostile world and his inevitable overthrow in Time'[7]—is an original variant of the 'struggle between good and evil'. Most later writers have approved it, but there have been some criticisms. Mr. T. M. Gang[8] noted that he used 'evil' in a range of meanings so wide that a large freedom of interpretation was assured. On the question of method I would add that it is unsafe to attach deep significance to things in which the poet has no choice. For example, if a proper name has to be introduced into a metre which it does not fit, abnormality is unavoidable and is not good evidence for the poet's voluntary treatment of that metre. The monsters Beowulf kills are inevitably evil and hostile because a reputation for heroism is not made by killing creatures that are believed to be harmless or beneficent—sheep for instance. So the fact that the monsters are evil does not require or favour the explanation that, in the poet's design, they are symbols of evil.[9]

But perhaps the strongest objection to this general interpretation arises from the number of ideas prominent in it that have to be read into the text. One is that Beowulf was defeated, that 'within Time the monsters would win'.[1] There is no word of his defeat in the poem. Wiglaf says, 'Yet God, the giver of victories, granted him that he, single-handed, avenged himself with steel' (2874 ff.); and, according to the poet, the Dragon Fight was 'his last victory' (2710). On the other hand, all the monsters are utterly defeated. The Dragon, the last and most terrible of them, is killed, robbed of his treasure, and his burnt-out carcass is shoved contemptuously into the sea (3131 ff.).

Another is the limitation of man's inevitable defeat to 'Time'. The contrast between life on earth and after-life, between Time and Eternity, was attractive to a Christian poet, yet it is not discussed in the text.

A third is the idea, often repeated, that the poet represents the courage of the Heroic Age as the courage of despair. It is hard to think of Beowulf as hopeless. He is praised by the poet because he has no fear of death.[2] He never broods on death or on life beyond it. When he surveys his own life on his last day, he has little to regret, much to recall with contentment.

These three ideas seem to be essential to the interpretation,

7. Op. cit., p. 18.
8. *RES*, n.s. 3 (1952), 6 f.
9. In some passages of Scripture and of Christian writings the Devil is represented by a 'dragon'. But our Dragon has no likeness to the dragon of the Apocalypse. Among patristic writers, none had greater authority in the West than St. Augustine of Hippo. With Psalm 90:13 in mind (*conculcabis leonem et draconem* ["You shall trample down the lion and the dragon"]) he says the Devil is represented by the lion *propter impetus*, by *draco propter insidias*. He is thinking of the traditional wiles of the serpent, not of an Anglo-Saxon fiery dragon who was formidable because of his furious assaults (*impetus*) rather than for his guile [*insidias*]. * * *

1. Op. cit., p. 22.
2. 'So shall a man do when he aims to win lasting praise in battle—he does not worry about his life' (1534 ff.; cf. 1442).

which invites the question: Why should a poet, having a great theme in mind, so conceal or disguise it that it has escaped 'the wisdom of a hepe of lerned men' in modern times? No reason has been given why an Anglo-Saxon audience should be more perceptive.

In a discussion which has been mentioned already,[3] Klaeber noted that the poem has 'a markedly edifying character which requires to be analyzed and explained'; and in a footnote he cites some far-fetched explanations as showing 'how urgently the necessity is felt of finding an additional, ulterior motive of some kind'. The existence of this feeling suggests that, for many modern critics, *Beowulf* in its plain meaning does not come up to the ideal standards they have set. Still, that does not compel us to search for some master-key, lost since Anglo-Saxon times. Possibly the standards assumed are inappropriate; certainly Anglo-Saxon taste and appreciation were very different from ours. Such reasons may account for the feeling that something essential to the understanding of the poem has been missed. It is questionable too whether a sense of 'urgent necessity of finding an additional, ulterior motive of some kind' makes for sound criticism, since it has brought writers who know the poem well to such strangely conflicting interpretations.

The uniqueness of *Beowulf* has its disadvantages. In Anglo-Saxon, or elsewhere in early Germanic literature, there is nothing comparable in age, content, and fullness of interest. So university teachers of Anglo-Saxon face a dilemma. Unless they neglect the greatest literary text in this field, they must, year after year, work over ground that has been very intensively worked already. The pressure to find something new is strong, and one of its consequences is a tendency to speculate on the things that are not expressed in *Beowulf*.

The kind of general interpretation that has been favoured in recent years[4] depends on two main assumptions. First, that the author of *Beowulf* was widely read in patristic writers: for this the text supplies no evidence in references or citations. Secondly, that he learned from patristic writers to use allegory; but though they, writing for learned readers, felt it necessary to explain their allegorical interpretations, he felt no need of explanation when composing poetry for an audience who preferred the vernacular. The divergent results that have already been derived from these assumptions should throw doubt on their validity.[5]

3. Above, p. 19, p. cxx of the third [Klaeber's] edition.
4. Note the preponderance of this kind in L. E. Nicholson's *Anthology of Beowulf Criticism*, Notre Dame, U.S.A., 1963.
5. Sisam's caveat against allegorical interpretations of *Beowulf* in terms of Christian patristics has gone pretty well unheeded. But his warning has been well taken—the approach must be used with great care and common sense. See the Kaske and Goldsmith essays that follow. *Ed.*

R. E. KASKE

[The Governing Theme of *Beowulf*] †

At the beginning of his famous paper on the thematic coherence of *Beowulf*,[1] now more than thirty years old, J. R. R. Tolkien remarks that the existing scholarship on the poem "is poor in criticism, criticism that is directed to the understanding of a poem as a poem" (p. 3). Though it is obvious that the past three decades have witnessed a spectacular improvement in our general intentions toward the poem *Beowulf*—in great part the result of Tolkien's essay itself—a survey of such attempts as have been made to interpret the poem *as a whole* leaves one with the impression that his comment is not altogether outdated. Let me add immediately that I do not intend to minimize the considerable progress which has in fact been made during this period toward a convincing interpretation of *Beowulf*. On the one hand, we have had countless interpretative studies of particular aspects or parts of the poem, many of them sensitive and well informed. Outstanding examples are a monograph by Anton Pirkhofer on the portrayal of characters in *Beowulf*;[2] and Adrien Bonjour's analyses of the digressions and other specific passages, which, while producing no overall interpretation beyond that of Tolkien, have made important contributions to our understanding of the poem.[3] On the other hand, there have been a number of major works which bear upon the interpretation of *Beowulf* with varying degrees of directness, though they cannot be thought of as primarily attempts to interpret it. Obvious examples are the metrical studies of John C. Pope, A. J. Bliss, and others;[4] the introduction and notes in the edition of C. L. Wrenn (London, 1953); Dorothy Whitelock's valuable exploration of the poem's intellectual background in *The Audience*

† Excerpted from "*Beowulf*," in *Critical Approaches to Six Major English Works*, R. M. Lumiansky and Herschel Baker, eds. (Philadelphia: University of Pennsylvania Press, 1971), pp. 3–40. Copyright © 1968 by the Trustees of the University of Pennsylvania. Reprinted by permission of the author and the publisher. Kaske, like most Christian allegorists, displays encyclopedic knowledge of the writings of the patristic tradition, i.e., of the early fathers of the Christian church. His copious notes are abbreviated here. Bracketed modern English versions of the OE are from Donaldson. I omit Kaske's lengthier Latin quotations and elevate his English from footnotes into the text.

1. "*Beowulf*: The Monsters and the Critics," *PBA*, 22 (1936), 245–95; references throughout are to the separate printing (Oxford, 1958) * * * [rpt. in *ABC*, p. 55–103, and *BP*, 8–56].
2. *Figurengestaltung im Beowulf-Epos* (Anglistiche Forschungen, 87; Heidelberg, 1940).
3. *The Digressions in Beowulf* (Medium Ævum Monographs, V; Oxford, 1950); *Twelve Beowulf Papers* (Université de Neuchâtel, Recueil de travaux publiés par la Faculté des Lettres, 30; Neuchâtel, 1962).
4. Pope, *The Rhythm of Beowulf* (New Haven, 1942); Bliss, *The Metre of Beowulf* (Oxford, 1958).

of *Beowulf* (Oxford, 1951); and Kenneth Sisam's *The Structure of Beowulf* (Oxford, 1965), in large part a reaction against the strenuous critical effort of the past thirty-odd years. Another example, perhaps less obvious, is Arthur G. Brodeur's admirable study *The Art of Beowulf* (Berkeley, 1959), which—despite keen individual analyses like those of the role of Unferþ (pp. 143–57), the passage on Freawaru and Ingeld (pp. 157–81), and the "subplot" depending on the fall of Hygelac (pp. 75–87)—is on the whole, as its title indicates, a descriptive treatment of various aspects of the poem rather than a comprehensive interpretation of it. We may notice in passing that any relation of the prolonged controversy concerning oral formulas to the interpretation of *Beowulf* seems thus far to be undefined and tentative, pending the development of a distinctive interpretative approach which can be convincingly applied to the poem as we have it.

Studies devoted to the interpretation of *Beowulf* as a whole during the past thirty years are, as I have suggested, fewer and in many cases less substantial than might be expected in an era enthusiastically committed to the intensive analysis of literary texts. Any account of them must of course begin with Tolkien's "*Beowulf:* The Monsters and the Critics" (note 1, above). As everyone now knows, Tolkien proposes that the monsters are at the center of the action precisely because their universality of meaning transcends what could be expressed through specific human antagonists, and that the resulting poem is "essentially a balance, an opposition of ends and beginnings . . . a contrasted description of two moments in a great life, rising and setting" (p. 29). Despite sporadic and, in my opinion, quite unsuccessful attacks,[5] this basic view of the poem seems to have gained for itself something like a core of general acceptance, and most subsequent interpretations will be found to rest on it in one way or another. To this deserved encomium, one should add that Tolkien's analysis is limited to the poem's broadest and simplest design, and makes no attempt to clarify its complex lesser patterns: the relation of episode to episode, the relevance of the digressive passages, and so on. To this extent his essay is not so much a comprehensive interpretation of *Beowulf*, as a brilliant indication of the direction in which such an interpretation is to be looked for. The same sort of distinction applies much more completely to another valuable pioneering study, Marie Padgett Hamilton's "The Religious Principle in *Beowulf*"[6] —which, though hardly offering a unified interpretation of the

5. *E.g.*, T. M. Gang, "Approaches to *Beowulf*," *RES*, n.s. 3 (1952), 1–12; J. C. van Meurs, "*Beowulf* and Literary Criticism," *Neophil*, 39 (1955), 114–30; Sisam (above) * * *.
6. *PMLA*, 61 (1946), 309–31 (reprinted in *ABC*, pp. 105–35).

poem, has increased radically our awareness of the possibilities for reading it in the light of patristic thought.

* * *

Nearly all the more recent attempts to interpret the poem as a whole are distinctively "Christian," though differing widely in their emphases. Maurice B. McNamee, S.J., in *Honor and the Epic Hero* (New York, 1960), maintains that "the character of Beowulf is such a complete verification of the Christian notion of the heroic or the magnanimous that it would almost seem to have been created to exemplify the virtue as Saint Paul and the early church Fathers sketched it—limited by the virtues of humility and charity" (p. 109). In his article *"Beowulf*—An Allegory of Salvation?"[7] Father McNamee suggests that "as an allegory of the Christian story of salvation the *Beowulf* poem both echoes the liturgy and reflects New Testament theological dogma" (p. 191). Beowulf's three major combats allegorize various aspects of the Redemption: the fight with Grendel reflects the essential story of salvation; the descent to the mere echoes the regenerative symbolism of baptism, as well as the Harrowing of Hell; the fight with the dragon allegorizes the death of the Savior. Besides containing a number of curious errors—for example, a reference to Beowulf as "expiring, like Christ, at the ninth hour" ("Allegory of Salvation," p. 204)—these studies consistently lack both the detailed documentation and the disciplined literary analysis normally needed to support such an interpretation, and so produce no really close correspondences of the kind that might be expected to carry conviction. * * *

* * *

A Christian poem of a different sort emerges from three articles by Margaret E. Goldsmith: "The Christian Theme of *Beowulf*," "The Christian Perspective in *Beowulf*," and "The Choice in *Beowulf*."[8] Central in all these studies (though it seems to become progressively milder and more qualified) is the view of Beowulf himself as less than an ideal figure—a noble though pagan hero, inevitably touched by the pride and avarice warned against in Hroðgar's sermon:

> . . . Beowulf is celebrated and yet, in a sense, found wanting, by the Christian poet. The hero, knowing nothing of Christ, is unregenerate man at his mightiest and most magnanimous. He conforms to the laws of his human nature, not to the laws of the

7. *JEGP*, 59 (1960), 190–207 (reprinted in *ABC*, pp. 331–52). * * *
8. *MÆ*, 29 (1960), 81–101; *Studies in Old English Literature in Honor of Arthur G. Brodeur*, ed. Stanley B. Greenfield (Eugene, Oregon, 1963), pp. 71–90

(abridged in *ABC*, pp. 373–86); *Neophil*, 48 (1964), 60–72. * * * [Goldsmith's *The Mode and Meaning of Beowulf* appeared after Kaske's essay; see the next selection in our text. *Ed.*]

Church. . . . In the first half of the poem the Christian ideal of loving service fuses with the Germanic ideal of love and loyalty to the lord. In the second part, the two ethics are in conflict in the person of the king, and here, by a subtle use of contrastive Christian allusion, the poet shows not only human strength and courage at their highest, but at the same time the weakness of unregenerate man alone in face of the Enemy ["Choice," pp. 63, 70].

A similar though more cogent distinction between the worthiness of Beowulf's actions in the two parts of the poem is drawn by John Leyerle in "Beowulf the Hero and the King."[9] According to Leyerle, the major theme of *Beowulf* is

the fatal contradiction at the core of heroic society. The hero follows a code that exalts indomitable will and valour in the individual, but society requires a king who acts for the common good, not for his own glory. The greater the hero, the more likely his tendency to imprudent action as king. The three battles with the monsters, the central episodes in the poem, reveal a pattern in which Beowulf's pre-eminence as a hero leads to the destruction of the Geats when he becomes king. . . . All turns on the figure of Beowulf, a man of magnificence, whose understandable, almost inevitable pride commits him to individual, heroic action and leads to a national calamity by leaving his race without mature leadership at a time of extreme crisis, facing human enemies much more destructive than the dragon [pp. 89, 101–2].

The studies of Goldsmith and Leyerle are full of illuminating points, and their general thesis concerning the hero—particularly as formulated by Leyerle—deserves serious consideration. My own opinion is that their arguments (especially that of Goldsmith) suffer continually from small distortions of emphasis, thus producing interpretations which, while difficult to "disprove," manage to be basically at odds with what will impress most readers as the governing attitude of the poem.

* * *

* * * it is evident that during the past twenty years or so the richest and most informative interpretations of *Beowulf* (apart from the question of their ultimate credibility) have been those employing Christian material and ways of thought. One reason, of course, is the comparative general neglect of Latin Christianity by earlier interpreters of medieval vernacular literature, and its recent enthusiastic rediscovery; another is the plethora of Christian writing which survives from the early Middle Ages, as against the almost complete lack of everything else; still another, I suspect, is

9. *MÆ*, 34 (1965), 89–102. * * *

the fact that any Christianity which can be convincingly revealed in *Beowulf*, with its pagan setting and essentially secular story, is likely to be present in unusually complex and interesting ways. Within the various Christian interpretations, the most important single critical question at the moment seems to be that of the poet's attitude toward Beowulf himself: to what extent is he an ideal heroic figure (possibly bearing some relation to Christ), and to what extent a somber portrayal of the inevitable doom that attends even the noblest of non-Christians? One possible answer will be suggested in my own interpretation of the poem, to which let us now turn.

The most profitable approach to *Beowulf* that I have found so far is by way of the old, widely recognized heroic ideal whose Latin formulation is *sapientia et fortitudo* ("wisdom and prowess").[1] In using this ideal as a basis for analyzing *Beowulf*, I do not of course mean to deny the existence or importance of other major themes and organizing principles in the poem. Interpretation of a work as early and isolated as *Beowulf* must of necessity be highly empirical; and the assumption that *sapientia et fortitudo* operates somehow as its thematic center seems to me to explain more about the poem —both its central narrative and its digressions—than any other theory I know of. In itself, of course, a series of direct references to such a formula, even at crucial points in the action, might be understood plausibly enough as an incidental interest of the poet; while, on the other hand, an apparent consciousness of it in the poem's larger patterns might in itself be reasonably discounted as inevitable. (In how many epics, for example, is the hero *not* depicted as wise and brave?) In *Beowulf*, however, the continual prominence of *sapientia et fortitudo* in both these ways seems to me to speak strongly for its being the governing theme.

Ernst Curtius has shown clearly the currency of this heroic ideal in authors possibly contributing to or reflecting aspects of the culture that produced *Beowulf*: Statius, "Dares" and "Dictys," Fulgentius, Alcuin, the *Waltharius*, the *Chanson de Roland*, and perhaps most explicitly Isidore's *Etymologiae*: "Nam heroes appellantur viri quasi aerii et caelo digni propter sapientiam et fortitudinem." ["For men are called 'heroes' (*heroes*) as if to say that they are 'aerial' (*aerii*), and worthy of heaven on account of wisdom and prowess."][2] Similar dichotomies occur frequently in the Old Testament, and

1. For a fuller and more completely documented version of the interpretation which follows, see my article "*Sapientia et Fortitudo* as the Controlling Theme of *Beowulf*," *SP*, 55 (1958), 423–56, here-after *SF* (reprinted in *ABC*, pp. 269–310).

2. I, xxxix, 9, ed. W. M. Lindsay (Oxford, 1911) * * *. Documentation for the present paragraph is included in *SF*, pp. 424–25.

occasionally in the *Disticha Catonis* and the Irish *Instructions of Cormac*. In the Germanic tradition as we have it, the ideal appears several times in the poems of the *Edda* as well as in Old English poems like *Widsiþ* (138–41) and the *Gifts of Men* (39–43, 76–77). There seems small room for doubt, then, that *sapientia et fortitudo* as a heroic ideal was familiar in the literature and the ways of thought most likely to have been available to the poet of *Beowulf*, and that there is no *a priori* unlikelihood about his having known and used the theme.

But if so, what did it mean to him? As the quality of a hero, *fortitudo* implies physical might and courage consistently enough. With regard to *sapientia*, we seem to have in *Beowulf* a general, eclectic concept including such diverse qualities as practical cleverness, skill in words and works, knowledge of the past, ability to predict accurately, and ability to choose rightly in matters of conduct. But there is a further, partly overlapping problem: Christian *sapientia* or pagan Germanic *sapientia*? I believe that in the theme of *sapientia et fortitudo* itself we may find (to misapply a remark of Tolkien's) "the precise point at which an imagination, pondering old and new, was kindled"[3]—that the poet has used this old ideal as an area of synthesis between Christianity and Germanic paganism. In a broad way, he seems first to draw on both traditions primarily as they relate to aspects of *sapientia et fortitudo*; and secondly, within this circumscribed area he seems to emphasize those parts of each tradition that can be made reasonably compatible with the other. We may notice that a core of this kind in the poem helps also to account for some of its apparent large ambiguities, like for example the co-existence of eternal salvation and earthly glory as the goals of human life; if Beowulf is deliberately made to behave wisely and bravely according to both codes, then the very ambiguity of both the *soðfæstra dom* ["judgment of the righteous"] and earthly *lof* ["praise, fame, glory"] is not only relevant but in a way demanded.

In Part I (1–2199), we find five key allusions to the *sapientia et fortitudo* of Beowulf, arranged symmetrically within the poem and themselves following a pattern of increasing elaborateness. The first is the poet's summarizing description of him as "snotor ond swyðferhð" ["wise and stout-hearted"] (826), immediately following the defeat of Grendel. The second is Wealhþeow's admonition, "cen þec mid cræfte on þyssum cnyhtum wæs/ lara liðe" ["make yourself known with your might, and be kind of counsel to these boys"] (1219–20), near the end of the festivities following Grendel's defeat. The third is Hroðgar's remark, "Eal þu hit

3. "*Beowulf*: The Monsters and the Critics," p. 27.

geþyldum healdest,/ mægen mid modes snyttrum" ["All of it, all your strength, you govern steadily in the wisdom of your heart"] (1705–6), following the defeat of Grendel's mother. The fourth is Hroðgar's similar remark, "þu eart mægenes strang ond on mode frod,/ wis wordcwida" ["You are great of strength, mature of mind, wise of words"] (1844–45), near the end of the festivities following her defeat. So far, I trust the symmetry is clear: a reference to Beowulf's *sapientia et fortitudo* as the thematic climax of each battle and of each celebration following his battles. The fifth and most elaborate statement occurs at the end of Beowulf's reception at the court of Hygelac, and seems to serve as the thematic climax of Part I as a whole. After praising Beowulf's *fortitudo* (2177–78) and summarizing the *sapientia* of his career (2179–80), the poet adds what sounds like an exact confirmation of Hroðgar's comment following the fall of Grendel's mother: "næs him hreoh sefa,/ ac he mancynnes mæste cræfte/ ginfæstan gife, þe him god sealde,/ heold hildedeor" ["His heart was not savage, but he held the great gift that God had given him, the most strength of all mankind, like one brave in battle"] (2180–83).

These five important passages are supported by Beowulf's speeches and actions in Part I. His *fortitudo* is obvious. His *sapientia* is variously illustrated by his skill and prudence in battle and a wisdom and foresight in the ways of violence generally; his skill in speech; his ability to predict accurately in his own and others' affairs; his respect for the counsels of the wise; his diplomatic ability, apparently including a grasp of situation and innuendo (1826–39); his realization of his dependence on higher powers; and by pagan Germanic standards, his properly high evaluation of glory. As a specific example, we may notice Beowulf's successive encounters with the coastwarden, Wulfgar, Hroðgar, and Unferþ, which form a series of confrontations designed to illustrate his *sapientia* in handling different types of questioners, and a broad parallel to the test of his *fortitudo* in the monster fights. The first three questioners are legitimate and courteous, and the success of Beowulf's answers to them is evident; the last, Unferþ, provides a hostile test of his *sapientia*, and can perhaps be interpreted in accordance with Gregorian psychology as the speaker of *sapientia* who is himself no longer *sapiens*.[4] Unferþ's taunt accuses Beowulf of recklessness—a lack of *sapientia*—and of a *fortitudo* inferior to Breca's. Beowulf defends his *sapientia* by emphasizing the formal *beot* ["boast, vow, promise"] (536) with its implicit purpose of attaining glory; the fitness of the venture for boys (535–37); and

4. Gregory, *Moralia in Iob*, XXVII, xlvi, 75, on Job 37:24 * * *. [For the Unferth episode see our text, pp. 9–11, and Morton W. Bloomfield, "*Beowulf* and Christian Allegory: An Interpretation of Unferth," *Traditio*, 7 (1949–51), 410–15 (rpt. in *ABC*, pp. 155–64, and *BP*, 68–75). *Ed.*]

their prudence in carrying weapons (539–41). To the reflection on his *fortitudo* he replies that he was not overcome; and that for him —unlike Breca—the exploit turned into an adventure worthy of a grown warrior; a fight against monsters, representing like Grendel the forces of external violence.

* * *

We are now confronted by the difficult second part of the poem. Like Part I, it is governed by the ideal of *sapientia et fortitudo*, though less obviously and with an important difference: Beowulf has progressed from hero to hero-king, and the ideal accordingly exists in relation to a different set of responsibilities and goals. Again, however, we find a somewhat symmetrical pattern of three major statements of the theme, all more elaborate than those in Part I, and all bearing a direct relationship to Beowulf's kingship. The first occurs at his real entry into Part II, following the announcement that his own hall has been burned. His *sapientia*, particularly his freedom from the pride warned against by Hroðgar, is illustrated by his wholesome fear of having transgressed the *ealde riht* ["old law"] (2327–32);[5] his *fortitudo* by his determination to meet the dragon (2335–36, 2345 ff.). The dichotomy is sharpened by the introductory epithets *se wisa* ["the wise one"] (2329) for the first part, and *guðkyning* ["the war-king"] (2335) for the second. The second major statement is Beowulf's own summary, following the fatal battle, of his career as king—emphasizing first his *fortitudo* by his protection of the realm (2732–36), then his *sapientia* by his avoidance of the major forms of Germanic wrongdoing (2736–43), all of them Christian sins as well. The third statement is in the concluding fourteen lines of the poem, where Beowulf is first praised for *fortitudo* (3169–74), then said to have been "manna mildust ond mon[ðw]ærrust,/ leodum liðost ond lofgeornost" ["mildest of men and the gentlest, kindest to his people, and most eager for fame"] (3181–82). The first three adjectives describe traits traditionally associated with *sapientia*—as for example in the Vulgate Old Testament, and in patristic statements of the ideal of kingly *sapientia*.[6] *Lofgeornost* I would interpret as the highest manifestation of Germanic wisdom, preserving a final and meaningful balance between Christian and pagan as well as between kingly and individual *sapientia*.

Omitting several lesser statements of the theme, I approach the interpretation of Part II with one important assumption: that in

5. Gregory, *Mor. in Iob*, XV, xxxvi, 42, on Job 21:4 * * *. See also *SF*, pp. 445–46. I would now incorporate, however, the convincing proposal of Morton W. Bloomfield, "Patristics and Old English Literature: Notes on Some Poems," *Brodeur Studies*, pp. 39–41 (reprinted in *ABC*, pp. 369–72), that the *ealde riht* is the *lex naturalis* ["natural law"].

6. E.g., Sap. 7:22–23 * * *.

view of the prominence given to Hroðgar's sermon in Part I, and the fact that it is addressed specifically to Beowulf, we may expect Part II to be in some way an account of how Beowulf does or does not live up to its precepts. The latter possibility—despite the recent arguments of Goldsmith, Leyerle, and others—seems to me to be contradicted by the total emphasis of the poem. Now Hroðgar's advice has consisted, briefly, of the admonition to cultivate *sapientia* and to combat its opposite, *malitia*, by checking the initial inner growth of pride and avarice. One notorious incitement to both pride and avarice is of course wealth, and the dragon's hoard is quite literally wealth, fought for by Beowulf; this I take to be the most important significance of the curse that is on the treasure, at least that aspect of it that seems to threaten Christian damnation. There is, to be sure, a certain amount of suspense concerning Beowulf's attitude toward the treasure, which might at first be thought to show a final pathetic gleam of avarice (2535–36, 2747–51, 2764–66). Not until he is at the point of death does he reveal his motive fully: as a wise king he has desired not the gold itself, but the good of his people to which it may contribute (2794–2801). The reburial of the treasure with Beowulf I would interpret as a final recognition of his irreplaceable prowess and wisdom. Just as there has been no one else among the Geats strong enough to win the treasure and wise enough to avoid its dangers, so there is no one left among them with the *fortitudo* to hold it and the *sapientia* to use it blamelessly and well. The treasure is *unnyt* ["useless"] (3168) because the rare ability to wield it has perished. Even Wiglaf, who is clearly described by way of the heroic ideal (*hæle hildedior* ["man brave in battle"], 3111; *se snotra sunu Wihstanes* ["the wise son of Weohstan"], 3120), is a model young retainer rather than a king, and seems pointedly contrasted with Beowulf in this very respect.[7]

And now at last, what of the dragon? First of all he is a real dragon, by defending his people against whom Beowulf gives final proof of kingly *fortitudo*. But there is more. Just as Grendel is an embodiment of external evil, or violence, so the dragon represents the greatest of internal evils, the perversion of the mind and will, *malitia*. As Grendel is *se ellengæst* ["the fierce spirit"] (86), so the dragon is an *atol inwitgæst* ["terrible malice-filled foe"] (2670); the roof of his lair is an *inwithrof* ["evil roof"] (3123), a detail so slenderly related to reality that it inevitably suggests allegorical intent; the identifications of both dragon and fire as *malitia* are patristic commonplaces;[8] and in a very real sense *malitia* does "sit

7. For a fuller discussion of Wiglaf, see *SF*, p. 454.
8. Gregory, *Mor. in Iob*, VII, xxviii, 36, on Job 6:18 * * *: ["For what is signified by the dragons except *malitia*? . . . In the perverted soul, therefore, the dragon lies down . . . because lurking *malitia* is cunningly covered over."]

on guard" over worldly treasure, in that the pursuer or possessor of it is subject to the constant initial dangers of pride and avarice. Grendel and the other perpetrators of violence in the poem must of course be thought of as themselves inwardly ridden by *malitia* (hence, I take it, Grendel's *glof* ["glove," or "pouch"] made of dragonskins, 2085–88); the dragon by contrast represents *malitia* itself, as a universal, and so comes a long step nearer to outright allegory than any other figure in the poem. As violence is the perversion of *fortitudo* and is combatted primarily by it, so *militia* is the perversion or abandonment of *sapientia* and is combatted by it, as in Hroðgar's sermon [pp. 30–31]. That some such idea of internal *malitia* and external violence as two great poles of evil did exist in the poet's scheme of things, seems evident from their mention by Hroðgar: "ne him inwitsorh/ on sefan sweorceð, ne gesacu ohwær/ ecghete eoweð" ["neither does dread care darken his heart, nor does enmity bare sword-hate"] (1736–38).

The dragon fight, then, is a brilliant device for presenting in a single action not only Beowulf's final display of kingly *fortitudo*, but also his development and his ultimate preservation of personal and kingly *sapientia*: first in combatting the ever-present danger of *malitia* in himself as a human being, and so fulfilling the theme announced in Hroðgar's sermon; and secondly, as king, in combatting an apparent spread of *malitia* among his people, typified by the action of the goblet-stealer and the later defection of his own retainers.[9] But if all this is so, why is the dragon allowed to kill Beowulf? The answer, I suspect, lies less in any one compelling reason than in an overall fitness of this ending. For one thing, the theme of Beowulf's defending the Geat nation (against both *malitia* and the ravages of a literal monster) certainly gains added significance from his not only facing death, but undergoing it bravely and willingly for his people's sake. Again, in both Germanic and Christian terms the fact of physical extinction is inevitable and relatively unimportant; what *is* of desperate importance is having fought the good fight. And the dragon fight, as I have interpreted it, is not only the climax but also the summary of Beowulf's kingship and of his life—in a sense, he has always fought the dragon. One may reflect also that an ending in which Beowulf won a final victory over the dragon of *malitia* and yet remained alive would leave him in a condition rather like that of Adam before the Fall; for man, the permanent victory over evil can be realized only through death. And finally, there is about Beowulf's death an air of inevitability that tends to remove it from the cause-and-effect of even symbolic dragon's tusks. Poetically, it is perhaps less

9. For a fuller discussion of Geatish *malitia* in Part II, see *SF*, pp. 452–53.

accurate to say that the dragon kills Beowulf, than that Beowulf dies fighting the dragon.

* * *

Before concluding * * * let us glance briefly at the question of a possible figurative association between Beowulf and Christ, which has troubled the minds of scholars for generations. While an allegorical correspondence of this kind strikes me as virtually out of the question, there does seem to be a real possibility for some sort of conscious analogy between Beowulf and Christ—a connection, that is, by which Beowulf is made not to serve as a figurative representation of Christ, but to remind us significantly of him in certain respects.[1] There is, for example, the familiar parallel between Hroðgar's laudation of Beowulf—"Hwæt, þæt secgan mæg/ efne swa hwylc mægþa swa ðone magan cende/ æfter gumcynnum, gyf heo gyt lyfað,/ þæt hyre ealdmetod este wære/ bearngebyrdo" ["Yes, she may say, whatever woman brought forth this son among mankind—if she still lives—that the God of Old was kind to her in her child-bearing"] (942–46)—and the remark of a woman to Christ in Luke 11:27: "Beatus venter qui te portavit, et ubera quæ suxisti" ["Blessed is the womb that bore thee, and the breasts that thou hast sucked"]. I do not think it has ever been pointed out that this speech occurs shortly after Christ has cast out a demon (11:14–18), while that of Hroðgar follows Beowulf's cleansing Heorot of the demonic Grendel. Again, Beowulf goes forth to fight the dragon accompanied by a band of twelve, one of whom is a culprit; during the fight the eleven retainers flee, and one (Wiglaf) returns. It would be difficult indeed to overlook the detailed parallel between this series of events on the one hand, and on the other the picture of Christ shortly before his death attended by the twelve Apostles; the treason of Judas; the flight of the eleven remaining Apostles; and the return of John at the crucifixion.[2]

In the light of my preceding interpretation, the most plausible thematic center for such an analogy between Beowulf and Christ would seem to be the ideal of *sapientia et fortitudo* itself. In accord with the familiar Pauline reference to "Christum Dei virtutem et Dei sapientiam" ["Christ the power and the wisdom of God"] (I Cor. 1:24), Christ is frequently represented by patristic writers as the *sapientia et fortitudo* of God—as for example in Gregory's exposition of Job 12:13: * * * "*With him [God] is wisdom and*

1. The distinction is essentially that drawn by Charles S. Singleton, "The Pattern at the Center," in *Dante Studies, I: Commedia, Elements of Structure* (Cambridge, Mass., 1957), pp. 45–60. Note the similar remarks of [Charles] Donahue, "*Beowulf* and Christian Tradi-

tion [: A Reconsideration from a Celtic Stance," *Traditio*, 21 (1965)], p. 116, in proposing a typological or figural significance for Beowulf.
2. Some further correspondences are suggested by Donahue, "*Beowulf* and Christian Tradition," pp. 107–8, 115–16.

might; he hath counsel and understanding. Not unfitly do we accept these words as referring to the Only-Begotten Son of the supreme Father, so that we understand him to be himself the wisdom and might [*sapientia et fortitudo*] of God. For Paul also bears testimony to our understanding of this verse, when he says, *Christ the power of God and the wisdom of God.*"³ In Old English literature, Christ is credited more simply with the possession of *sapientia et fortitudo.* A Vercelli Homily, for example, remarks of his early life that "mægene & syntero he wæs gefylled mid gode & mid mannum" ["he was filled with might and wisdom before God and before men"] (cf. Luke 2:40, 52); and the poetic "Descent into Hell" describes him at the Resurrection as "modig . . . sigefæst ond snottor" ["brave . . . victorious and wise"] (22–23).⁴ In addition, medieval interpretation of parts of Ps. 90:13 (Vulgate), "et conculcabis leonem at draconem" ["and thou shalt trample underfoot the lion and the dragon"], produces an image of Christ triumphing over a pair of creatures whose exegetical meanings bear a strong resemblance to the violence and *malitia* that I have proposed for the Grendel family and the dragon respectively; witness a sermon by Caesarius of Arles, traditionally attributed to Augustine:

> But the devil is called a lion and a dragon: a lion because of his violence, a dragon because of his snares; as a lion he rages openly, as a dragon he lies secretly in wait. In earlier times the church did battle against the lion; now she fights against the dragon. But even as the lion was conquered, the dragon is conquered. What might of the lion can stand against that lion [*i.e.,* Christ] of whom it is written: *The lion of the Tribe of Juda has prevailed* [Apoc. 5:5]? And what might of the dragon can stand against the death of the Lord, who hung the serpent upon a tree?⁵

The portrayal of a warlike and victorious Christ with his feet resting on a prostrate lion and dragon is also a commonplace in early medieval iconography.

But if the poet has indeed seen fit to establish such an analogy on the basis of *sapientia et fortitudo,* to what purpose? And in particular, what are we to make of the apparently fatal objection that whereas mankind is saved by the death of Christ, the Geats are doomed by the death of Beowulf? I would suggest that in this final decisive difference we are to see the *raison d'être* of the entire

---

3. *Mor. in Iob,* XI, viii, 11 * * *. See also patristic commentary on I Cor. 1:24 generally.
4. Hom. VI, ed. Max Förster, *Die Vercelli-Homilien* (Bibl. der ags. Prosa, XII; Hamburg, 1932), p. 137. "Descent into Hell," ed. G. P. Krapp and E. V. K. Dobbie, *The Exeter Book* (Anglo-Saxon Poetic Records, III; New York, 1936), p. 219.
5. Serm. LXIX, ed. G. Morin, *Sancti Caesarii Arelatensis sermones* (CCL, 103; Turnhout, 1953), I, 291–92. * * *

analogy: the champion Beowulf, in life reminiscent of the champion Christ in various aspects of his wisdom and power, is in the end revealed to be not God-man but man, his death not a supernatural atonement but a calamitous natural phenomenon. We may notice in passing that an analogy of almost any kind between Beowulf and Christ might in itself account for the notorious absence of explicit references to Christ in the poem.

Whatever one may think of this proposed analogy, there remains for our consideration one great theme hovering over the poem rather than active in it: that of the infinite *sapientia et fortitudo* of God as the source of all finite human *sapientia et fortitudo*. The idea is a familiar one in the Old Testament, particularly in Job: * * * ["In ancient men is wisdom, and in length of days prudence. with him (*i.e.*, God) is wisdom and might . . ."] (12:12–13). The frequency of similar brief allusions in *Beowulf* is obvious. Against this greater reality, the limited *sapientia et fortitudo* of the people in the poem are continually being projected, in a variety of ways. There are for example more or less explicit references, like the poet's remarks on the Danes' idol-worship (175–88) and the passage preceding the Finn Episode (1056–62). By way of less explicit comparison, there is the whole texture of allusion to the giants and their works, the scop's unusual knowledge of the distant past, the forgotten past of which the treasure is a dim reminder, and so on— all suggesting the limitations of individual human *sapientia*. Its limitations are expressed again in what might be called the "men know not—" theme, usually though not always applied to the forces of evil (e.g., 50–52), (162–63).[6] Still subtler contributions are the repeated mentions of the awe with which the people in the poem behold evidences of a mysterious evil imperfectly comprehended (e.g., 980–90).

Finally, there is a broader way in which the action of *Beowulf* is projected against this higher *sapientia et fortitudo*. Vital as human *sapientia et fortitudo* is for the very survival of peoples in the heroic age, the total impression left by the poem is that it is a rare enough combination in a world full of possibilities for error and weakness. Even the infrequent combinations of the two heroic virtues are not guaranteed to last; Hroðgar's decline in *fortitudo* invites Grendel, and Heremod's decay in *sapientia* as well as *fortitudo* brings on his own destruction and the dreaded lordless time. And finally, beyond his own control, man himself is mortal, as the elegy of the Last Survivor (2247–66) emphasizes to good purpose; even Beowulf, the persevering combination of both heroic

6. "Men cannot truthfully say who received that cargo [Scyld's burial-ship], neither counsellors in the hall nor warriors under the skies;" and "men do not know where hell-demons direct their footsteps." *Ed.*

virtues, must die at last, leaving to his people the unlikely chance of finding the ideal embodied in a new ruler. And above the imperfection, the mutability, and in any case the final impermanence of human *sapientia et fortitudo*—and heightening its poignancy—there towers the *sapientia et fortitudo* of God, perfect, unchanging, everlasting. In that contrast lies, at its deepest and most inclusive, the tragedy of *Beowulf*.

MARGARET E. GOLDSMITH

[Beowulf's Spiritual Vulnerability]†

The last voyage of Ulysses, as Dante describes it,[1] is a great triumph of the human will. Ulysses dares to use his powers to the uttermost without regard for safety or policy, pressing on into unknown waters until 'death closes all'. The modern reader responds with admiration to the magnificent gesture, finding it difficult to understand how Dante could imaginatively conceive this great hero and yet present him as a lost soul shrouded in everlasting flame. Ulysses, like Satan in *Paradise Lost*, and also, I would say, like Beowulf, embodies his author's impulse to defy his destiny. Yet in these poets themselves the impulse is subdued, as they follow what they believe to be a nobler ideal. There is something of this defiant spirit in Beowulf as he goes upon his last adventure; the decision to fight alone is foolish and splendid at once, like Ulysses's decision to press on into the uninhabited world. The comparison of these heroes suggests that modern interpreters of *Beowulf* may be misled by the poet's evident admiration of the hero's unfaltering courage into the supposition that he is drawn as a pattern of conduct to the end. In the case of Ulysses, the portrait is of a noble lost soul; in the case of Beowulf, the portrait is somewhat enigmatic and the manner of his death a paradox of defeat in victory. Hrothgar's admonition, as we have seen, prepares the audience for a conflict between the hero and the Devil. If he becomes spiritually negligent, the Enemy will have an initial advantage, as happened at Heorot when Grendel attacked the Danish king. Whether or not Beowulf becomes arrogant in later life, the conflict is inescapable. The appearance of the Dragon is prepared for, but the kind of retaliation the old king will make is left uncertain, and when he fights his motives and his spiritual strength are in doubt.

† From *The Mode and Meaning of Beowulf* (London: Athlone Press, 1970), chap. 7, "The Nature of the Hero," pp. 210–16, 221–25; chap. 8, "Structure and Meaning," pp. 245–48, 254–57, 265–66, 268–69. Copyright © 1970 by Margaret E. Goldsmith. Reprinted by permission of the author and the publisher. All notes are included, though some are abbreviated; *Beowulf* quotations are from Donaldson.
1. *Inferno*, 26, 112–20.

For this reason, those who read the poem may disagree about the poet's attitude to his hero's end.

Both Ulysses and Beowulf are epic heroes inherited by a poet whose values are very different from those of the warrior society which brought the hero into being. The traditional hero both entertained and exhilarated the community whose admirable qualities he epitomized. He was remembered for his military successes and for his adherence to a code of honour which opposed certain loyalties to self-interest and a system of donation to personal greed. A Christian society could still admire the loyalty and generosity of such a hero, but could not accept him as the epitome of all the manly virtues. As the social symbols of the community were transformed, so the symbolic persons had to change their allegiances[2] or cease to be the source of inspiration they had been during their legendary life. Could Beowulf be a source of inspiration for a Christian prince?

It will be useful to examine the degree to which Beowulf is given personality, and in what areas of human activity he has his being. There is a prevalent opinion that the poet created in him a mirror of kingship,[3] but I think it can be shown that the kinds of royal behavior which interested this author are narrowly circumscribed, and even a conflation of all the kingly acts described in the stories would not make a rounded portrait.

It is not difficult to demonstrate that the poet gives scant attention to Beowulf's private personal relationships. The hero does not speak of his parents, and his marriage is not mentioned, though it is inferred from the presence of a mourning woman at his funeral (3150). As he is dying he briefly regrets that he has no son and heir (2729 ff.); he gives his personal possessions to Wiglaf; to whom he uses the affectionate form of address *Wiglaf leofa* ["beloved Wiglaf"] (2745), but it is hard to estimate what kind of feeling the word *leofa* implies. It is used by Hrothgar (1758, 1854), Wealhtheow (1216), and Hygelac (1987) in addressing the hero, by Beowulf towards Hrothgar (1483) and Wiglaf (2745), and by Wiglaf to Beowulf in his peril (2663). Hrothgar is filled with strong fatherly affection for the young champion who has delivered him from the destroyers; he kisses and embraces him and weeps at his departure (1870 ff.), but Beowulf gives no sign of reciprocal grief. Brodeur has made much of the mutual love of Beowulf and his uncle Hygelac:[4]

2. A prince's change of aim in life is clear-cut in the OE *Guthlac A*; and even more explicit in the *Vita Guthlaci* * * *.
3. See particularly Levin L. Schücking, 'Das Königsideal im *Beowulf*' [*MHRA Bulletin*, 3 (1929), 143–54; rpt. in English in *ABC*, pp. 35–49], and also in J. Leyerle, 'Beowulf the Hero and the King' [*MÆ*, 34 (1965), 89–102].
4. A. G. Brodeur, *The Art of Beowulf* (Berkeley: University of California Press, 1959), pp. 80 ff. *Ed.*

The demonstration of this love through Beowulf's words and acts gives warmth and depth to the hero's personality, and an additional dimension to his actions. It is his strongest and most enduring emotion, and exerts its influence as long as he lives. In Part I, Hygelac is the center of Beowulf's world; in Part II, the recollection of Hygelac remains, a living, moving force, in his heart.[5]

There follows a good deal more in the same vein, but the text does not wholly support it. Loyalty and trust between uncle and nephew are indeed mentioned more than once, the relationship of these two is held up as an example (2166 ff.), and a strong feeling of kinship warms the words with which Beowulf hands his rewards to his king (2148 ff.). This is the expression of an ideal relationship between man and lord, strengthened by the family tie.[6] Much or little may be made of Beowulf's *Hygelac min* ["my own Hygelac"] (2434) in his recollections of youth. To Brodeur it means that Beowulf is 'thinking first and always of Hygelac',[7] but it might only imply that Beowulf took up arms in Hygelac's service. If Brodeur's reading were valid, some expression of sorrow at Hygelac's death would surely be demanded? Beowulf served faithfully, and avenged his lord's death, an action which according to his own philosophy was better than much mourning (cp. 1384 f.); nevertheless, Beowulf's last reminiscences, which include a sympathetic account of Hrethel's grief for Herebeald (2444 ff.), do not mention Beowulf's own early loss of Hygelac as such, though there is an oblique reference to the battle in which he died (2501 ff.). Brodeur reads between the lines a 'passionate resolve (lines 2497 ff.) to be worthy, in his last fight, of his beloved Hygelac'.[8] I do not find this personal element in the speech; it seems to be a recollection of past victories meant to hearten the great warrior,[9] countering the 'dark thoughts' (cp. 2332) which fill his breast: *beotwordum spræc/ niehstan siðe: 'Ic geneðde fela/guða on geogoðe; gyt ic wylle,/ frod folces weard, fæhðe secan,/ mærðu fremman'* ["for the last time he spoke words in boast: 'In my youth I engaged in many wars. Old guardian of the people, I shall still seek battle, perform a deed of fame'"] (2510–14).

It could be argued that Beowulf's reticence about his personal bereavements (cp. 2150 f.) is fitting for a martial hero, in whom the softer emotions are cloaked. But the truth is that Beowulf, in spite of his recollection of so many battles in the speech just

5. *Ibid.*, p. 83.
6. Cp. *The Battle of Maldon*, 223 f.
* * *.
7. Brodeur, *Art*, p. 85.
8. *Ibid.*
9. The four references to Hygelac's last

battle are of some structural importance in the poem; the event is a pivotal point in the history of the Geats, and this fact rather than interest in Hygelac as a person accounts for the repetition of it.

quoted, is not actually presented as a campaigner. No battle in which he took part is fully narrated. One is particularly conscious of an opportunity missed in the account of Hygelac's last battle, in which Beowulf's part is a feat of swimming bearing in his arms thirty trophies of war (2359 ff.) and a wrestling with Dæghrefn the Frankish champion, briefly mentioned in his reminiscences (2501 ff.); there is no display of Beowulf's valour against great odds on the banks of the Rhine. He provides no model here for a royal commander or for a swordsman.

In what activities could Beowulf be considered a pattern of princely behaviour? First I would place his courteous speech and behaviour at court, which provide a counterbalance to the savagery of the wrestling with Grendel, assuring the audience that though he can at need match ferocity with merciless violence, he is himself neither aggressive nor uncouth. His controlled rejoinder to Unferth's scornful mockery, which might have brought a challenge or a blow from an irascible man,[1] and his reported forbearance with his drunken retainers (2179 f.) consort well with the brief statement that the Geatish warriors thought him *sleac* ["slack"] and *unfrom* ["unbold"] in his youth.[2] As his courage is never in question, their poor estimation of him as a young warrior is most reasonably taken as a sign that his temperament was equable and peace-loving; his anger and the full use of his strength were reserved for retaliation against aggressors (cp. 423 f.).

His motives for fighting are important. He is more the knight than the adventurer in his early exploits, first fighting the giants and *niceras* ["water-monsters"] who attacked the Geats (420 ff.), and then sailing to the help of the Danish king, *þa him wæs manna þearf* ["since he had need of men"] (201). When he and his men arrive in Denmark, Wulfgar guesses from their bearing that they have come *for wlenco, nalles for wræcsiðum, ac for higeþrymmum* ["for daring—not for refuge, but for greatness of heart"] (338 f.). Hrothgar gives other reasons than these for Beowulf's appearance at his court; the first, unfortunately, is in some doubt, because of textual corruption, but the second lays to Beowulf's credit an unselfish desire to help: *for arstafum* ["for past favors"] (458). This bears out the laconic indication of line 201, and implies that Beowulf's great adventure at Heorot was not begun in a spirit of self-glorification as Wulfgar's words suggest, but to put his services at the disposal of the unfortunate

1. Schücking (op. cit., p. 153) suggests that the Unferth digression was introduced principally to show Beowulf *continens in ira* ["self-controlled in wrath"]. I think this is one among several functions of this episode.

2. No doubt the trait was traditional, but it need not have been included by the poet in his eulogy of the hero.

Hrothgar. The other phrase used by Hrothgar about Beowulf's intentions reads in the manuscript *fere fyhtum* (457); the editors are divided in their choice of emendation; some read *for were-fyhtum* 'for defensive fighting',[3] which is palæographically probable and semantically in accord with what has been said above concerning Beowulf's successes as a deliverer of the afflicted. Klaeber, Dobbie and others adopt Trautmann's proposal *for gewyrhtum* 'because of deeds wrought in the past', an allusion to Hrothgar's generosity towards Beowulf's exiled father, now to be repaid by the son.[4] Though this reading is harder to defend on palæographical grounds, I think it undoubtedly makes better sense in the context. In a rather similar way, Beowulf's own generosity is repaid when he in his turn is in danger from a monster, as Wiglaf remembers all that he owes to his lord (2606 ff.) and urges his companions to think of Beowulf's deserts (*ealdgewyrht* 2657).[5] Whichever interpretation of Hrothgar's words is preferred, this speech ascribes honourable and unselfish motives to Beowulf. He certainly also desires to win fame at Heorot, but less for self-glorification than to deserve well of his king and reflect honour upon him[6] (cp. 435 f.). He does not set out for Denmark to enrich himself: he receives the great rewards Hrothgar offers him with natural pleasure, but he shuns the treasure he finds in the giants' hall (1612 f.), and on his return home he presents the costly gifts to King Hygelac and Queen Hygd (2145 ff.). His motives for fighting the dragon are more complex and I will defer consideration of them to later in the chapter.

The hero's relations with his followers are treated in the most general terms. His companions in the first adventure are a shadowy band, among whom he has no particular friend; he betrays no grief for Hondscioh as Hrothgar does for Æschere in similar circumstances.[7] The Geat warriors are not created as individuals; they share a corporate sorrow at the thought of never seeing their homes again (691 ff.), and an equal keenness to protect their lord's life (794 ff.). The death of one of them emphasizes both Grendel's savagery and, by contrast, Beowulf's extraordinary prowess; if the man had been introduced to the hearers as a living person, Beowulf's failure to try to save him would be intolerable.[8] The hero is conscious of his duty towards his men collectively (1480 f.) and

3. So Grundtvig, Wrenn, and von Schaubert.
4. For other less likely suggestions, see Dobbie's note, *Beowulf* [New York: Columbia University Press, 1953], p. 140.
5. I follow Klaeber and Wrenn in the interpretation of *ealdgewyrht*; for other possibilities, see Dobbie's note, *Beowulf*, p. 253.
6. The warrior's duty to ascribe his own successes to his lord is an often-quoted feature of Germanic life as Tacitus records it (cp. *Germania*, c. 14).
7. In his report to Hygelac, Beowulf does indeed speak briefly of him in terms of esteem and affection, but without mention of personal sorrow (2076 ff.).
8. For further comment on this incident, see p. 264, below.

he shows some magnanimity in sharing the honours of victory with them in his report to Hrothgar (958 ff.).[9] In these relationships, therefore, he worthily fills the office of a leader of men, but no private feeling is described.

This limited private portrait is consonant with the portrayal of an ideal ruler, but when the poem is scrutinized it becomes clear that the poet is silent about all the public duties of a king relating to law-making and the administration of justice. It is said that he ruled well, but there are no instances to show how he protected the helpless or kept peace within the land. It would seem, therefore, that the poet did not use the opportunities provided by the story to show Beowulf's private loves or friendships, or to create a complete portrait of an able commander or a just king. Apart from the monster-fights, few of the hero's specific deeds are mentioned. His goodness and success as a king are stated rather than illustrated, and one must turn to what he says and what is said about him to discover more of his character.

I have already discussed Hrothgar's estimation of him in the great admonitory speech. I now turn to the summing-up of his character at the end of the first part of the poem (2177 ff.), in which he is praised for self-control (2179 f.),[1] as by Hrothgar. The first sentence of the passage reads, *Swa bealdode bearn Ecgðeowes,/ guma guðum cuð godum dædum,/ dreah æfter dome* ["Thus Beowulf showed himself brave, a man known in battles, of good deeds, bore himself according to discretion"] (2177–79). The phrase *godum dædum*[2] appears to be in strange company if the rest of the sentence is interpreted in purely secular terms. But it is to be remembered that the battles in which Beowulf has shown bravery up to this point in the story are not the campaigns of his king, but early combats against *eotenas* and *niceras* ["giants" and "water-monsters"] and the exploits at Heorot for which he is being honoured by Hygelac. *Dom* no doubt means the good estimation of his king and his fellows, but it also has connotations of righteousness, as in the compound *domfæst*.[3] I interpret this sentence, in accord with what follows, as an allusion to Beowulf's use of his strength in the service of God and man, never in brawling or in aggressive fighting. This is the only eulogy of Beowulf in the poet's own voice, but two other passages enumerate his virtues.

9. His generous distortion of what actually happened may be compared with Wiglaf's equally honourable distortion of the end of the dragon-fight in his report of it (cp. 2875 f.).

1. One trait included in this speech has already been mentioned, namely, his forbearance towards his retainers in their cups.

2. ["of good deeds"] Klaeber's note,

Beowulf [Boston: Heath, 1950], Suppl. pp. 457 f., suggests that this is a Christian phrase (cp. *bona opera*) which has here undergone what Tolkien calls 're-paganization'. I should prefer to look upon it as a nodal point where secular story and moral allegory meet.

3. Note the use in the OE *Genesis* of *domfæst* (1510) and *godum dædum* (1507) of Noah.

One is his own appraisal of his life as he lies dying, the other is his followers' praise of him in their funeral lament. Neither of these can be assumed to present objectively the poet's estimation of the hero, since the former may also disclose the limitations of a pagan moral philosophy, and the latter will present the dead king in the best possible light according to the *ethos* attributed to that time and country. * * *

* * *

Beowulf's recollections cover fifty years in which all his enemies were kept at bay. These words naturally recall Hrothgar's similar experience before Grendel came, and bring Hrothgar's observations about his life back into mind (cp. 1769 f.). The rather vague lines, *Ic on earde bad/ mælgesceafta, heold min tela* ["In my land I awaited what fate brought me, held my own well"] (2736 ff.), perhaps suggest that King Beowulf did not journey abroad like Hygelac, leaving his people unprotected. A similar thought—that he did not engage in aggressive fighting—might lie behind *ne sohte searoniðas* ["I sought no treacherous quarrels"] (2738), but it is rather more likely that the poet's mind has turned to domestic affairs; Beowulf was not drawn into intrigue or treachery such as marred the lives of Unferth, Finn and Ingeld, for he speaks of false oaths, and as the climax of the list of evil acts eschewed he puts the murder of kinsmen.

It appears from this speech that Beowulf's life as ruler has fulfilled its promise. He has not fallen into the evil ways of Heremod or any of those other kings in the stories who came to violent ends. Kaske says that this speech 'illustrates his *sapientia* by his avoidance of the major forms of Germanic wrongdoing (2736–43), all of them Christian sins as well'.[4] If so, it is a curiously limited sort of *sapientia*. As Augustine said of another such list of negative virtues, the qualities of the just man in Psalm 14: *ista non sunt magna* 'these are not great'.[5] Augustine was not disposed to believe that it was enough to avoid certain kinds of malicious or dishonest dealing to reach God's holy hill; these must be the prerequisites to the attainment of higher virtues. Both the psalm and Beowulf's speech include rather universally-admired personal and social virtues; the form of the speech readily evokes remembrance of the psalm, which would seem to the Anglo-Saxon Christian more pertinent to Beowulf's situation than it does today, since the *tabernaculum* of the first verse suggested a military tent in which God's soldiers went

4. P. 446 [R. E. Kaske, "*Sapientia et Fortitudo* as the Controlling Theme of *Beowulf*," *SP*, 55 (1958), 423–57; rpt. in *ABC*, pp. 269–310. See also Kaske's preceding essay in our text; *sapientia*, "wisdom."].

5. Augustine, *Enarr. in Ps.*, *CCSL* 38, 89.

campaigning with him. The Pseudo-Bede commentary on the psalm therefore calls the list of the just man's good qualities *nobilium militum descriptio* 'a description of noble soldiers'.[6] Moreover, the fourth verse of the psalm: *ad nihilum deductus est in conspectu eius malignus* 'in his sight the malignant one is brought to nothing'—is referred by the commentator (following Augustine) to the Evil One, who can establish no hold over a man unless the rational soul *Creatorem neglegit . . . et terrena appetit* 'disregards the Creator . . . and desires earthly things'.[7] Thus the underthought of Psalm 14 has the same tenor as Hrothgar's sermon and concerns the conquest of the Enemy by the just soul. It seems to me that Beowulf's enumeration of these lesser virtues was meant to call up such thoughts as underlie the description of God's soldier in the psalm, harking back to Hrothgar's admonitory speech and thus bringing the allegorical significance of the dragon-fight to the fore. But before I turn to the allegory, I must complete the secular portrait.

The last lines of the poem praise the dead king in the words of his followers: as kind and gentle to all men, and as *lofgeornost* ["most eager for fame"]. That final controversial word leaves the hearers with a tacit question: did Beowulf do right to challenge the dragon alone? Apart from this doubt, the picture is highly favourable. The nearest analogue I have found is the eulogy of Emperor Constantine in the *Life* by Eusebius, which shows a similar combination of warlike fierceness towards the enemy and gentle benevolence of nature.[8] I do not know whether this *Life* was available to the *Beowulf* poet as a model, but it is interesting to find an earlier example of a kind but terrifying ruler in Christian literature. In other respects the eulogy notably lacks mention of Christian qualities, such as humility, piety, righteousness, justice for the weak and sternness towards the malefactor.[9] Some of these virtues would come strangely from the mouths of a pagan *heorðwerod* ["body of retainers"], and the poet shows a sense of artistic propriety in allowing the funeral itself to be the last word upon the hero. Granting this, one may still note that the poet's praise in his own voice is of Beowulf as prince, at the end of the first part of the poem (2177–99), so that there is in fact no complete eulogy of Beowulf as king.

6. Ps. Bede, *In Ps. Lib. Exegesis, PL* 93, 556.
7. Ibid., 557.
8. Eusebius, *The Life of Constantine*, trans. A. C. McGiffert, Bk. I, ch. 46, p. 495. It may also be noted that ch. 45 praises Constantine's forbearance with those who were exasperated with him.
9. These qualities all occur in Ælfric's eulogy of the martyr-king Edmund, which is quoted by Schücking (op. cit., pp. 148 f.) without any indication that the portrait of Beowulf is substantially different. Schücking also speaks of 'das ideal eines milden Friedensfürsten' ["the ideal of a gentle prince of peace"] (p. 149) though there are no instances at all of Beowulf in the role of peace-maker; he terrifies his enemies into quiescence, but that is hardly the same thing; he also seems to have a poor estimation of Hrothgar's attempts to make peace by compact.

It has sometimes been argued that the word *lofgeornost* carries implications of excess,[1] but one would not expect the king's followers to review his faults in their lament for him. This consideration, and the parallelism of the other superlative expressions, make the translation 'too eager for fame" inappropriate. Nevertheless, the word is double-edged, and may well be meant as dramatic irony, in view of Wiglaf's earlier censure of Beowulf's decision to go after the dragon (3077 ff.) and the forecast of a wretched future for the Geats as a consequence of his fatal combat (3018 ff.). Beowulf's zeal for fame quite evidently proved calamitous to his people, and it may reasonably be thought an example of *desmesure*, the opposite of the ideal of *mensura* which Schücking rightly recognized to be present in the poem.[2] Strangely, Schücking did not consider the possibility that Beowulf in the end fell short of the ideal. Yet the hero was at the best tragically wrong to suppose that his single combat with the dragon would benefit his people. If a worse construction is placed on his decision to fight alone for the treasure, it may be said that his heroic desire for glory was selfish and imprudent. The poet does not say this, nor does he praise him unequivocally for this act of heroism. In this way he brings the code of personal heroism into question.[3]

In the first part of the poem no questioning of ethical ideals is apparent. It is said to Beowulf's credit, *dreah æfter dome* ["he bore himself according to discretion"] (2179). But his early fame was won in willing service of his fellow-men, accompanied by trust in God, so that his heroic deeds did not contravene God's law. If he endangered his own life, he harmed no other person by so doing. After fifty years, he is in the very different situation of a man with power and responsibility. In secular terms, the heroic gesture may prove detrimental to his subjects.[4] From a religious point of view, the search for fame which in the young prince was a part of loyal service to God and king, has become in the old ruler a much more selfish quest in which God is not acknowledged as the author of his strength and upholder of his power. Following this train of thought, one can see that the heroic gesture and its calamitous effects are what one would expect to stem from the spiritual deterioration described by Hrothgar. The unrecking challenge *per se* is a symptom of arrogant self-confidence, and if there

---

1. See Tolkien's observations on '*Ofermod*', printed as an appendix to 'The Homecoming of Beorhtnoth Beorhthelm's Son', *Essays and Studies* (1953), 13–18. Leyerle, who states his indebtedness to Tolkien (op. cit., p. 97), translates *lofgeornost* 'too eager for praise' (p. 101).
2. [*mensura*, "temperance"; *desmesure*, "intemperance"] Schücking, op. cit., pp.
151 f.
3. The word *wyruldcyning* ["world-king"] has the same double-edged significance as *lofgeornost*; see also my earlier comments on this word in *Neophil*, 1964, 71, n. 21.
4. Leyerle, op. cit., pp. 98 ff., stresses this aspect of the poem.

is added to it a desire for gain, the hero's bold action is spiritually perilous.[5]

* * *

Beowulf, as I have said * * *, is portrayed first and foremost as a just man who nobly fought a losing battle against the evil powers. Because he was also a king with responsibility to defend and protect a people, the consequences of his overthrow brought sorrow to a whole nation. God might pardon Beowulf's fault ultimately, but the temporal effects of his fatal fight could not be undone. The king's interior struggle was vital not only to himself, but to all those whose lives came into contact with his. The setting of actual wars and feuds was necessary to give Beowulf solidity and to present the truth, as the poet understood it, that the miseries of earthly life were caused by the subjection of mankind to the Devil.

The very influential study of the subsidiary stories and digressive elements in *Beowulf* by Professor Bonjour[6] shows, I think, a characteristically modern attitude to the relation of the historical to the symbolic fighting in the poem. I quote his general view of the value and function of the digressions:

> First, the very number and variety of the episodes renders the background of the poem extraordinarily alive; they maintain a constant interest and curiosity in the setting and, by keeping continuously in touch with 'historical' events, represent the realistic note serving as a highly appropriate foil to the transcendental interest of the main theme with its highly significant symbolic value. The way in which many digressions are presented, the allusive manner that so often suggests rather than describes, the light and subtle undercurrent of implications and connotations that runs beneath the vivid pageantry of many scenes, all contribute to create the 'impression of depth' which, as pointed out by Professor Tolkien, justifies the use of episodes and makes them so appealing.[7]

With Bonjour's general valuation of the episodes in themselves I warmly concur, but I cannot accept that they 'represent the realistic note, serving as a highly appropriate foil to the transcendental interest of the main theme'. The word 'foil' implies opposition and contrast, but in the thought-world of the poem the meaning of life lies in the interpenetration of the visible and the supernatural worlds. Unless Beowulf were a 'real' man implicated in the affairs of nations the 'highly significant symbolic value' of the central

5. Note that the Carolingian writers on kingship quoted by Leyerle (ibid., pp. 98 f.) are more concerned with 'the consequence of pride as damnation of the soul' than 'the destruction of the nation'. * * *

6. A. Bonjour, *The Digressions in 'Beowulf'* [Oxford: Blackwell, 1965]. * * *

7. Bonjour, ibid., p. 71. * * *

action would not be shown to have relevance to other men in positions of authority. The 'historical' digressions which do not directly
impinge on Beowulf's life I take to be examples which are chosen
to point and elaborate certain elements in the central story, to make
them more prominent and memorable. These elements have to do
with human feuds and the motives which cause and perpetuate
them. The motives are the Devil's own motives which he was
thought to have insinuated into human nature, his daily business
being to stir them into activity, to the detriment of the individuals
concerned and the progress of mankind at large. The view of
human nature in the stories is pessimistic, in accord no doubt with
some of the author's own experience and his knowledge of history,
but also in accord with his philosophy, in that the people of the
stories had ordinarily no means of grace and were easily dominated
by the unruly impulses which Adam's sons inherited.

The Christian historians from Eusebius onward taught that God
governed human life, but that the Devil and his cohorts, including
those human beings whom he had suborned, were permitted to
cause strife and suffering, for reasons which remained inscrutable:[8]

> Manifestly the one true God rules and governs these things as
> he pleases; and if his motives are hidden, are they therefore
> unjust? So it is, even with the duration of wars, as it is in his will
> and just judgment and mercy either to afflict or to console the
> human race, so that some wars come to an end sooner, some
> later.[9]

Augustine and his disciple Orosius[1] also believed that in the pre-
Christian era the world was even more unhappily riven with contention than in their own troubled times. It is small wonder that
an Anglo-Saxon Christian poet, who received besides in his native
poetry a memorial to the legendary past of feuds and violent
deaths, should himself portray the imagined world of his ancestors
in a rather one-sided fashion. Like Augustine, he was able to believe
that a beneficent Creator had ordered the universe and still
watched over it, though men were given the freedom to act against
the eternal law and cause suffering to themselves and others, even
as Cain was permitted to kill his innocent brother. A Christian poet
of that period would certainly not have expected to find in existence
in the unregenerate world the *ordinata concordia* ["harmonious
order"] which was, as Schücking says, the ideal of a Christian
state in its internal and external relations.[2] The world which

---

8. See R. L. P. Milburn, *Early Christian
Interpretations of History* (London,
1954), especially chaps. 4 and 5.
9. Augustine, *De civitate Dei, CCSL* 47,
158. [The Latin is omitted.]

1. Paulus Orosius, *Historiarum adversum
paganos libri* VII, *CSEL* 5, passim.
2. Cp. Schücking, 'Das Königsideal im
Beowulf', p. 147. * * *

Beowulf is imagined as inhabiting had no pattern of brotherly love to oppose to the spirit of self-interest which haunted it, and in it the natural goodness of the wise was all too easily marred by the Devil's persistent attempts to make men more like himself.

The history of the world according to the Christian historians began with a brother-murder and the building of a city.[3] The central story of *Beowulf* begins with the building of Heorot, which shelters the fratricide Unferth and is taken over by the posterity of Cain. These things and the foreshadowing of the destruction of the place by fire are signs that the poet wished his hearers to see in his history a microcosm of the story of carnal man, his technical achievements, his destructive antagonisms and his ultimate ruin. He portrays the ruthless ferocity of the forces of evil, opposed and for a time held off by the power of natural goodness in one man, and the way in which the corruption of the race itself nullifies the effects of that victory. He then shows, with more terrifying effect, how the evil powers sap the hero's strength from within, so that he too follows Adam's errant steps to the way of all the earth, leaving the people once more in the power of the forces of destruction.

* * *

The digressions and episodes of the poem are divided by Bonjour into two main groups: those which concern the background and those which are connected with the main theme.[4] The division is an artificial one, as Bonjour himself reveals by putting the Finnsburg and Heathobard episodes in both groups, and by separating the Swedish-Geatish wars (in the second group) from the Danish wars involving the destruction of Heorot (placed in the first group). These peripheral parts of the poem all reinforce the central theme, which Bonjour has conceived too narrowly. He follows Tolkien in defining the main theme, quoting the latter's statement 'In its simplest terms it is a contrasted description of two moments in a great life'.[5] This definition goes some way to explain the structure of the poem, but it leaves out a great deal, notably the part played by the treasure-winning in Beowulf's life and the importance given to the hero's death. In another place, Tolkien over-emphasizes the theme of death: the author, he says, 'is still concerned primarily with *man on earth*, rehandling in a new perspective an ancient theme: that man, each man and all men, and all their works shall die'.[6] Again it is a partial truth. Bonjour, accepting Tolkien's theories, is driven to speak of a 'main theme' and a 'fundamental theme', the latter being 'the transience of all earthly things, even

3. Cp. Augustine, *De civitate Dei, CCSL* 48, 457–65.
4. Bonjour, *Digressions*, pp. 72 f.
5. Tolkien, *Monsters*, p. 29; quoted by Bonjour, op. cit., p. 70.
6. Tolkien, *Monsters*, p. 265.

the most beautiful'.[7] Both scholars miss the significance of Beowulf's involvement with the dragon's hoard. This is the point where these themes meet: man chooses the things that must die, and he must die with them.

The beauty of the earth and man's handiwork is deeply felt by the poet, as Bonjour's phrase implies, but it would be a great mistake to infer on this account that his preference for the *invisibilia* ["immaterial," spiritual, hence eternal] is spurious. The conflict within Beowulf externalized in the fight with the dragon is one which the poet can present poignantly because he himself knows the delight of the eyes. Augustine too shows the same keen sense of the beauty of physical things, and the same confidence that what he sees gives only an inkling of the beauty of the immaculate eternal world. Like the *Beowulf* poet, far from disparaging the wonderful work of the craftsman, he can describe it in all its burnished elegance:

> If someone were to show you a decorated vessel, overlaid with gold, delicately wrought, and you were free to gaze at it, and the desire of your heart were drawn towards it, and the skill of the craftsman, the weight of the silver and the lustre of the metal delighted you—would not every one of you say, if only I might possess that vessel?[8]

This passage leads to a contrast with *charitas* ["charity," love of God and neighbor], a more desirable possession and free to all men. The *Beowulf* poet, I suggest, has the same attitude towards the dragon's *dryncfæt deore* ["precious drinking vessel"]. It is beautiful, and any man might wish to buy it or steal it, but it is a poor exchange for the chalice of God. The golden cup symbolized all the satisfactions the world can offer, not simply material wealth, as my quotations from Gregory's interpretation of the *calix aureus Babylon* ["golden cup of Babylon"] showed.[9] There could be no more fitting object to signify the *temporalia* [the fleeting, material things of this world] for which the aged Beowulf was willing to sell his life; in the allegory of mankind it merges with Adam's *poculum mortis*[1] as the Dragon merges with the Serpent.

Here, unmistakably, in the dragon's cup and pile of gold is the missing link between the themes of glory, transience and death. The opposition between the two halves of *Beowulf* is that between life and death: life imagined as a campaign against the foes of God, or, in other language, as a series of temptations—*tentatio itaque*

7. Bonjour, *Digressions*, p. 70 and p. 74.
8. Augustine, *In Ep. Joan. ad Parthos*, *Tract.* 7, *c.* 4, *PL* 35, 2034. [The Latin is omitted.]
9. Cp. p. 144, above.

1. Cp. p. 86 and p. 201, above. For the literary use of the symbol see Carleton Brown, '*Poculum mortis* ["goblet of death"] in Old English', *Speculum* 15 (1940), 389–99.

ipsa militia est[2]—and death imagined as the final battle with the *bana,* the death-bringer, who tempts men to grasp the things that perish.

It can be seen that for the pagan Beowulf there could be only limited victory in life and at best partial defeat in death, because he inherited Adam's spiritual vulnerability. The historical story makes a satisfying moral allegory in terms of the beliefs of the author's time, but he wanted, I believe, to make it both particularly relevant to his audience and also spiritually significant to all men. For the first purpose, he had chosen a story localized in a time just beyond the compass of living memory and in a place associated with ancestral heroes of the English kings. For the second purpose, he enriched each half of his composition with a tangential theme which is not kept within the progress of the narrative but leads off from it. The theme of life in the first half has as its upward tangent the life-giving contest of Christ with the Devil, hence the hints of the harrowing of hell and of baptism. The theme of death has a downward tangent in Adam's delusion by the Dragon and his drinking of the bitter cup, the poisoning of his race and the captivity of his people.[3] The poem ends, as Tolkien perceived 'looking back into the pit'.[4] The story was all in the past: Heorot and Beowulf and their gold had been swallowed up in the fire. But in the perspective of eternity the great cosmic war still raged and could only end in a universal conflagration; God still had need of heroes who would fight in his service.

* * *

There were among the Anglo-Saxon kings a few who gave away their crowns and their possessions to embrace monastic poverty; it is by no means impossible that *Beowulf* encouraged one or other of them to make this choice, but I do not think the author's purpose was to turn his king into a monk. He appears to have been anxious for the welfare of both the king and the people, a welfare which in his philosophy depended essentially upon the spiritual health of the ruler. He therefore composed *Beowulf,* as I believe, both as a fitting entertainment for a Christian court and as a prophylactic for the souls of men, especially those in high places.

---

2. I.e., "and temptation itself is warfare." *Ed.*

3. The curious lines upon the thief (2291–93) imply that he was one *se ðe Waldendes hyldo gehealdeþ* ["who holds favor from the Ruler"], in spite of his sinfulness (cp. 2226); they have reference to the tangential theme, as a reminder of the penitent thief upon the cross who, in spite of a life of cupidity, was wholly pardoned and released from the sentence of eternal death placed upon mankind after Adam's sin: the Dragon could not harm him. Since Adam's losing contest with the Adversary was a contrastive figure for the coming victorious contest of Christ, the images even in the second half are not wholly dark. (Cp. p. 269, below.)

4. Tolkien, *Monsters,* p. 265.

It is no longer necessary to ask, 'Why was *Beowulf* preserved?'[5] In its large compass, its parables touch upon all the great questions which troubled that age, and succeeding ages: it speaks of God's ordering of the world and the causes of wars and violence, the relation of destiny and human responsibility, the inheritance of sin and its consequences, and, above all, of the dependence of the human being, however great, upon his Creator. It considers the right and the wrong use of power and wealth, reminding the listeners that these things are lent, not given. It sounds a battle-call, *memento belli* ["be vigilant against warfare"], to a society beginning to exchange the arts of war for the arts of peace, because the poet believes that the invisible hosts will take possession of an unguarded city and that the king is deceived who thinks he has no enemy.

* * *

A reader who can imaginatively enter the thought-world I have been describing will, I am confident, find the large structure of the poem simple and satisfying. Both the literal narrative and the moral allegory are closely knit and well-balanced in the two parts,[6] though one will perhaps still concede with Hulbert that the composition is 'clumsy in some details of development and too compressed and allusive'.[7] On the level of what I have called the tangential themes, in which Beowulf becomes a type of mankind opposing the diabolical powers, there is not, nor could there be, a progress similar to the movement through the three stages of trial in the personal allegory of the hero. For this transcendental purpose, the natural sequence of time had to be reversed, to move backward from Christ to Adam. I do not think this regress could be avoided, since Beowulf as man victorious in God-given strength must bring to mind human nature made invincible in the incarnate Christ: hence the symbolic acts of the wrestling, going down into the water, cutting off the great head, and so on, which evoke remembrance of the divine warrior, belong naturally to the first part of the poem. But Beowulf as man deluded by the Dragon's gold, rashly striving for independence and greatness, and discovering death, carries our minds back to the beginning of human time and the myth of Adam's rebellion against the law of his being. Though the poet

5. The argument was advanced by K. Brunner, *Études Anglaises*, 1954, I ff., in an article under this title, that *Beowulf* was preserved for its moral teaching. He * * * thought that the *Beowulf* codex was 'one primarily devoted to Christian heroes'. My findings vindicate and go beyond his argument: it will be seen that *Beowulf* has something in common with *Judith* and even with *The Passion of St. Christopher*.

6. The work of Brodeur and more recently of Carrigan has sufficiently shown that the historical stories are cleverly interlaced across both parts of the poem. * * * (Cp. E. Carrigan, 'Structure and Thematic Development in *Beowulf*', *Proc. R. Irish Academy*, 66, sec. C, no. I [1967], p. 2.)
7. J. R. Hulbert, '*Beowulf* and the Classical Epic', *MP* 44 (1946–47), p. 74.

can and does take great liberties with chronological sequence in the story of Beowulf's life and the events which touch upon it, he would surely have found it impracticable to treat the hero's death in the first part and his crowning achievements retrospectively in the second. There could be no more fitting end to the poem than the interment of the hero's ashes together with the gold. From every point of view, Beowulf's death and burial, as an image of man's encounter with the *bana*—the cause, as was then believed, of the mutability and transience so movingly described at several places in the work—is a proper culmination of all that the poet has had to say about life on earth. It is a melancholy, but by no means a despairing conclusion to the work. For even here, because Adam's fatal contest with the Serpent-Dragon had a typological significance, the thoughts are once more turned forward. The second Adam, the divine warrior, is shadowily foreseen when the Dragon is struck down, as the Lord piercing Leviathan with his sword in the day of ultimate victory.

ALVIN A. LEE

Symbolic Metaphor and the Design of *Beowulf*[†]

* * *

In my examination of the mythical design or structure of Old English narrative romances I tried to show how the constant remembering back to an ancient time, designated as *ær* or *in geardagum*, that is, to a primordial beginning, often associated with the myth of Creation, balances a complementary tendency to look forward to an apocalyptic Doomsday when human or earthly history will be annulled. We saw also that the heavenly fulfillment of man's quest is his starting point transformed, the celestial dryht[1] being the perfect, eternal model of the guest-hall of the earthly Paradise. Such a pattern is of course precisely in harmony with the traditional Christian idea (whether Anglo-Saxon or not) that the work of Christ both abolishes and renews history. It establishes a term for history but periodically renews the Church and the individual soul in the liturgical cycle of the Christian year. Renewal takes place through the sacramental repetition of the archetypal acts of Christ and the saints, since these, by virtue of their divine

† From *The Guest-Hall of Eden: Four Essays on the Design of Old English Poetry* (New Haven and London: Yale University Press, 1972), pp. 174–77, 211–23. Copyright © 1972 by Yale University. Reprinted with permission. Lee's line references are to Klaeber's edition. 1. I.e., celestial society. See pp. 13–14 for Lee's discussion of the dryhts of heaven, middle-earth, and hell. *Ed.*

source or cause, do not bear the burden of time and are therefore capable of freeing a Guthlac or a Juliana or the dreamer in *The Dream of the Rood* from that bondage to sin and death which is the chief determinant of man's fate in the *læne* world. The poets' insistent harking back to the old or the traditional is witness to the belief that the old is the new; the ancient Creation is the newly redeemed order emerging from the depths of the Red Sea or from the waters of Baptism.

But *Beowulf* is unique among Old English longer poems in several important respects, the most obvious being the large amount of its story materials that derive from a Scandinavian milieu rather than from a biblical or Mediterranean or even English one. Despite a measure of agreement nowadays about its having something of a Christian character, it is not as clearly and unmistakably shaped and informed by Christian myth and symbol as are most of the poems examined in the first three essays of this book. The apparent obliqueness of its Christianity poses a whole set of questions that continue to puzzle most thoughtful readers. Is Beowulf, in any demonstrable sense, an imitation of Christ, as some have surmised? What really is the meaning in the poem of the references to Cain and the Deluge? Are they simply mythological embroidery, or do they have a deeper purpose? Why has the poet associated the building of Heorot with God's Creation of the world? If Beowulf is to be thought of as a redeemer figure based implicitly on Christ, why does the poem give so much attention to his physical death and to the social desolation surrounding it, with scarcely a hint of anything in the bleak closing scenes to suggest resurrection or redemption? How can a poem so resolutely engaged, even while recounting heroic triumphs, in the depicting of death, disintegration, treachery, loss, and the waste of human effort be construed as Christian, especially since so many of the human acts described, not only the hero's, are represented as bound by time in a way that we have seen to be foreign to the Christian belief in the possibility of escape from time, even during earthly existence? These questions, and others like them, do not admit of simple or easy answers, but I should like at least to make certain suggestions, working with the patterns already described as constituting the Old English poetic mythology and also with the definition of myth as symbolic metaphor.

Standing back mentally from the whole text and thinking of it in terms of its abstract design, one can see that *Beowulf* is about two earthly kingdoms, Denmark and Geatland, that go down to defeat, despite the deeds of the man whose heroic acts are deeply involved in their corporate lives. The story of the house of the Scyldings is sketched in its entirety, from the mysterious emergence from the sea of the eponymous ancestor, Scyld Scefing, to the final conflagration in which Heorot is destroyed. The main focus is on the reign of Hrothgar, during which Grendel takes possession of the royal gold-hall and along with his monstrous mother has to be destroyed by the hero who has come across the sea from Geatland. The story of Beowulf's own people, the Geats, does not emerge so completely. Although we hear several times of Hygelac's reign and its disastrous conclusion in the land of the Franks, and although we can piece together, from various references, Beowulf's own life among the Geats, from "dummling" youth to venerable king, the story of this kingdom does not emerge into the foreground of the poem with the clarity and definition characteristic of the scenes in Denmark. The reasons for the difference of treatment are deeply embedded in the structure of the poem, in the fact that Heorot, for all the gloomy foreboding about its ultimate fate, is the scene of the youthful hero's major achievement and recognition as a champion against the forces of darkness. Hrothgar's kingdom is the setting for the romance and the marvels that are central to a tale of how God works, through his chosen hero, to rescue a doomed people. Geatland, whose gold-hall is never visualized in the poem, is, on the whole, the setting for tales of death, confusion, and social chaos. Aside from that part of the narrative in which Beowulf tells Hygelac the story of his Danish adventures— the imaginative focus there is almost exclusively on Denmark—the kingdom of the Geats appears as one wracked by wars and feuds, except during Beowulf's reign, when he manages to hold an insecure peace against threatening forces. In brief, Geatland is the main symbolic setting for the poem in its tragic aspect.

Moving a little closer to the text but still thinking of it in terms of its overall design, one can recognize four major myths or symbolic episodes, each of which is concentrated at appropriate points in the narrative but also extends its effect, with varying emphases, throughout the whole poem. In the emergence of the Scylding dynasty, climaxed by the construction of Heorot, we have a *cosmogonic myth* explicitly connected by the poet with the Christian biblical account of the origins of the created world. This in turn is followed by *the myth of the Fall and the beginnings of fratricide and crime,* as the Grendel kin of the race of Cain begin to lay waste Hrothgar's hall. Next comes the account of the advent of the hero and *the myth of the heroic redeemer,* and finally as the poem moves into its decisively tragic phase, we have *the myth of the hero's death and the return to chaos.*[2]

* * *

2. Lee treats the first three myths on pp. 178–81, 181–96, and 196–211, respectively. On pp. 211–23 he deals with the fourth myth, and this is reprinted here. *Ed.*

The *Beowulf* poet's sense of the fleeting or mutable character of everything in middle-earth inevitably extends in Part 2 to the person of the hero. In Part 1, as a figure of vitality and superabundance, as the heroic vehicle of divine grace, Beowulf was enabled to abolish that destructive time as duration into which Heorot—this poem's main *imago mundi*—had fallen and to restore the hall to its original freshness and radiance: "the hall rose high above him, vaulted and shining with gold; inside, the guest slept . . ." (1799b–1800). The twelve years of bondage to Grendel were in a sense canceled in favor of that sacred time contemporary with Creation, and Hrothgar appropriately gave twelve symbolic treasures to his deliverer at the end of the twelve years of misery. Now in Part 2, as the central organization of images takes on the shape of *the myth of the hero's death and the return to chaos,* we find that time and *yldo* (age) have worn the hero and his kingdom. Hrothgar was described by Beowulf as "a peerless king, altogether blameless" (1885b–1886a), defeated only because of that age which toward the end of his fifty-year reign took from him the joys of power. Now Beowulf, also an exemplary king, is first threatened and then destroyed by a fifty-foot serpent, also at the end of a fifty-year reign. The tragedy of Hrothgar's life, only temporarily relieved by Beowulf's deeds, has now become the hero's own, but no heaven-sent champion appears who can act effectively on his behalf.

There is no escape from the ruins of time in this elegiac tragedy, for the basis of the tragic vision is being in time. Even as we move through the poem's romance, through its myths of creation and heroic deliverance, we are constantly made aware that death and human defeat in middle-earth are what give tragic shape and form to the lives of the Scyldings. It is death that defines the life of Scyld, of Beow, of Heorogar, and, finally, of Hrothgar. Now, in the account of the end of Beowulf's *lændagas* (loan-days, fleeting days), again it is death that defines the shape of the heroic life. Throughout Part 2 the poet carefully establishes a sense of imminent and nearly total disaster, a disaster partly realized by the end of the action. But the catastrophe described is not apocalyptic, as in the Old English Doomsday poems. In these latter, time as duration is brought to an end, history is abolished, and what is pure and faithful within God's Creation is taken back into eternity. But *Beowulf* does not show an end of the world, a Ragnarok or Doomsday. It shows the defeat of heroic effort in the world of time. At the very end of the narrative the Geats are still struggling against time; they build a great barrow on the headland called *Hronesnæs* (the Headland of the Whale) that will keep alive for other seafarers the memory of their king. Within the barrow lie an ancient, useless treasure and the ashes of the hero. Outside, twelve horsemen, warriors bold in battle, sons of chieftains, circle round, uttering an ancient lament. Beowulf has died, haunted by the memory of those marvelous times when he displayed in almost godlike manner his greatest powers; Hrothgar earlier was forced to admit defeat at the hands of Grendel but also looked back nostalgically, *in geardagum* (in former days), to a time when he subdued all enemies of the Danes and doled out treasures in almost godlike manner. It is fundamental to the elegiac nature of the poem that the acts of strength, of superabundance, and of creativity are constantly pushed back into that legendary earlier and better time indicated by the hoary phrase *in geardagum*.

The poet uses various materials to convey his theme of human defeat in time-dominated middle-earth. We have seen how the myth of Cain can be used as an illuminating aid to interpretation in Part 2, even though the poem no longer explicitly mentions it by name. The dryht of hell and the confused, chaotic society of Cain and Babylon have gained the ascendant. But the memory of something more in accord with heaven's purposes must never fade entirely from the poetry, or the tragic effect will give place to unrelieved irony. In the poet's use of the Lay of the Last Survivor (2247–2266), we have a vivid illustration of the way human splendor and achievement are made to recede into the past even as they are clung to in human memory.

This set piece, an elegy within an elegy, is a melancholy vision of vanished kinsmen and comrades uttered by the one survivor of an ancient race, who has just deposited his ancestral treasure in the earth and now laments his own fate, along with that of his people. The human tragedy presented is of a splendor two degrees removed into the distant past, a vision of pluperfect things. From the poet's perspective, the guardian of the rings is "an unknown man in days gone by" (2233); from the perspective of the lone survivor, the subject of the lament—that is, his own noble race—is also something from a glorious past that no longer exists. The immediate context of the foreground narrative, the disintegration of Beowulf's kingdom, deals with exactly the same theme in a less oblique way. The lone survivor tries briefly to enjoy "the treasure slowly accumulated through the years," but the same fate that has destroyed his kinsmen removes him as well, leaving only a memory. So too with the dying Beowulf, himself a "guardian of rings" who lives on "after the fall of heroes" (3005a); the aim is to restore an ancient treasure to its former use, but this desire is frustrated, at the cost of the hero's life.

The point of time in Geatish history at which Beowulf dies signals an imminent end for the Geats as a unified dryht society. It is true that Beowulf leaves behind him Wiglaf as the *endelaf* (last remnant) of his people, placing the young hero in somewhat the same position as that of the lone survivor in the elegy, but the social disintegration is now so far advanced that there is, so far as we are told in the poem, little hope for Geatland in the fact that Wiglaf remains. The last words of the aged Beowulf, as he gives his bright helmet, his golden circlet, his ring, and his corslet to the young spear-warrior, clearly signal the end of a race: * * * "You are the last of our race,/ Of the Wægmundings. Fate has swept away/ All my kinsmen to their destiny,/ Men in their power; I must follow after them" (2813–2816).[3]

We have seen how in this poem, as in other Old English poems, each creative human act—the emergence of Scyld from the sea, the building of Heorot, the cleansing of Heorot, the quelling of the mere—has its archetype in the creative and redemptive acts of God or Christ. Hrothgar's throne may be only an approximate reproduction of its transcendent model existing *in æternum*, but its reality and significance derive from that model. When this reality is threatened or hidden, as in the devil worship, tragedy ensues. Similarly, Beowulf's works of cleansing and delivering may be only imitations of those of Christ, who is never named in the poem, but much of their genuine significance for a Christian audience must surely have derived from their oblique but unmistakable association with their archetype. The Grendel kin as well, however much they may be trolls with Scandinavian associations still clinging to them, have—unless we assume the Old English poetic mythology to be largely irrelevant to *Beowulf*—their main symbolic resonance in the archetypal monsters of the dryht of hell. Now in Part 2 of the poem, we observe the victory, on the level of middle-earth, of those same destructive forces symbolized by the monsters and their human associates in Part 1; the outlaws and traitors of Part 2 who now make up the race of Cain are the logical successors to Unferth, Hrothulf, and the combatants of the Finn episode. There is, however, a development. Human murder is now presented in a narrative context in which the death-bringing dragon is central and succeeds in destroying the hero.

Considerable discussion has taken place among *Beowulf* scholars as to whether the Grendel kin and the dragon are monsters of a similar kind or kindred significance. The question is important, even crucial, in any consideration of the overall tragic structure and unity of the poem, and I should like now, in terms of the concept of symbolic metaphor operating in the four essays of this book, to attempt an answer.

We have seen how Grendel's mere is a complex fusion of images

3. The OE is omitted. *Ed.*

from the conventional fallen world described throughout the canon, a fusion which involves the motifs of both the wasteland and the chaotic sea as these are brought into intimate association with traditional hell images. Grendel is deprived of the joys of the dryht, both heavenly and earthly, and lives in a hostile hall or death dwelling where a hoarded, unused treasure (1613) is only one indication of his membership in the demonic dryht. Like Moses in *Exodus*, leading his troop along a symbolic narrow and unknown road through the moorlands to the Red Sea in anticipation of a new creation, Beowulf has to take his troop and the Danes along the same *enge anpaðas, uncuð gelad*, to make possible the decisive encounter of God's champion with the dryht of hell and the resultant restoration of the dryht of Heorot.

The dragon's barrow is not as elaborately described as the mere, but it too is presented as a hall—*eorðsele* (2410, earth-hall); *hringsele* (2840, ring-hall); *sele* (3128, hall). It is a vault beneath the earth (*hlæw under hrusan*) near the welling sea and the struggling waves (2411–2412a). In addition, it is described as "the serpent's den" (*þæs wyrmes denn*, 2759; *dennes*, 3045) and as "an earth-grave" (*eorðscrafa*, 3046). In this barrow for many years the dragon has guarded the "ornaments of a hall" (*recedes geatwa*, 3088) which here lie utterly useless (*læne licgan*, 3129), the symbols of a vanished dryht. Like the mere, the dwelling of the treasure guardian is difficult of access: "beneath lay a path unknown to men" (2213b–2214a). Like the Grendel kin, the fire-dragon lives in "a no man's land" ("ne ðær ænig mon/ on þære westenne," 2297b–2298a), from which he comes at night to harass the world of the dryht. Finally, this hall deep in the earth is called the "secret dryht-hall" (*dryhtsele dyrnne*, 2320) of the guardian of the treasure, indicating quite clearly that, despite certain obvious differences, the central imaginative idea here is that of another demonic dryht. The fact of the dragon's aloneness, like that of his hoarding, is a clear indication of the way in which he symbolizes a perversion of those dryht values championed by Beowulf.

The immediate conflict between the Geats and the fire-dragon begins with the theft by an outlaw of a cup from the serpent's hoard. Similarly, in the *Reginsmál*, the baleful influence of the Niflung hoard begins to work from the moment the mischievous Loki steals the treasure. One is reminded, as well, of how in *Elene*, when the marvelous "hoard" is unearthed, the devil appears, enraged, in Jerusalem and complains loudly about the theft of his treasure by a second Judas. His fury over the fact that the loss of treasure means the end of his possession of human souls is relevant to *Beowulf*, a poem in which human societies engaged in the free dispensing and receiving of treasure are consistently presented as spiritually healthy, as living in the way God intends. A hoarded treasure is spiritual death or damnation.

The fact that the *Beowulf* dragon does not attack until the rifling of the hoard is not an adequate reason for deducing that he does not represent general hostility to the world of the dryht in which man lives. For three hundred years "the foe of the people" (*se ðeodsceaða,* 2278, 2688) has been hoarding the rich treasure of a human society and now, when provoked, sets out to destroy every living thing in the land of the Geats (2314b–2315). Whatever his motivation (its inadequacy in terms of cause and effect is another mark of the nonnaturalistic character of the poem), the results of the dragon's attack are very similar to those of Grendel, except that his ravages are more nearly complete: Beowulf's hall and gift-throne are utterly and immediately destroyed. It is worth remembering that the poet explicitly connects the hero's final battle with all those that have gone before, in two different places (2345 ff., 2518 ff.), even as he stresses that this final struggle will be *in extremis.*

Beowulf's last monstrous foe is designated by the word *wyrm* (serpent, worm) more frequently (fifteen times) than by any other; the word *draca* (dragon) occurs several times, as do *draca* compounds: *ligdraca* (2333, 3040, fire-dragon); *frecne fyrdraca* (2689, terrible fire-dragon); *se eorðdraca* (2712, the earth-dragon); *egeslic eorðdraca* (2825, horrible earth-dragon). In Old English poetry the worm or dragon, in any of its three aspects, always represents enmity to mankind: the worms who devour man's corpse after death; the dragons and serpents who receive his soul in hell; and the dragon of sin and mortality who rules over middle-earth until Christ cancels for all time the work of the tempter. In the fallen world under the threefold curse on Adam, Eve, and the serpent, it is the wyrm that triumphs, for, like the wolf and the raven, he claims the human body. In hell it is serpents and dragons who receive human souls. In the elegiac signature to *The Fates of the Apostles,* Cynewulf anticipates the day when he must leave behind his "earthly part or corpse as a comfort for worms," and similarly, in *The Grave* it is the worms who conquer as they divide between them the decomposing body. In *Soul and Body I* again we find the idea of the worm as the devourer of the human body and of the serpent as the lowest of earthly creatures. The soul, spitefully haranguing the body, says, "Now in the earth you will feed worms." He then goes on to damn the body utterly, by saying it would have been better for the body to have become a fowl, or a fish, or a beast of burden, or a cow wandering witless in the field, or a fierce wild beast, or, finally, the basest of serpents. In *Christ and Satan* (97–98) and in *Judith* (115), to name only two examples of a recurrent motif, there is mention of the dragons and serpents who wait in hell to embrace the souls of the damned. It is the form of these last wyrmas that Satan assumes when he prepares to destroy the joy of the dryhtsele of Eden.

The serpent or dragon which destroys Beowulf's body but not his soul appears to me to have a somewhat oblique symbolic connection with the traditional idea of the four elements from which all mortal things are composed: he is an ancient *"earth*-dragon" who guards an accursed hoard in an "earth-hall" by day and by night flies through the *air* spewing out venomous *fire*, until he is killed and pushed over a cliff into the embrace of the sea *waters*. To notice this—in a poem where symbolism of fire and water and comparisons between "fleeting" middle-earth and eternal reality loom large—may not be overly fanciful, especially since the dragon obviously represents the elemental fact of death for the aged hero and for other living things in his kingdom. Like the fateful treasure over which he keeps jealous watch, he has a ringed or coiled form (*hrinboga*, 2561, and *wohbogan*, 2827), and however malignant his effect, again like the treasure, he has a certain fatal, demonic splendor: *syllicran wiht* (3038, strange or wonderful creature).

The Grendel kin and the dragon share some of the descriptive words and epithets used for monsters in the poem—*bona* (slayer), *feond* (enemy), *lað* (hostile one), *mansceaða* (evil destroyer), *aglæca* (wretch, monster, demon, or warrior), *grim* (fierce, angry), *atol* (horrid), *freca* (bold one). They all live in demonic halls; they wage war on the world of the human dryht; they are all enemies of societies championed by Beowulf, the "greatest of men in the days of this life." The giants and the "wondrous serpent" (891) or "dragon" (892) killed by Sigmund are clearly meant to be analogous to the Grendel kin; they are mentioned following the victory over Grendel, not following the fight with the fire-dragon. It is true that each monster is individualized to a considerable degree and presented as distinct from the others; perhaps the dragon differs from the Cain-descended monsters of Part 1, even as the evil which impinges on age differs from that encountered by youthful energy. But in a poem in which metaphorical identification brings together logically separate entities as much as in *Beowulf* this should be no reason for not seeing obvious connections, especially when the poet himself points them out. To say that the dragon is "a mere participant in a tragedy that started many ages before"[4] certainly minimizes the significance of a creature that dominates much of the latter part of *Beowulf* and has close connections with the other monsters in the poem. The fact that Satan has been the foe of

---

4. See T. M. Gang, "Approaches to *Beowulf*," *RES*, 3 (1952), 1–12.

Adam's sons ever since his visit to the guest-hall of Eden does not make him any the less guilty; nor does the fact that the dragon in Christian iconography is always identified with forces hostile to men and God make an individual but typical representative of the species any the less guilty. *Beowulf* is a tragedy about the world of the golden or paradisal dryht going down to defeat. The dragon has jealously kept to himself many of the treasures of that world for three hundred years.

There is another aspect of the conflict with the dragon which indicates the intricacy and cunning of the poem's metaphors. We have seen that the "halls" inhabited by the monsters are parodies or perversions of those inhabited by the Danes and the Geats. The dryht-hall as such, then, is a double image, existing in both ideal and "un-ideal" forms, as well as in an ambiguous mixture of the two. We have seen, moreover, how certain aspects of the society of Heorot, most notably the fratricide and the devil worship, have their metaphorical significance in the Grendel kin and the mere. An identification of the same kind is working in Part 2, between the old king, Beowulf, and the dragon.

At the time of their encounter each is represented as an aged protector of his hall: Beowulf is "frod cyning/ eald eþelweard" (2209b–2210a, "a venerable king, old guardian of the homeland") and "frod folces weard" (2513, "old and wise keeper of the people"); the dragon is *wintrum frod* (2277, old in years); Beowulf has ruled for fifty years (2733); the dragon is fifty feet in length (3042). Beowulf has a splendid dwelling (2326) and gift-throne (2326–2327); the dragon has a mighty treasure house (2279b–2280a) and dryht-hall (2320). Both are presented as warriors who rejoice in battle: Beowulf is called *har hilderinc* (3136, hoary battle warrior), and a few lines earlier the poet has described the monster as *hilderinc* (3124, a battle warrior). Early in the poem when the hero is fighting triumphantly with Grendel's mother, the poet uses the formula *secg weorce gefeh* (1569, the man rejoiced at his work); a similar phrase is applied to the dragon, *wiges gefeh* (2298, he rejoiced in the war). The hero is called *niðheard cyning* (2417, a king brave in battle), and his foe is a *gearo guðfreca* (2414, alert fighter). The adjective *stearcheort* (stouthearted) is used in describing both of them, Beowulf at line 2552 and the dragon at line 2288. So also is the term *aglæca*, at line 2592, where they are both included in the phrase *þa aglæcan* (the warriors). Each, moreover, is similar in his impact on the other: "æghwæðrum wæs/ bealohycgendra broga fram oðrum" (2564b–2565, "each of the hostile pair was an object of horror to the other").

If only one or two words, phrases, or ideas were used in common to describe the assailants, one could conclude that nothing very much was implied, especially since each is a fighter in a tale of conflict and the language of the poem is formulaic. But when several expressions are used for both, one begins to recognize a closer metaphorical relationship between the protagonist and his last enemy. In some mysterious and illogical way the poet's mythical mode of imagining has managed to bring the two into a relationship both of antithetical tension and of partial identification. There is never any doubt that the old king will die in the struggle with the fiery monster, because the poet tells us from the beginning of Part 2 that this will happen. It is also true that the monster has been roused to seek vengeance by the theft of a goblet. But in some more comprehensive way than that the dragon is the foe of man who brings death and destruction to the land of the Geats. The hoard he guards is under an ancient curse that extends its deadly power to Doomsday. (Is this strange and much-discussed curse the ancient biblical one placed on man and nature and fated to last through all history until the Judgment?) The guardian of the treasure who reluctantly gives up the hoard is, in his reluctance, similar to Beowulf, unwilling to surrender the treasure of his soul to death (2422). The corpse of each is only a ruin of former power: Beowulf's is separated from his soul, crumbles in the flames of the pyre, and is buried as ashes; the dragon's body is separated from the hoard and pushed from a cliff into the surging waters of the sea. The fact that the physical treasure is consigned to the ground "as useless as it was before" is set against the more important fact that the only real treasure in Beowulf's life, his soul, faithful to the heavenly Dryhten, has gone to the Judgment of the just.

In the metaphorical design of the poem, the dragon, at certain points of the narrative, *is* the body of death, of Beowulf's death and, by extension, of the Geatish people as a unified society. If, moreover, Beowulf's gold-hall, like Heorot, is another *imago mundi*, the dragon is also the body of man's mortality. The coils of the serpent surround the warrior-king while the thanes who should be shoulder to shoulder with their lord turn away and retreat into the woods. Loyalty dies, protection vanishes, and the good society disintegrates. It is the twilight or coming winter of a society's life that we see in Part 2, as destructive fire and social chaos succeed the joys of the wine-hall, the order of the dryht. The dragon is the central unifying symbol in the whole poem for the elemental power of death; the symbols of life and divinely sanctioned human activity are the gold-hall, circulating treasures, and the hero.

Where most other Old English poetic narratives show an intensely otherworldly loyalty, *Beowulf* reveals a tension between courageous devotion to that heroic work which is necessary and good in the tragic context of middle-earth and the realization that, ultimately, human loyalty must focus elsewhere. The contempt-of-the-world theme is kept in restraint in *Beowulf*, however, * * * with the result that sustained elegy and tragedy remain possible. The guest-hall of Eden and the Promised Land gleam most splendidly near the beginning and in the central parts of the poem, but they are never entirely lost sight of, to the point where homiletic strictures on the worthlessness of earthly endeavor can take over. The basis of the poem's tragic nature is its account of being in time, the fact that the fifty years respectively of Hrothgar's and Beowulf's reigns are measured by the fifty-year habitation of a demonic dryht by murderous monsters and by a fifty-foot dragon of destruction who guards a rich treasure of the world of the dryht.

If one presses very far a rigorous Augustinian doctrine of extra-terrestrial reality with this poem, one is bound to conclude that a life like Beowulf's, deeply involved in the wars and the gift-dispensing rituals of Denmark and Geatland, is less ascetically pure than that of Guthlac or Juliana, but such thinking cannot absorb the kind of experience described in the poem. To see this and accept it does not, in my view, mean that *Beowulf* is an intractably pagan poem somewhat influenced by a Christian sensibility. It means that it is a tragedy and that the experience of the tragic—Christian, pagan, or whatever—cannot be moralized or comprehended within any conceptual world-view. Hrothgar is a tragic figure whether or not he in any way is culpable in the fate of Heorot; Beowulf is consistently admirable throughout the poem, despite the old king's sermon to him on the dangers of pride and despite the possible suggestions later in the text that he is somehow caught by a worldly interest in a fated treasure.

What makes Beowulf a tragic figure is his superabundance, his capacity for superhuman acts, his strength of thirty men, his exalted sense of social obligation, and his generosity—all these being characteristics that place him above ordinary human experience, to the point where, finally, he is destroyed by a dragon. It is this heroic energy, first visible in the sea passage from Geatland to Heorot and in his account of the swimming contest with Breca, and continued in the fights with Grendel and his mother, that is the basis of the poem's romance. Heaven's plenitude has extended in extraordinary measure to this greatest of men between the seas, and his experiences show him as constantly bursting the confines of normal earthly life. His energy is directed to the protection of the most ideal form of heroic life and society in middle-earth—Heorot in its unfallen aspect. In contrast to Beowulf, his king, Hygelac, though reputed in Germanic historical monuments to have been almost a giant, falls dead in the land of the Franks while Beowulf swims away, carrying the armor of thirty men.

But Beowulf, like Heorot, becomes simply a memory. The close alignment of aged hero and dragon in Part 2 is the poem's decisive reminder that in the tragic vision even the most heroic form, perhaps most especially the heroic form, is defeated by the elemental facts of existence in time. The world that remains after Beowulf has died contains two sorts of people, cowards and outlaws, on the one hand, and those faithful to dryht loyalties (Wiglaf, the weeping woman, and the circling horsemen), on the other. By this point we have been shown the impact of heroic energy on the world of the fallen dryht and have been shown also that in such a world it is heroic energy that is destroyed while the fallen creation continues in time. The golden dryht of middle-earth and the youthful Beowulf are poetic images of the kind of joy and reality the *hæleð*[5] want, but the irony of the tragic vision decrees that life is not shaped according to human desires. The poet, with the quiet assurance of great artistry, follows his account of the roaring flames and raging winds of Beowulf's cremation with a description of the disposal of physical things: the hero's ashes are sealed in a great barrow; the rings, necklaces, and armor of the ancient treasure are returned to the earth, hidden again and useless to men. Twelve riders circle the mound, ritually containing the grief of the Geats: they eulogize the greatness and glory of their dead king, and they mourn his passing. The closing scene expresses a pronounced tragic sense of confinement, of the putting into dark places of all that is splendid in this world. It shows the stilling of heroic energy.

JOHN LEYERLE

The Interlace Structure of *Beowulf*†

* * *

I

Beowulf is a poem of rapid shifts in subject and time. Events are fragmented into parts and are taken with little regard to chrono-

---

5. I.e., "heroes." *Ed.*

† A memorial lecture for the late Professor Norman Garmonsway; reprinted from *University of Toronto Quarterly*, 37 (Oct. 1967), 1–17, by permission of the author and University of Toronto Press. I regretfully omit here Leyerle's discussion on pp. 2–3 of stylistic interlace exemplified by such artifacts as the Bewcastle Cross, Abingdon Brooch, Gandersheim Casket, and others, and their respective notes and ten illustrative plates. Readers especially interested in Anglo-Saxon art should see Leyerle's original essay, which convincingly demonstrates the validity of the general statements on the pervasiveness of stylistic interlace in OE art which I retain in this excerpt. *Ed.*

logical order. The details are rich, but the pattern does not present a linear structure, a lack discussed with distaste by many.[1] This lecture will attempt to show that the structure of *Beowulf* is a poetic analogue of the interlace designs common in Anglo-Saxon art of the seventh and eighth centuries. *Beowulf* was composed in the early eighth century in the Midlands or North of England, exactly the time and place where interlace decoration reached a complexity of design and skill in execution never equalled since and, indeed, hardly ever approached. Interlace designs go back to prehistoric Mesopotamia; in one form or another they are characteristic of the art of all races.[2]

* * *

From the early Anglo-Saxon period there are thousands of interlace designs surviving in illuminations of manuscripts, in carving on bone, ivory and stone, and in metal work for weapons and jewellery. They are so prolific that the seventh and eighth centuries might justly be known as the interlace period. In one artifact after another the complexity and precision of design are as striking as the technical skill of execution. Recognition of this high level of artistic achievement is important for it dispels the widely held view, largely the prejudice of ignorance, that early Anglo-Saxon art is vigorous, but wild and primitive. As the interlace designs show, there is vigour to be sure, but it is controlled with geometric precision and executed with technical competence of very high order. Apart from such direct analogies as the one presented in this lecture, study of Anglo-Saxon art is most useful as an aid to the reassessment of early English literature because it is an important reminder that the society was capable of artistic achievements of a high order which can be looked for in the poetry as well.

II

The pervasive importance of interlace designs in early Anglo-Saxon art establishes the historical possibility that a parallel may be found in poetry of the same culture. The historical probability for the parallel, a rather more important matter, can be established from seventh- and eighth-century Latin writers in England. There is ample evidence that interlace design has literary parallels in both style and structure.

1. For example, see F. P. Magoun, Jr., "*Beowulf* A¹: A Folk-Variant," *ARV: Tidskrit för Nordisk Folkminnesforskning*, 14 (1958), 95–101, or *Beowulf and the Fight at Finnsburg*, ed. Fr. Klaeber 3rd edition (Boston, 1950), li–lviii. All quotations are from this edition.
2. For an account of the origin of these designs, see Nils Åberg, *The Occident and the Orient in the Art of the Seventh Century*, Part I, *The British Isles*, Kungl. Vitterhets Historie och Antikvitets Akademiens Handlingar, Del. 56: 1 (Stockholm, 1943). An admirable account of such designs is given by R. L. S. Bruce-Mitford in *Codex Lindisfarnensis*, ed. T. D. Kendrick, *et al.* (Olten and Lausanne, 1956–60), II, iv, vii–x, 197–260.

Stylistic interlace is a characteristic of Aldhelm and especially of
Alcuin. They weave direct statement and classical tags together to
produce verbal braids in which allusive literary references from the
past cross and recross with the present subject.[3] The device is self-
conscious and the poets describe the technique with the phrases
fingere serta or *texere serta*, "to fashion or weave intertwinings."
Serta (related to Sanscrit *sarat*, "thread" and to Greek σειρά,
"rope") is from the past participle of *serere*, "to interweave, en-
twine, or interlace." The past participle of *texere*, "to weave, braid,
interlace," is *textus*, the etymon of our words text and textile. The
connection is so obvious that no one thinks of it. In basic meaning,
then, a poetic text is a weaving of words to form, in effect, a verbal
carpet page.

The passage in *Beowulf* about the scop's praise of Beowulf describes a recital in which a literary past, the exploits of Sigemund
and Heremod, is intertwined with the present, Beowulf's killing of
Grendel. This episode is extended and might equally be considered
as an example of simple structural interlace. The scop is said to
wordum wrixlan, "vary words" (874); the verb *wrixlan* is found
elsewhere in this sense, for example in Riddle 8 of the Exeter Book.
Klaeber calls such variation "the very soul of the Old English
poetical style" (lxv); it involves multiple statement of a subject in
several different words or phrases, each of which typically describes
a different aspect of the subject. When variation on two or more
subjects is combined, the result is stylistic interlace, the inter-
weaving of two or more strands of variation. This may be what
Cynewulf refers to in *Elene* when he writes *ic . . . wordcræftum wæf*,
"I wove words" (1236–37). An example from *Beowulf* will serve to
illustrate stylistic interlace:

<pre>
                      No þæt læsest wæs
hondgemot[a]   þær mon Hygelac sloh,
syððan Geata cyning   guðe ræsum,
freawine folca   Freslondum on,
Hreðles eafora   hiorodryncum swealt,
bille gebeaten.   [2354–59]
</pre>

Although awkward in modern English, a translation following the
original order of phrases shows the stylistic interlace.

> That was not the least
> of hand-to-hand encounters where Hygelac was killed,
> when the king of the Geats in the rush of battle,
> the beloved friend of the people, in Frisia,
> the son of Hreðel died bloodily,
> struck down with the sword.

3. See Peter Dale Scott, "Alcuin as a Poet," *UTQ*, 33 (1964), 233–57.

Hygelac, Geata cyning, freawine folca, and *Hreðles eafora* make one strand,[4] *mon . . . sloh, hiorodryncum swealt,* and *bille gebeaten* make a second strand;[5] *þær, guðe ræsum,* and *Freslondum on* make the third.[6] Three strands are woven together into a stylistic braid. This feature of style is familiar to readers of Anglo-Saxon poetry and is the literary counterpart for interlace designs in art that are decorative rather than structural. Designs on a sword, coffer or cross are decoration applied to an object whose structure arises from other considerations.

At a structural level, literary interlace has a counterpart in tapestries where positional patterning of threads establishes the shape and design of the fabric, whether the medium is thread in textile or words in a text. Unfortunately cloth perishes easily and only a few fragments of Anglo-Saxon tapestry survive although the early English were famous for their weaving and needle work which was referred to on the continent simply as *opus Anglicum* with no other description. Since tapestry examples are lost, decorative interlace must serve here as graphic presentation of the principle of structural interlace, a concept difficult to explain or grasp without such a visual analogue.

Rhetoricians of the classical period distinguished between natural and artificial order, but emphasized the former as being especially effective for oral delivery since they were chiefly concerned with the orator. In the *Scholia Vindobonensia,* an eighth-century commentary on the *Ars Poetica* of Horace, there is a passage on artificial order of great interest to the subject of interlace structure in Anglo-Saxon poetry. The authorship of the *Scholia* is unknown, but its editor attributes it to Alcuin or one of his school.[7] The passage is a comment on four lines of the *Ars Poetica.*

> Ordinis haec virtus erit et venus, aut ego fallor,
> ut iam nunc dicat iam nunc debentia dici,
> pleraque differat et praesens in tempus omittat,
> hoc amet, hoc spernat promissi carminis auctor. [42–45]

Of order, this will be the excellence and charm, unless I am mistaken, that the author of the long-promised poem shall say at the moment what ought to be said at the moment and shall put off and omit many things for the present, loving this and scorning that.

The commentator was particularly interested in the last line, which he regards as having the force of an independent hortatory

---

4. "Hygelac," "the king of the Geats," "the beloved friend of the people," and "the son of Hreðel." *Ed.*
5. "Hygelac was killed," "died bloodily," and "struck down with the sword." *Ed.*

6. "where," "in the rush of battle," and "in Frisia." *Ed.*
7. *Scholia Vindobonensia ad Horatii Artem Poeticam,* ed. Josephus Zechmeister (Vienna, 1877), iii.

subjunctive; he takes *hoc . . . hoc* in the strong sense of "on the one hand . . . on the other" which would have been expressed by *hoc . . . illo* in classical Latin.

Hoc, id est, ut nunc dicat iam debentia dici quantum ad naturalem ordinem; *amet auctor promissi carminis*, id est, amet artificialem ordinem. *Hoc*, id est, contrarium ordinis artificialis, id est, ordinem naturalem *spernat auctor promissi carminis*; hoc breviter dicit. Nam sententia talis est: quicumque promittit se facturum bonum carmen et lucidum habere ordinem, amet artificialem ordinem et spernat naturalem. Omnis ordo aut naturalis aut artificialis est. Naturalis ordo est, si quis narret rem ordine quo gesta est; artificialis ordo est, si quis non incipit a principio rei gestae, sed a medio, ut Virgilius in Aeneide quaedam in futuro dicenda anticipat et quaedam in praesenti dicenda in posterum differt.[8]

Hoc, that is, he should say now what ought to have been said before according to natural order; *amet auctor promissi carminis*, that is, should love artificial order. *Hoc*, that is, the opposite of artificial order, that is, *spernat auctor promissi carminis* natural order; Horace says this briefly. For the meaning is as follows: whoever undertakes to make a good poem having clear order should love artificial order and scorn natural order. Every order is either natural or artificial; artificial order is when one does not begin from the beginning of an exploit but from the middle, as does Virgil in the *Aeneid* when he anticipates some things which should have been told later and puts off until later some things which should have been told in the present.

This comment extends the source into a doctrine on the suitability of artificial order for poetry concerned with martial material (*res gesta*) and takes an epic (the *Aeneid*) as an example. What I have called interlace structure is, in more general terms, complex artificial order, with the word complex in its etymological sense of woven together. Interlace design is a dominant aspect of eighth-century Anglo-Saxon visual art and the *Scholia Vindobonensia* present convincing evidence that the same design principle was applied to narrative poetry.

Alcuin's two lives of St. Willibrord provide instructive examples of natural and artificial order.[9] The prose version begins with an account of Willibrord's parents and gives a chronological account of the Saint's life, death, and the subsequent miracles at his tomb. The poem, on the other hand, plunges *in medias res* with an

8. Zechmeister, 4–5, repunctuated.
9. *De Vita Sancti Willibrordi Archiepiscopi*, ed. B. Krvsch and W. Levison, *MGH, Scriptores Rerum Merov.* (Hanover and Leipzig, 1919), VII, 113–41; this is the prose version. *De Vita Willibrordi Episcopi*, ed. E. Dümmler, *MGH, Poetarum Latinorum Medii Aevi*, I (Berlin, 1881), 207–20.

account of Willibrord's visit to Pippin; the details of the Saint's early life are placed at the end. The poem is in simple artificial order, and in the Preface Alcuin states that it is for private study but that the prose version is for public reading. The same logic is followed in Alcuin's *Disputatio de Rhetorica* which deals only with natural order since it is intended for instruction in public oral discourse.[1] On the basis of this preference for natural order in work intended for oral delivery, an argument might be made that *Beowulf* was meant for private study since it has complex artificial order.

Before I turn to the poem, a brief summary of my argument thus far may be helpful. In the visual arts of the seventh and eighth centuries interlace designs reached an artistic perfection in England that was never equalled again. Interlace appears so regularly on sculpture, jewellery, weapons, and in manuscript illuminations that it is the dominant characteristic of this art. There is clear evidence that a parallel technique of word-weaving was used as a stylistic device in both Latin and Old English poems of the period. Finally there is the specific statement of the *Scholia Vindobonensia* that artificial order was preferred for narrative poetry. Such artificial order I have called interlace structure because the term has historical probability and critical usefulness in reading *Beowulf*.

III

Beowulf is a work of art consistent with the artistic culture that it reflects and from which it came, eighth-century England. It is a lacertine interlace, a complex structure of great technical skill, but it is woven with relatively few strands. When *Beowulf* is read in its own artistic context as an interlace structure, it can be recognized as a literary work parallel to the carpet pages of the Lindisfarne Gospels, having a technical excellence in design and execution that makes it the literary equivalent of that artistic masterpiece.

Examples of narrative threads, intersected by other material, are easy to perceive in the poem once the structural principle is understood. The full account of Hygelac's Frisian expedition is segmented into four episodes, 1202–14, 2354–68, 2501–9 and 2913–21, in which chronology is ignored. The poet interlaces these episodes to achieve juxtapositions impossible in a linear narrative. In the first episode the gift of a precious golden torque to Beowulf for killing Grendel is interrupted by an allusion to its loss years later when Hygelac is killed. Hygelac's death seeking Frisian treasure foreshadows Beowulf's death seeking the dragon's hoard. The transience of gold and its connection with violence are obvious. In the second episode Beowulf's preparations to face the dragon

---

1. Ed. and trans. Wilbur S. Howell (Princeton, 1941), sec. 22.

are intersected by another allusion to Hygelac's expedition; each is an example of rash action and each ends in the death of a king. The third episode comes as Beowulf recalls how he went in front of Hygelac

> ana on orde,   ond swa to aldre sceall
> sæcce fremman,   þenden þis sweord þolað.
>
> [2498–99]
>
> alone in the van and so will I always
> act in battle while this sword holds out.

He had needed no sword to crush Dæghrefn, the slayer of Hygelac; against the dragon his sword Nægling fails. The pattern is the same as for the fights with Grendel whom he had killed with his hands and with Grendel's mother against whom the sword Hrunting fails. Beowulf's trust in a sword against Grendel's mother had nearly cost him his life; against the dragon it does. The last episode comes in the speech of the messenger who states that the fall of Beowulf will bring affliction to the Geats from their enemies. Among them, the messenger warns, are the Frisians seeking revenge for Hygelac's raid years before. Hygelac's death led to the virtual annihilation of his raiding force; Beowulf's death leads to the virtual annihilation of all the Geats. The four Hygelac episodes, like all the narrative elements in the poem, have positional significance; unravel the threads and the whole fabric falls apart. An episode cannot be taken out of context—may I remind you again of the etymology of the word—without impairing the interwoven design. This design reveals the meaning of coincidence, the recurrence of human behaviour, and the circularity of time, partly through the coincidence, recurrence, and circularity of the medium itself—the interlace structure. It allows for the intersection of narrative events without regard for their distance in chronological time and shows the interrelated significances of episodes without the need for any explicit comment by the poet. The significance of the connections is left for the audience to work out for itself. Understatement is thus inherent in interlace structure, a characteristic that fits the heroic temper of the north.

The Hygelac episodes contribute to what I believe is the major theme of *Beowulf*, "the fatal contradiction at the core of heroic society. The hero follows a code that exalts indomitable will and valour in the individual, but society requires a king who acts for the common good, not for his own glory."[2] Only two periods in Beowulf's life are told in linear narrative; they are the few days, perhaps a week, when he fights Grendel and his mother and the

---

2. John Leyerle, "Beowulf the Hero and the King," *MÆ*, 34 (1965), 89.

last few days when he fights the dragon. This treatment emphasizes Beowulf's heroic grandeur, his glorious deeds, and his predilection for monster-fighting. However, this main narrative is constantly intersected by episodes which present these deeds from a different perspective. The Hygelac episodes show the social consequences of rash action in a king and they become more frequent as the dragon fight develops. Hygelac's Frisian raid was a historical event; the history of this age provides many parallels. In 685 Ecgfrið, King of Northumbria, led a raiding party against the advice of his friends deep into Pictish territory. Caught in mountainous narrows at a place called Nechtanesmere on May 20, he and most of his army were killed, a disaster that ended English ascendency in the north. The main theme of *Beowulf* thus had relevance to a major recent event in the society that most probably produced it. Ecgfrið's brother Aldfrið, a man famed for his learning and skill as a poet, ruled from 685 to 704; Bede says that he re-established his ruined and diminished kingdom nobly,[3] a stable reign that made possible the learning and scholarship of eighth-century Northumbria, the golden age of Bede and Alcuin.

At first the episodes give little more than a hint that Beowulf's heroic susceptibility may have calamitous consequences for his people. The references to Sigemund and Heremod after Beowulf kills Grendel foreshadow Beowulf's later career as king. He kills a dragon, as Sigemund did, and leaves the Geats to suffer national calamity, as Heremod left the Danes to suffer *fyrenðearfe* (14), "terrible distress."[4] In the second part of the poem Beowulf's preparations to fight the dragon are constantly intersected by allusions to the Swedish wars, ominous warnings of the full consequences to the Geats of Beowulf's dragon fight. In this way the poet undercuts Beowulf's single-minded preoccupation with the dragon by interlacing a stream of more and more pointed episodes about the human threats to his people, a far more serious danger than the dragon poses. Beowulf wins glory by his heroic exploit in killing the dragon, but brings dire affliction on his people, as Wiglaf quite explicitly states.

> Oft sceall eorl monig   anes willan
> wræc adreogan,   swa us geworden is.   [3077–78]

> Often many men must suffer distress
> For the willfulness of one alone, as has happened to us.

Of particular interest to my subject is the way in which the interlace design, in and of itself, makes a contribution to the main

3. *Historia Ecclesiastica*, ed. C. Plummer (Oxford, 1896), IV, xxiv, vol. I, 268. See F. M. Stenton, *Anglo-Saxon Eng-*land, 2nd edition (Oxford, 1950), 85–89.
4. See "Beowulf the Hero and the King," 101.

theme. Because of the many lines given to the monsters and to Beowulf's preparations to fight them, they are the largest thread in the design, like the zoomorphs on the Windsor dagger pommel or the dragons on the Gandersheim casket. Monster-fighting thus pre-empts the reader's attention just as it pre-empts Beowulf's; the reader gets caught up in the heroic ethos like the hero and easily misses the warnings. In a sense the reader is led to repeat the error, one all too easy in heroic society, hardly noticing that glorious action by a leader often carries a terrible price for his followers.

The monsters are the elongated lacertine elements that thread through the action of the poem making symmetrical patterns characteristic of interlace structure. Beowulf's fights against Grendel's mother and against the monsters in the Breca episode are clear examples. During the swimming match Beowulf, protected by his armour, is dragged to the ocean floor. Fate gives him victory and he kills *niceras nigene* (575), "nine water monsters," with his sword; this prevents them from feasting on him as they intended. After the battle, light comes and the sea grows calm. This is almost a *précis* of the later underwater fight against Grendel's mother; the pattern is the same, though told in greater detail.

Once the probability of parallel design is recognized, the function of some episodes becomes clearer. The Finnesburh lay, for example, is probably a cautionary tale for the Danes and Geats. Beowulf and his Geats visit Hroðgar and his Danes in Heorot to assist in defending the hall against an *eoten*, Grendel. During the first evening they share the hall Unferð issues an insulting challenge to which Beowulf makes a wounding reply stating that Unferð had killed his own brothers. This deed associates him with Cain, the archetypal fratricide, and Cain's descendant, Grendel. The defence of the hall is successful and Grendel is killed. At the victory celebration the scop recites a lay about the visit of Hnæf and his Half-Danes to Finn and his Frisians in Finnesburh.[5] They fall to quarrelling and slaughter each other. In this episode the word *eoten* occurs three times in the genitive plural form *eotena* and once in the dative plural *eotenum*. These forms are often taken as referring to the Jutes, although no one can say what they are doing there or what part they play. More likely the references are to monsters.[6] At line 1088 the Frisians and Danes surviving from the first battle are said each to control half of the hall *wið eotena bearn*, which probably means "against the giants' kin." Quite possibly the Half-Danes go to Finnesburh to help the Frisians hold their hall against monsters, a situation which would explain why Finn did not burn out the Half-Danes when the fighting started.

5. *Beowulf*, pp. 19–21. *Ed.*
6. For more on this, see R. E. Kaske,   "The *Eotenas* in *Beowulf*," *OEP*, pp. 285–310. *Ed.*

The hall was their joint protection against the monsters. After the lay Wealhþeow makes two moving pleas (1169–87 and 1216–31) for good faith and firm friendship in Heorot, especially between the Geats and the Danes. She clearly takes the scop's lay as a warning and fears being afflicted like Hildeburh. Just before she speaks, Unferð is described as sitting at Hroðgar's feet; he is a figure of discord as shown by his name, which means "mar-peace", and by his behaviour. The queen might well be concerned lest insults between Dane and Geat be renewed and lead to fighting. From all this emerges an interesting connection. In *Beowulf* monsters are closely associated with the slaying of friends and kinsmen.[7] They function in part as an outward objectification and sign of society beset by internecine slaughter between friend and kin.

The Finnesburh episode and the situation in Heorot are part of another theme that forms a thread of the interlace design of *Beowulf*—visits to a hall. A guest should go to the hall with friendly intent and be given food and entertainment of poetry by his host. Grendel inverts this order. He visits Heorot in rage, angered by the scop's song of creation, and makes food of his unwilling hosts. Hroðgar cannot dispense men's lives in Heorot, but Grendel does little else. He is an *eoten*, or "eater," and swallows up the society he visits almost as if he were an allegorical figure for internecine strife. In a similar way Grendel's mother visits Heorot and devours Æschere; in return Beowulf visits her hall beneath the mere, kills her, and brings back the head of Grendel. The Heaþobard episode concerning Ingeld and the battle that breaks out when the Danes visit his hall is another appearance of this thematic thread. Hroðgar gives his daughter Freawaru to Ingeld in marriage, hoping to end the feud between the two tribes, but an implacable old warrior sees a Dane wearing a sword that once belonged to the father of a young Heaþobard warrior. He incites the youth to revenge and the feud breaks out again; in the end the Heaþobards are decimated and Heorot is burnt. Other hall visits may be noted briefly. A slave visits the hall of the dragon and steals a cup; the dragon burns halls of the Geats in angry retribution, a token of the fate in store for Geatish society soon to be destroyed by war. Beowulf attacks the dragon who dies in the door of his hall fighting in self-defence.

Another theme of the poem is that of women as the bond of kinship. The women often become the bond themselves by marrying into another tribe, like Wealhþeow, Hildeburh, and Freawaru. This tie often has great tension put on it when the woman's blood relations visit the hall of her husband and old enmities between the

---

7. Heremod's story fits this context, too, for he kills his table companions and dies *mid eotenum* (902).

tribes arise, as happens in the Finnesburh and Heaþobard episodes. The marriage then gives occasion for old wounds to open, even after an interval of years, and produces a result exactly opposite to its intent. On the other hand, women can be implacable in revenge as Grendel's mother is. Þryð (or Modþryð)[8] is also implacable at first in resisting marriage; she causes her would-be husbands to be killed. Afterwards her father sends her over the sea as wife to Offa who checks her savage acts and she becomes a *freoðuwebbe*, "peace-weaver," knitting up her kinsmen rather than refusing all ties. In general the women are *cynna gemyndig*, "intent on kinship," as the poet says of Wealhþeow (613). They preserve the tie of kin or revenge it when given cause.

Another tie that binds society is treasure, especially gold; but, like kinship, it is also a cause of strife. Treasure is not sought for selfish avarice, but to enable a hero to win fame in gaining treasure for his lord and his lord to win fame dispensing it as a *beaga bryttan*, as "dispenser of treasure," from the *gifstol*, "gift throne." The gift and receipt of treasure are a tie between a lord and his retainer, an outward sign of the agreement between them. The strength and security of heroic society depend on the symbolic circulation of treasure. A lord offers support and sustenance to his retainer who agrees in turn to fight unwaveringly for his lord, a bond of contractual force in heroic society. Injury or slaughter of a man had a monetary price and could be atoned by *wergild*, "man payment." The monsters are outside this society; for them treasure is an object to be hoarded under ground. They receive no gifts and do not dispense them. The poet states ironically that none need expect handsome recompense for the slaughter that Grendel inflicts. Hroðgar is the one who pays the *wergild* for the Geat, Hondscio, killed by Grendel in the Danish cause. The relation of the monsters to *gifstolas* presents an interesting parallel in the interlace design. The dragon burns the *gifstol Geata* (2327), an act that implies his disruption of the entire social order of Beowulf's *comitatus*. The full extent of this disruption appears when all but one of Beowulf's chosen retainers desert him in his last battle. Grendel, on the other hand, occupies Heorot, but he is not able to cause complete disruption of Hroðgar's *comitatus*, however ineffective it is against him. The sense of lines 168–9, a much disputed passage, thus seems likely to be that Grendel cannot destroy Hroðgar's *gifstol* (168), thought of as the objectification of the Danish *comitatus*.[9]

The poem is also concerned with a society's gain of treasure as well as its loss. When a king seeks treasure himself, the cost may be ruinous for his people. Hygelac's Frisian raid and Beowulf's

8. See *Beowulf*, p. 34. *Ed.*
9. *Comitatus*, the social unit of retainers and lord bound by a strong commitment of mutual trust. *Ed.*

dragon fight are examples. Although Grendel's cave is rich in treasure, Beowulf takes away only a golden sword hilt and the severed head of Grendel; his object is to gain revenge, not treasure. Hroðgar's speech to Beowulf after his return contains warnings on pride in heroic exploits and on the ease with which gold can make a man stingy, hoarding his gold like a monster; either way the *comitatus* is apt to suffer. Heremod, who ended *mid eotenum*, is an example. When treasure passes outside the society where it is a bond, it becomes useless. The treasure in Scyld's funeral ship, the golden torque lost in Frisia, the lay of the last survivor, and the dragon's hoard buried with Beowulf are examples. Treasure had some positive force in heroic society, but it casts a baleful glitter in the poem because it is associated with monsters, fighting, the death of kings, and funerals.

These various themes are some of the threads that form the interlace structure of *Beowulf*. Often several are present together, as in the Finnesburh episode or in the final dragon fight. The themes make a complex, tightly-knotted lacertine interlace that cannot be untied without losing the design and form of the whole. The tension and force of the poem arise from the way the themes cross and juxtapose. Few comments are needed from the poet because significance comes from the intersections and conjunctions of the design. To the *Beowulf* poet, as to many other writers, the relations between events are more significant than their temporal sequence and he used a structure that gave him great freedom to manipulate time and concentrate on the complex interconnections of events. Although the poem has to be lingered over and gives up its secrets slowly, the principle of its interlace structure helps to reveal the interwoven coherence of the episodes as well as the total design of the poem in all its complex resonances and reverberations of meaning. There are no digressions in *Beowulf*.

The structural interlace of Beowulf, like the visual interlace patterns of the same culture, has great technical excellence, but is not to be regarded as an isolated phenomenon. The term is specifically applied to literature in the late middle ages. Robert Manning states in his *Chronicle* (1338) that he writes in a clear and simple style so that he will be readily understood; others, he says, use *quante Inglis* in complicated schemes of *ryme couwee* or *strangere* or *interlace*.[1] *Entrelacement* was a feature of prose romances, especially those in the Arthurian tradition, as Eugène Vinaver has recently shown.[2]

---

1. Ed. F. J. Furnivall (London, 1887). See lines 71–128.
2. "Form and Meaning in Medieval Romance," The Presidential Address of the Modern Humanities Research Association (1966). See also Eugène Vinaver, *The Rise of Romance* (Oxford, 1971), chap. 5, "The Poetry of Interlace," pp. 68–98.

The term interlace may be taken in a larger sense; it is an organizing principle closer to the workings of the human imagination proceeding in its atemporal way from one associative idea to the next than to the Aristotelian order of parts belonging to a temporal sequence with a beginning, middle, and end. If internal human experience of the imagination is taken as the basis, the Aristotelian canon of natural order as moving in chronological progression is really *ordo artificialis*, not the other way around as the rhetoricians taught. The human imagination moves in atemporal, associative patterns like the literary interlace. *Don Quixote* presents a useful illustration. The Don, supposedly mad, is brought home in a cage on wheels at the end of Part I. He could be taken as the interlacing fecundity of the associative mind, caught in the skull-cage, reacting with complex atemporal imagination, weaving sensory impressions with literary experience. The Canon of Toledo who rides along outside mouthing Aristotelian criticism of romances is, as his name suggests, an uncomprehending set of external rules, or canons, sent to bedevil and torment the poetic imagination.

There is a substantial amount of literature having interlace structure, if I may extend the term without presenting evidence here. Mediaeval dream poetry, such as *Le Roman de la Rose* and *Piers Plowman*, is largely a mixture of literary and imaginative experience with an atemporal interlace structure as are many complex romances, especially those with allegorical content like the *Faerie Queene*. The allegorical impulse in literature is often presented with an interlace structure because it is imaginative, literary and atemporal. Stream-of-consciousness novels frequently have something like interlace structures as well, for the same reasons.[3]

Like the poem, this lecture will make an end as it began. Scyld's glorious accomplishments and ship funeral at the opening of the poem mark the start of a dynasty and a period of prosperity for the Danes after the leaderless affliction they suffer following the death of Heremod. The funeral in the Finnesburh episode begins the period of affliction of the Half-Danes and presages the destruction of Finn's dynasty. At the end of the poem Beowulf's death begins a period of affliction for the Geats. The poem ends as it began with a funeral, the return of the interlace design to its start. The sudden reversals inherent in the structure as one theme intersects another without regard to time give to the whole poem a sense of transience about the world and all that is in it as beginnings and endings are juxtaposed; this is the much remarked elegiac texture of *Beowulf*. Scyld's mysterious arrival as a child is placed beside his mysterious departure in death over the seas. A descrip-

---

3. Interlace structure in later texts will be the subject of a larger work now in preparation [to be entitled *The Visual Imagination. Ed.*].

tion of Heorot's construction is followed by an allusion to its destruction. The gift of a golden torque, by its loss. Beowulf's victories over monsters, by his defeat by a monster. With each reversal the elegiac texture is tightened, reminding us of impermanence and change, extending even to the greatest of heroes, Beowulf, a man mourned by those who remain behind as

> manna mildust ond mon(ŏw)ærust,
> leodum liŏost ond lofgeornost.   [3181–82]

> the most gentle and kind of men,
> most generous to his people and most anxious for praise.

A bright and golden age of a magnanimous man vanishes, even as it seems hardly to have begun.

> The jawes of darkness do devoure it up:
> So quicke bright things come to confusion.
> [*Mids.* I. i. 148–49][4]

FREDERIC G. CASSIDY
AND RICHARD N. RINGLER

Oral-Formulaic Theory†

As long ago as 1912, H. M. Chadwick discussed *Beowulf* in terms of what was then known about Yugoslavian oral poetry and decried "the chimæra of a literary Beowulf."[1] He was politely ignored. Then in recent years two classical scholars at Harvard, Milman Parry and Albert P. Lord, investigated this Yugoslavian poetry intensively for the light which it might shed on the authorship and composition of the Homeric poems.[2] Their results were extended to OE verse in a very important article by Francis P. Magoun, Jr., which makes clear his debt to Parry and Lord.[3] According to this oral-formulaic theory, the oral poet does not first memorize by rote and then subsequently perform and reperform an unvarying text; rather he creates at every performance a fresh verbal realization of the skeletal and basically stable narrative pattern. He does this by having learned, over a long period of

4. Shakespeare, *A Midsummer Night's Dream*. Ed.

† From *Bright's Old English Grammar and Reader*, 3rd ed., edited by Frederic G. Cassidy and Richard N. Ringler, pp. 270–72. Copyright © 1891, 1894, 1917, 1935, 1961, 1971 by Holt, Rinehart and Winston, Inc. Reprinted by permission of Holt, Rinehart and Winston, Inc. See also Ann Chalmers Watts, *The Lyre and the Harp: A Comparative Recon-**sideration of Oral Tradition in Homer and Old English Epic Poetry* (New Haven: Yale University Press, 1969).
1. H. Munro Chadwick, *The Heroic Age* (Cambridge, 1912), p. 76.
2. See Albert B. Lord, *The Singer of Tales*. (Cambridge, Mass., 1960).
3. "Oral-Formulaic Character of Anglo-Saxon Narrative Poetry," *Speculum*, 28 (1953), 446–67 * * * [rpt. in *ABC*, pp. 189–221, and *BP*, 83–113. Ed.].

apprenticeship to his art, a number of what we may call "formula frames."

Each of these frames is an abstract verbal pattern whose metrical and syntactic contours are fixed, but whose constituent verbal elements may, in any concrete manifestation (an actual "formula" as it occurs in the verse), vary according to the demands of alliteration and/or context. This requires elaboration. Take the second halfline of *Beowulf*, *in geārdagum*, "in days of yore." This is a formula, as indicated by the fact that we find precisely the same form of words in *The Wanderer* * * *. But in *Christ and Satan* (367a) we find *on geārdagum*, and in *The Phoenix* (384a) *æfter geārdagum*. These are not precisely the same formula as *in geārdagum* but clearly they are closely related. We can express the relationship of these concrete formulas by an abstract frame: "[preposition] + *geārdagum*." Notice that the variation permitted by this free substitution of prepositions enables the members of this frame to be used in different contextual situations. Glancing through the poetry we now come upon *on fyrndagum* (*Andreas* 1b), *in ǣrdagum* (*Christ* 79a), *in ealddagum* (*Christ* 303a)—all of which mean precisely the same thing as *in geārdagum*. We can now adjust our abstract frame to the form: "[preposition] + x-*dagum*." The variation permitted by free substitution of first elements in the compound "x-*dagum*" enables the members of this frame to be used in different alliterative situations. All members of the frame "[preposition] + x-*dagum*" have the same rhythm (x-́ úx) and the same syntax (prepositional phrase used adverbially); hence the definition at the beginning of this paragraph.

Language itself supplies a useful parallel. The child learns his language by abstracting recurrent patterns out of the apparent chaos he hears in the speech of adults. He learns how to substitute within grammatical "frames"—substitute one noun for another, etc. The frames themselves remain constant. The oral poet learns, in a similar way, the grammar of formulaic substitution—and will ultimately be as flexible and spontaneous at oral poetical composition as we are at speaking our native language.

The development of this system of formula frames among the Germanic peoples must have been concurrent with the development of alliterative verse itself. It took place long before the Anglo-Saxons migrated to England. Hence we find the same frames and often the same formulas in the extant verse of all the Germanic languages—ON for example yields the now familiar *í árdaga*, "in days of yore."

The great question, of course, is this: how much, if any, extant OE poetry is directly oral in origin—i.e., a written record, taken down by dictation, of an oral performance by an unlettered *scop*?

How much of it, on the other hand, is a literary reflex of earlier oral tradition—i.e., the written production of literate clerics and poets who used and imitated the ancient oral style simply because it was the only style in which poetry in the vernacular was known to exist? Sometimes external evidence strongly suggests oral composition—as for example Bede's account of Cædmon and the genesis of his hymn.[4] Bede himself on his deathbed, in addition to quoting a good bit of Latin, spoke in *nostra quoque lingua, ut erat doctus in nostris carminibus* ("also in our own language, seeing as how he was skilled in our vernacular songs")—which has been taken by many scholars to imply that he was composing rather than simply quoting. On the other hand, internal evidence often argues conclusively against oral origin. It was no illiterate oral singer who ended *The Phoenix* with what he conceived to be a fine macaronic climax: according to him, after death we shall all *gesēon sigora Frēan   sine fine/ ond him lof singan   laude perenne/ ēadge mid englum   Alleluia* ["see the Lord of victories   without end/ and sing His glory   in eternal praise/ blessed with the angels   Alleluia" Ed.]. Nor could anyone trained only in the "formula frames" of oral composition, those syntactic units ready to hand for fitting into easy paratactic syntax, have come up with the Latinate disjunction and involution of *Judith* 52b–4a.

While recognizing, then, that the corpus of OE verse unquestionably includes some orally composed poetry along with some literary poetry written in imitation of the oral style (and possibly also some transitional pieces), at the present moment we have not developed techniques which will in every case enable us to distinguish between the different types.

Finally it is important to note that in the broader narrative, too, the oral-formulaic theory calls attention to the use of formulaic "themes," characterized and identified by their having conventional subject-matter and expressing conventional attitudes.[5] Neither the occurrence of a theme nor the point of its appearance can be predicted, nor are any two presentations of the same theme identical; yet there is enough similarity from one version to another to justify (in a broad sense) the word "formulaic." We may feel certain both that an audience would have expected the oral poet to bring into his heroic narrative at appropriate points certain accustomed themes, and that the poet, while satisfying that expectation, would yet have been free to present the theme in his own way.

4. See Francis P. Magoun, Jr., "Bede's Story of Caedman: The Case History of an Anglo-Saxon Oral Singer," *Speculum,* 30 (1955), 49–63.
5. See F. P. Magoun, Jr., "The Theme of the Beasts of Battle in Anglo-Saxon Poetry," *NM,* 56 (1955), 81–90; also S. B. Greenfield, "The Formulaic Expression of the Theme of 'Exile' in Anglo-Saxon Poetry," *Speculum,* 30 (1955), 200–206.

PAULL F. BAUM

The *Beowulf* Poet†

* * *

A poem assumes readers, but since in the eighth century the *Beowulf* poet could hardly expect any considerable number of readers and since then poetry was commonly recited, read aloud with some sort of musical accompaniment—þær wæs hearpan sweg, swutol sang scopes [there was the sound of the harp, the clear song of the minstrel (*Beowulf*, p. 3. *Ed.*)]—it is usually taken for granted that the *Beowulf* poet cast himself in the role of *scop* and both recited his poem to a group of listeners and hoped that others would do the same. Miss Whitelock has computed that the poem "could easily be delivered in three sittings," and it only remains to inquire who the listeners would be.[1] This question she has faced with courage and great learning; she presents her case with shrewd caution, avoiding over-confidence: "it would be unsafe to argue that any part of England was in the eighth century insufficiently advanced in intellectual attainments for a sophisticated poem like *Beowulf* to have been composed there and appreciated." Most admirable caution, though one might have hoped for a more positive conclusion. "The audience," she says, "would doubtless consist of both veterans and young men" in the royal retinue, as well as "an audience of sportsmen." They would probably be Christians. Remembering Alcuin's *Quid Hinieldus cum Christo* [What has Ingeld to do with Christ], she seems not to have included a monastic audience. (One wonders how much Alcuin knew about Ingeld. Saxo's spelling is Ingellus.) The men on the meadbench are slightly disguised as veterans and young men: they would have to be more temperate than the celebrants in Heorot.

For such an "advanced" audience two requisites must be met: one, a group both interested in the fearless exploits of a heathen hero, modified for Christian ears, who fought ogres and a dragon in the long ago, and sufficiently familiar with Geatish and Swedish feuds and with continental legends and sagas—Sigemund and Heremod, Hengest and the Heaðobards, and so forth—to be able to absorb easily and with pleasure the poet's somewhat abrupt allusions; and secondly, a group capable of the concentrated attention necessary to follow, while listening, a narrative as involved and circuitous ("circumambient," "static" with the illusion of forward

† Originally appeared in *Philological Quarterly*, 39 (1960), 394–99; published by the University of Iowa (reprinted in *ABC*, pp. 359–65). Reprinted by permission of the publisher.
1. Dorothy Whitelock, *The Audience of Beowulf* (Oxford: Clarendon Press, 1951), p. 20. *Ed.*

movement), in a style as compressed and often cryptic, as that of *Beowulf*. The reasoning assumes not only a group of listeners knowledgeable on all the many topics to which the poet points and passes, as well equipped as the poet himself, and sufficiently able to fill in all that he leaves out or hints at, but *a fortiori* nimble-minded enough ("alert") *while listening* to, say, three sequences of about 1000 lines each, to pick up and drop at need the several allusions historical and traditional without losing the main pattern, to adjust and readjust their attention in rapid alternation to diverse matters without sacrificing their interest in the principal concern. Could such a listening audience ever have existed? Did ever a poet before or since ask so much of one?

The 'argument' was succinctly put, long ago, by Gummere: "The style of reference to the death of Hæthcyn shows how familiar the whole story must have been."[2] Miss Whitelock elaborates this. At every turn she insists that the poem would not be intelligible unless the audience was well informed—on Christian doctrine, for example, to understand a Biblical reference (the giants of *Exodus*), or on the subsequent history of Hroðgar's strife with his own son-in-law to catch the hint of *þenden* (1019),[3] and so on. "To an audience that did not know that Hrothulf killed Hrethric, the whole section [1164 ff.] would be pointless." She dwells at length on the fourfold account of Hygelac's Frisian raid. It would ask a good deal for the audience to pick up the second hint eleven hundred and forty lines after the first unless they were well acquainted with Frankish tradition and Geatish history. It assumes "the likelihood that the poet could rely on his hearers' previous knowledge of the Geatish kings as on that of the Danish kings, and could leave it to them to supply more than he chose to tell them" — while they listened for what was coming next. And finally, "if even a few of the claims I have made are true, we must assume a subtle and sophisticated poet, and an alert and intelligent audience" later than the age of Bede.

Those elements of the minstrel style which the poet made use of, and his picture of the improvising scop at Hroðgar's court will not have deceived him, or us. He was not composing an enlarged tripartite 'lay.' "The first concern of heroic poetry," says Bowra, "is to tell of action, . . . bards . . . avoid . . . not merely moralizing comments and description of things and places for description's sake, but anything that smacks of ulterior or symbolic intentions"; "the listening audience requires single moods and effects, without complications." A bard has to hold the audience's attention, "to make everything clear and interesting."[4] This hardly

2. *The Oldest English Epic* (New York, 1910), p. 129.
3. *Þenden*, i.e. "then." See *Beowulf*, p. 18, XV, par. 2, "the Scylding-people had not then (*þenden*) known treason's web," and note 1. Ed.
4. C. M. Bowra, *Heroic Poetry* (London, 1952), pp. 48, 55, 215.

describes the *Beowulf* poet and his work. The "discontinuity of action" (Tolkien) and the calculated double movement of Part II especially, with its rapid interchange of present (Beowulf and the Dragon) and the historical past is the last thing a scop would submit to a group of listeners. Miss Whitelock's "we must assume" is therefore circular: if the poet wrote for an audience, the audience must have been waiting.

> Who will, may hear Sordello's story told.

We are still in the dark about the poet's intentions. If we knew anything precise about those lost 'lays' we might guess a little about his originality. Did he invent Grendel's Mother, for instance? and why did he give her no name? The supernatural elements were, one assumes, in the 'lays' and he accepted them; they are the folklore coefficient of heroic saga. The Scandinavian settings were, one assumes also, in his 'lays' and he had to accept them and try his best to make them interesting to his Anglian 'audience.' He would celebrate a hero whose life was dominated by a (pagan) desire for fame, who won fame by overcoming superhuman opponents, and whose last act was to order a burial mound on a conspicuous head-land as a monument to his fame, and whose epitaph was *lofgeornost* [most eager for praise, glory]. But he would raise what might seem like a tale of adventure "above mere story telling"; he would make it a *poem* and load every rift with ore. So he avoided continuous narrative, intercalated fragments of story with recondite, enriching, sometimes teasing, allusions and with forward and backward glances into the historical backgrounds, and arrayed it all in a highly ornate, alembicated style, with some vestiges of the minstrel formulas to set it off. These have an odd look alongside his methods of "syntactic correlation, parallel and antithetic structure, parenthesis, and climactic progression" (Klaeber). His *style* is one of the poet's glories—and impediments. It makes his poem a tour de force, which he must have enjoyed writing and hoped others would enjoy— enjoy the peculiar strain he put upon language and relish the tension of keeping pace with his structural convolutions. But this combination is so curious, so original, in the sense of being contrived, that the whole seems more like an artifact than a poem created out of the artist's experience.

When, finally, one thinks of the modern reader, *Beowulf* suffers the drawbacks of all subjects drawn from Northern myth and legend. The Greek and Roman world is too much with us. The subject of the poem is unsympathetic to our taste and the cultivation of a taste for it is a burden. Its people are alien to us. The tribal conflicts of sixth-century Danes and Swedes have no recognizable

place on our stage of history. Their names have no familiar associations; and for our confusion there are twenty-six personal names
beginning with H——. We have some acquaintance with literary
dragons, but our imagination can do little with ogres and trolls;
and what is more, none of the characters in the story makes an
emphatic appeal to us. Only by intervals is there a touch of human
feeling or anything that speaks directly to us. There is no conception of character tested in significant human situations or any clear
sense of tragic conflict, man against man or man against fate, with
a catharsis which ennobles the victim through his sacrifice and the
reader through contemplation of victory in death. (The hero's end
is confused, for the reader, by his involvement with the heathen
hoard.) The divided spirit of Hroðgar; the plight of that terrible
old Ongenþeow, his queen captured and rescued and his death at
the hands of a young man; the graciousness of Wealhþeow; the
pathos of Hildeburh and the indecision of Hengest; the little
comedy (if it be comedy) of Unferð—these seem to us undeveloped
possibilities. We can see them but they are offered in passing. Like
the tragic glimpses of Heremod and young Þryð, and all the
so-called digressions, they are absorbed into the main 'narrative'—
smaller or larger pieces of color, purple or crimson or black—with
little attention to their emotional or psychological interest. Whether
functional or decorative or both at once, they appear suddenly and
are gone quickly, and one hardly has time to enjoy them. The poet
evidently set great store by them, but his touch-and-go use of them
robs them of their power. The one major character for whom we
are invited to feel sympathy is the Dragon.

All this and more would make for the dullness and dimness which
the late Middleton Murry saw in the poem.[5] But dullness and
dimness are relative terms, and it is worth recalling that to some
Racine is dull, his characters a seeming vehicle for rhetorical
declamation. To your French critic Shakespeare is chaos. Even
Prometheus Bound is a strange work unless one brings to it the
right kind of sympathetic understanding; Prometheus on his rock
and the Oceanides singing would be, if we were not brought up on
them, as remote as Hroðgar and his trolls or Beowulf and his
Dragon. The language of Aeschylus is as difficult, until one has
learned it, as the language of *Beowulf*.

As literature, said Mr. Murry, *Beowulf* is "an antediluvian
curiosity," and Professor Gilbert Highet, speaking as a classicist,
says that "artistically *Beowulf* is a rude and comparatively unskilled
poem."[6] Well, it must be conceded that *Beowulf* is a foreign

5. J. Middleton Murry, a review of the
translation by C. K. Moncrieff, in *The
Nation and the Athenæum*, 22 October

1921.
6. Gilbert Highet, *The Classical Tradition* (Oxford, 1949), p. 24.

masterpiece, as foreign to modern taste in subject and manner as in language. It has, however, affinities with much of Donne and some of Browning, and it looks forward, curiously, to the very modern handling of time-sequence. But it cannot be translated to our idiom because we have no language corresponding to its ideas and emotions and we have no ideas and emotions to fit its peculiar language. The poet seems to have created many of his own difficulties. He had, one surmises, his own taste of chaos and in his fashion revived it, recreated it, while at the same time he looked back to a time of ideal loyalties and heroism. Simplicity, clarity, and elegant organization were luxuries he could not afford if he was to communicate what he felt the need of expressing. Why did he try? He could expect few silent readers in his own day. He adopted a tense crowded style and a convoluted method of narration, the very antithesis of a minstrel's, most unsuited for oral recitation, and if he looked for an audience of listeners he was extraordinarily, not to say stubbornly, sanguine. But all the signs point (they can hardly be called evidence but they are all we have) to a very individual man, a serious and gifted poet, steeped in the older pagan tradition from the continent, moved perhaps by a pious desire to compromise his two religions, and above all delighting in his unusual skill with language (as all poets do)—all the signs point to such a poet sitting down to compose a quasi-heroic poem to please himself, in the quiet expectation of pleasing also just that "fit audience though few." Shelley said of *Prometheus Unbound* that it was "never intended for more than five or six persons." It may seem odd to picture such an ivory-towered poet in the eighth century, but *Beowulf* is unique in every sense, and in the balance of probabilities the scales incline to even this unlikely assumption: a poet as individual and apart as his style, his plan, and his subject.

E. V. K. DOBBIE

[The Geats and the Swedes]†

* * *

The earliest of the Geatish kings mentioned in the poem is Hrethel, the father of Hygelac and Beowulf's grandfather on his mother's side (ll. 373–75a). We learn that Herebeald, the eldest

† From *Beowulf and Judith*, vol. 4 of his and George P. Krapp's edition of *The Anglo-Saxon Poetic Records*, 6 vols. [vol. 4 by Dobbie alone] (New York: Columbia University Press, copyright © 1953), pp. xxxix–xl. Reprinted by permission of the publisher. See also Jane Acomb Leak, *The Geats of Beowulf: A Study in the Geographical Mythology of the Middle Ages* (Madison: University of Wisconsin Press, 1968), and Appendix II, "Tribes and Genealogies," in our text.

son of Hrethel, was accidentally killed by his brother Hæthcyn (ll. 2435–43) and that the king died of sorrow over the death of his heir (ll. 2462b–71).

During the reign of Hæthcyn began the first of the two Swedish wars (ll. 2472–89, 2922–98). Whether hostilities were begun by Hæthcyn or by Ongentheow, who then ruled over the Swedes, it is difficult to decide, since ll. 2476b–78, in which a hostile intent is attributed to the Swedes, seem inconsistent with ll. 2926–27. But we are probably to understand that the first invasion was made by the Swedes, who attacked the Geats at Hreosnabeorh in Geatland (ll. 2472–78), and that shortly thereafter Hæthcyn initiated a war of retaliation and invaded Sweden (ll. 2479–89). The first results of the campaign were favorable to the Geats, who captured the Swedish queen. But Ongentheow, in a counterattack at Hrefnawudu,[1] liberated his queen (ll. 2930b–32) and killed Hæthcyn (ll. 2482b–83, 2924–25). The leaderless Geats were faced with extermination, but Hygelac, Hæthcyn's younger brother and successor, brought reinforcements and attacked the Swedes (ll. 2933–60). Ongentheow was killed by the two brothers Wulf and Eofor (ll. 2961–81), and the victory rested with the Geats.

Of the two sons of Ongentheow, Ohthere and Onela, we are not told which was the elder; but the narrative makes sense only if we assume that Ohthere was the older son and his father's successor.[2] How long he ruled we are not told, but it was apparently during his reign, while the Geats and Swedes were at peace, that Hygelac was killed in his unsuccessful expedition against the Franks.

After the death of Ohthere, his brother Onela usurped the Swedish throne to the exclusion of Eanmund, Ohthere's elder son and the rightful heir. Eanmund and his brother Eadgils, after an unsuccessful revolt, fled the kingdom and took refuge among the Geats (ll. 2379b–84a). Onela, pursuing them, invaded the land of the Geats and killed Heardred, Hygelac's son and successor; he then withdrew to his own country, allowing Beowulf to succeed Heardred as king of the Geats (ll. 2202–6, 2384b–90).[3] In this campaign Eanmund was killed by Weohstan, Wiglaf's father (ll. 2611–16a), who was in the service of Onela. At a later time Beowulf supported the destitute Eadgils, now the rightful heir to the Swedish throne, invaded Sweden, and killed Onela (ll. 2391–96). This is the last of the hostile encounters between Geats

---

1. I.e., Ravenswood. *Ed.*
2. See [Kemp] Malone, *PQ*, 8 (1929), 406–7.
3. It is not clear whether we are to understand from ll. 2389–90a that Beowulf became a puppet king under the overlordship of Onela, or merely that

Onela withdrew entirely, permitting the Geats their own choice of Heardred's successor. Beowulf's freedom to initiate the later campaign which resulted in the death of Onela supports the latter alternative.

and Swedes which are referred to in the poem as past events; but after the death of the childless Beowulf, Wiglaf predicts a renewal of hostilities (ll. 2999–3007*a*).[4]

* * *

EDWARD B. IRVING, JR.

The Feud: Ravenswood[†]

It is not necessarily over-ingenious to see a progression in the poem from the story of Finn to the Ingeld scene and then to the battle of Ravenswood, which is described by the Messenger near the end of the poem. The poem does seem to have something of a Yang-Yin structure to it, after all: as the kind of heroic achievement that Beowulf represents nears its end in Beowulf's own death, the kind of self-destructiveness the feuds represent—the negative side of the heroic ideal—comes into clearer and clearer focus.

The story of Finnsburg,[1] told as an integral part of the celebration of Beowulf's defeat of Grendel, is offered to us ostensibly as a rousing minstrel's tale intended to entertain the feasters. It has no direct and explicit relevance to the audience that hears it, other than in the fact that Danes of a previous generation were involved in the story, although, as we have seen, it is certainly true that there is an important implicit or analogical relevance to the situation of Wealhtheow and the Danish court. Again, the Finn tale, for all its intensity, is not presented in specifically dramatic terms by the poet but rather in the form of narrative summary; the episode, for example, contains no speeches.

The Ingeld story,[2] on the other hand, has somewhat more immediacy. In form, what makes it particularly memorable is the direct presentation of the old warrior's speech. It is more immediate also because we have more interest in the characters. We have come to know Hrothgar well, and this is the story of what will probably happen to Hrothgar's daughter, in a feud that will lead to the destruction of Heorot itself. Yet in spite of this, the Ingeld story is still somewhat removed from a full degree of reality by the very fact that it is presented not as historical fact but as Beowulf's prediction of the future, and it is told not to the Danish

---

4. This prediction evidently refers to the war which, as we know, resulted in the extinction of Geatish independence and the absorption of the Geats into the Swedish kingdom.

† From *A Reading of Beowulf* (New Haven and London: Yale University Press, 1968), pp. 179–91. Copyright © by Yale University. Reprinted with permission. The longer OE quotations are omitted. Modern English versions are Irving's.

1. Lines 1068–1159. *Ed.*

2. Lines 2021–69. *Ed.*

participants themselves but to the detached though curious Geatish king Hygelac.

Ravenswood is quite another matter. Here we have what Klaeber calls "the only detailed account of a real battle in *Beowulf*."[3] It is very detailed, and very real; it is presented in the form of a masterly scenic narrative full of suspense. To be sure, this battle took place in the past, but it was a past accessible to the human imagination, two generations back, not in the half-legendary past of the fight at Finnsburg or of the story of Sigemund's killing of the dragon. It is a past, moreover, that has the greatest importance for the Messenger's Geatish audience, not only because their own grandfathers and fathers were in the battle but because the battle was an early stage of the same long-lived feud that is certain to break out again in the very near future after the news of Beowulf's death has spread north to the Swedes. Indeed no story could have more harsh relevance.

Because the Ravenswood battle is presented as a scene, it differs from the numerous other references in Part II of the poem to the Geatish-Swedish wars. These references are typically condensed summaries of the ups and downs of the hostility, often describing in rather abstract terms a rapid series of events. The following passage is a fair example:

> Then there was hatred and conflict of Swedes and Geats over the wide water, and fighting on both sides, and sharp battle, after Hrethel died; Ongentheow's sons were bold and aggressive, with no intention of keeping the peace across the sea. Instead, again and again, they carried out atrocious and vindictive raids near Hreosnabeorh.   [2472–78]

Lines like these suggest very effectively the unending *heard ceap*, the rugged economics, of the vendetta: exile, rebellion, pursuit, revenge, conspiracy, the precarious peace, counterplot, massacre. We should note here that this passage follows a description of the death of King Hrethel; it is typically a king's death that releases such anarchic savagery. The frequency with which such passages as these occur in Part II serves to make us more and more conscious of the world of feud, and to prepare us for the climactic scene at Ravenswood.

The Messenger begins his report to the waiting Geats, a report that immediately follows Wiglaf's reprimand to the cowardly retainers, by offering for their contemplation a compact picture, almost an icon, composed of three figures: Beowulf dead, the dragon dead beside him, and Wiglaf sitting motionless over both.

3. Fr. Klaeber, *Beowulf and the Fight at Finnsburg* (3rd ed., Boston: D. C. Heath, 1950), p. 223.

Now the bountiful lord of the Geats is fast in the bed of death, lies in his slaughter-couch, victim of the dragon's deeds. Beside him lies his deadly opponent, brought down by dagger-wounds; with his sword Beowulf was never able to make any wound at all in the monster. Wiglaf son of Weohstan sits over Beowulf, one good man sitting over another no longer alive; in his exhaustion he keeps guard over the head of friend and foe.
[2900–2910a]

The dominant impressions we receive from this heroic Pietà are those of immobility and helplessness. The verbs in these lines fall into the same pattern of meaning: is deaðbedde fæst, · wunað wælræste, ligeð, siteð, healdeð.[4] The scene is composed as a static picture: nothing moves. But even though he is motionless in this tableau of grief, Wiglaf has an intense vitality. He has just ended his vehement speech of reproach to the retainers, and the echo of it is still in our ears. In his role here as "guardian" he suggests a surviving spirit of heroic dedication and loving responsibility; by his own attitude he dramatizes concretely the love and loyalty Beowulf has inspired, and he further dramatizes the possibility of their survival after Beowulf's death.

The relevance of this tableau to the main theme of the Messenger's speech is made plain in the references in the quoted passage to the wilgeofa Wedra leoda,/ dryhten Geata.[5] Dominating the entire speech by the Messenger is the master-image of the fyll cyninges, the King's Fall. Beowulf's death is national disaster. The audience must see the death scene clearly before the Messenger moves on to interpret the political meanings of the picture in terms of its predictable effects on others: on the Franks and Frisians, the Hugas and the Hetware, on the Swedes, and finally on the Geats themselves. The strong pattern of cause and effect is emphasized at the outset by the correlative rhetorical pattern. The nu is of the opening lines is to be taken together with the lines that follow:

[Now that the king is lying dead . . .] now the people may expect a time of troubles, after the fall of the king becomes widely known among the Franks and Frisians.   [2910b–13a]

As the Messenger goes on to predict the reaction of neighboring nations to the news of Beowulf's death, the image of the King's Fall is expanded greatly in importance. As the shock waves of the event radiate outward, the Geats come to realize more fully that only the strength of Beowulf's heroic reputation has protected them

4. "Fast in the bed of death," "lies in his slaughter-couch," "lies," "sits over," "keeps guard over." Ed.

5. I.e., 'the bountiful lord of the Geats." Ed.

for decades. But now, as the other nations, enraged by Geatish attacks in the past, in their turn come to "read" the picture that was held up for contemplation, the ring will begin to close.

The mention of Hygelac's death at this point further expands the range of meaning of the master-image.

> That fierce quarrel with the Hugas was started when Hygelac sailed with an armed fleet to the lands of the Frisians, and there the Hetware attacked him in battle and, since they outnumbered him, quickly succeeded in making the armed warrior give way; he fell among his men—that lord gave no treasure to his loyal retainers. Ever since then, the favor of the Merovingian [king] has not been granted us. [2913*b*–21]

Since the importance of Hygelac as a central and unifying figure in the poem as a whole has been recognized and well described by Professor Brodeur, there is no need to discuss it at length here.[6] But we should recognize that this particular passage is a climax to the story of Hygelac as it has been slowly developed throughout the poem. Here we have the fourth and final mention of Hygelac's disastrous expedition to the continent, and here, for the first time, the political rather than the personal implications of the raid are made clear.

We are certain that Hygelac's raid, in the early years of the sixth century, is historical fact.[7] Perhaps we might guess that it was, even in the absence of knowledge from outside the poem, for it has something of the puzzling intractability of history in the context of *Beowulf*. This attempt at political aggrandizement may have been Geatland's proudest and most ambitious moment, but it may also have sealed its doom. But it is too easy, and perhaps misleading, to cast this event into the black-and-white patterns of moral lessons to be drawn from history. When the raid is first mentioned, at the time of the Great Banquet, it is true that the poet seems to blame Hygelac for his arrogance in seeking out trouble (*syððan he for wlenco wean ahsode*, 1206).[8] But it might be a little nearer the truth to say that Hygelac could not have loved his people so much loved he not glory more. From one point of view, Hygelac's adventurous raid is the fine excess of a truly heroic character. If the poet reproves Hygelac for his action, it is in much the same tone that a later poet reproves Earl Byrhtnoth of Essex for allowing the Viking invaders to come ashore and fight in the battle of Maldon.

But the poet's attitude toward the raid is still ambivalent. Perhaps

6. *The Art of Beowulf* (Berkeley and Los Angeles: University of California Press, 1959), pp. 71–87.
7. The relevant excerpts from Gregory of Tours may be found in Klaeber's Appendix, pp. 267–68.
8. I.e., "when for pride he sought trouble." *Ed.*

this ambivalence finds expression in the very role he assigns Beowulf in this expedition. Nothing anywhere in the poem suggests that Beowulf's devotion to Hygelac is ever anything but absolute and unqualified. He accompanies his king on this raid and later avenges his death on the Franks. Yet we are never told that Beowulf was involved in the planning of the raid or in the looting and fighting that took place in its early stages; he is somehow kept disengaged from all aspects of it except the simple obligations to follow his lord and to avenge him when he falls in battle. Moreover we are not told elsewhere in the poem that Beowulf himself engages in aggressive warfare of this kind when he becomes king.[9]

In the context of the Messenger's speech, in any event, we are probably to see the raid as an instance of Geatish arrogance, if only because here the account of the raid forms one half of a rhetorical parallel, when it is taken together with the Geatish attack on the Swedes, which the Messenger mentions next.

> Nor do I expect any peace or faith on the part of the Swedish people; on the contrary, it was common knowledge that Ongentheow took life away from Hæthcyn son of Hrethel at Ravenswood, that time the Geatish people, in their arrogance, first went to meet the warlike Swedes. [2922–27]

Here the symmetrical pattern (attacks from both north and south in reaction against past Geatish aggression) seems to be established at the expense of consistency. We were told earlier (2475 ff.) that this particular series of wars was originally launched by the Swedes and that the Geatish expedition to Ravenswood was actually a countermeasure of revenge, almost an act of self-defense.

The Messenger has told us that King Beowulf has fallen, and King Hygelac; now we hear also of the fall of King Hæthcyn. The master-image has been expanded to include incidents of the past and portents of the future. But the presentation up to this point has been essentially static. The development and restatement of the theme of the King's Fall into terms of real dramatic power await the juxtaposition of this static form of presentation with the explosive scene of violence that follows.

For it is just at this point in the speech that the word *sona*[1] introduces abruptly a series of sudden actions, bursting upon us after all the slow and mournful building up of somber expectation:

> Instantly the aged father of Ohthere, old and terrible, struck a counter-blow, felled the sea-king [Hæthcyn]; the old man rescued

9. Unless one considers him very deeply involved in Eadgils' expedition of revenge against his uncle Onela, which he may be, but the text is not very clear on this point (lines 2391–96).

1. I.e., "soon," "at once," "instantly." *Ed.*

his wife, that old woman of a former day, mother of Onela and Ohthere, now bereft of gold; and then pursued his mortal enemies until they got away painfully into Ravenswood, lordless.[2]

[2928–35]

Here is a series of events almost too rapid for the hearer to take in. The invading Geats, momentarily triumphant, run head-on against the fury of Ongentheow—a fury given expression here by the hammering consecutive verb phrases—and are sent reeling back into a desperate position in Ravenswood. The action begins in fury and continues without pause. Cowering in the shelter of the wood, the beaten Geats face certain extinction at the hands of this grim old devil who howls his threats of hanging and massacre at them all through the long night. For there is certainly no moral ambiguity in Ongentheow's motivation at this point. That he is rescuing his wife and protecting his land from invaders adds to the very force of his onslaught: it is the uncomplicated release of righteous indignation.

What the poet shows us here is Ongentheow playing the role of the strong king, vigorously defending his beloved people against foreign attack. His very presence underlines the fact that the Geats are (temporarily at least) *hlafordlease*, a defenseless people without a king. They are saved from their dangerous situation by the sudden arrival of Hygelac:

> Comfort came once more to the sadhearted men together with early dawn, after they recognized the sound of Hygelac's horn and trumpet, when the brave one followed after the track of the picked body of retainers. [2941*b*–45]

Their emotional response to Hygelac's arrival is dramatized by the very word order. Comfort, security, relief flood back with the light of dawn after that night of horror and with the welcome daylight of Hygelac's name, then the sound of his trumpets, and finally the sight of him hurrying to their rescue.

The rest of the battle is presented in the same terms of swirling and tumultuous action. The poet immerses us in the desperate seesaw action of the fighting. Now it is Ongentheow's turn to place his back grimly against the wall. He is pursued by the Geats with the same headlong violence with which he pursued them and is at last brought to bay like a trapped animal. He goes down fighting savagely and gallantly in an unequal battle against two young Geatish warriors, Wulf and Eofor. In this fight we may believe that he would have had the audience's sympathy. Patriotic

2. The reading *gomela*[*n*] *iomeowlan* ["that old woman of a former day" *Ed.*] (2931) and its translation here follow the interpretation suggested by John C.

Pope, "*Beowulf* 3150–3151. Queen Hygd and the Word 'Geomeowle,' " *MLN*, 70 (1955), 77–87.

or nationalistic feeling is usually ignored by the poet of *Beowulf*, although not always by the characters themselves.

It is of vital importance to our experience of the poem that we live through the action of this battle and feel all its emotions. The gripping narrative ensures that we do. We perceive that these are men released from any burden of rational choice or self-discipline by the animal necessity of survival. Brought to bay, they fight like animals. Is the poet not inviting us to think of the story in just those terms? Two men named Wolf and Boar drag down the mighty Ongentheow in the Wood of the Ravens, and the Messenger's speech ends with a dialogue between Raven and Eagle.[3]

To share this experience is to know at the same moment why it is that men fight—beyond any question there is tremendous excitement and exhilaration in this scene—and what it is that Beowulf has resisted all his life. Perhaps not resisted consciously, except insofar as he has tried to keep the peace with his neighbors as best he could, but resisted by the force of his own massive and silent example. The Ravenswood battle is pure heroic poetry, for all its ferocity. It ends traditionally with Hygelac showing his emphatic approval of the actions of Wulf and Eofor by giving them munificent rewards. Yet here, as everywhere in the poem, we can perceive the central tragic fact about the society that heroic poetry reflects: that in its very strength and beauty, in its cohesive loyalties and allegiances, lie inevitable forces of destruction and anarchy. Hygelac's action in honoring the slayers of Ongentheow is impeccable heroic etiquette, yet it plants the seed of disaster; the greater the Geatish triumph, the more violent the predictable vengeful reaction on the part of the Swedes. Like the story of Finnsburg, the account of the battle of Ravenswood has an ostensibly happy ending, but both stories are fundamentally tragic prophecies in their contexts. The Geatish audience's temporary euphoria would have been shattered by the implications of the Messenger's comment:

> *That* [i.e. what I have just shown you in the violence of Ravenswood] is the feud and hostility, the murderous hatred of men, with which I fully expect the Swedish people will come looking for us when they hear our lord is dead, the lord who once guarded wealth and kingdom against enemies. [2999–3004]

Ravenswood is only the ultimate development of the world of feud. As such, it is the greatest of all the many negative images in the poem: it is placed opposite the figure of the hero. We have not seen Beowulf involved in this world of feud; the poet has

---

3. See Hans Weyhe, "König Ongentheows Fall," *ES*, 39 (1908), 14–39, especially pp. 35–36 [, and *Beowulf*, lines 3024–27. *Ed*.].

never placed him in the distressing situations of Hengest or Ingeld. Consistently Beowulf's energies are directed outward and away from the world of human violence and warfare, directed outward with the purpose of preserving human community by fending off threats from the outside. All through the poem Beowulf's is the embodiment of a moral discipline so perfect as to seem instinctive and effortless. His tremendous strength, both physical and spiritual, is applied to precise objectives for the good of other men: it is never wasted, never turned on itself, never beyond the control of his calm heroic will.

Ravenswood is Beowulf's absence. It is what the world is like without him and without the almost superhuman values he asserts. It is ironic that for the Geats the story of the battle is superficially one of rescue and salvation. Their experience of being helpless and lordless during the battle is acute and frightening, but brief: Hygelac rides melodramatically over the hill to save them. But they were saved then only by the arrival of Hygelac, and saved later from the dragon's attacks only by the courage of Beowulf. But the Messenger's speech was prefaced by an elaborate reminder of the deaths of these two kings. That was the last rescue; there will never be another.

Ravenswood, as a vision of the perpetual violence which is man's lot, moves out of history into a timeless world. That battle of the far past is now, and it is the future for the Geatish nation. The scene suddenly and vividly fuses *wen*, the expectation of the probable future, with *geo*, the distant but inescapable past, and both with the insistent verbs of driving action in the present. The startling sense of life and reality in the narrative of the battle, its greater vividness and concreteness of detail in a poem where so much is half-veiled in misty hints, its exposure of basic universals of human experience in a scene that is both specific and half-allegorical—all these go far to give the Messenger's later prophecy of unending warfare and ultimate extinction for Beowulf's people the solid impact of fact, not fantasy. We know that it was, and if it was it will be.

FREDERICK R. REBSAMEN

[*Beowulf*—A Personal Elegy]†

* * *

* * * The question of whether *Beowulf* is a Christian or a pagan poem will be forever clouded by the fact that the best qualities of

† From *Beowulf Is My Name* by Frederick R. Rebsamen, pp. ix–x. Copyright © 1971 by Rinehart Press. Reprinted by permission of Rinehart Press.

both these traditions overlap in such a way that no clash is felt, and it must ultimately be decided by reference to the whole, its aggregate effect upon the emotions. But this question, as well as others, should first be directed at that feature of the poem which is the most fascinating thing about it: Beowulf himself.

It seems clear to me that the poet has here created for his purpose a character who would not have been recognized in the poet's day as any particular figure from history or legend or folklore or mythology—though this assumption must ultimately be accepted on faith. Beowulf is neither human nor superhuman, Christian nor pagan, English nor Geatish, heroic nor humble, but something of all of these and much more besides. To the standard Germanic heroic attributes, all of which Beowulf has, the poet has added a measure of compassion and understanding and meditative restraint which, although these same qualities were certainly to be found to one degree or another in some real-life Germanic heroes, has made of Beowulf as a *literary* character something approaching Chaucer's knight. *Approaching*, I say, for the differences are of course enormous and the cultures eight hundred years apart—yet Beowulf, to a reflective reader familiar with both cultures, really does come across as, in his own day and way, "a verray parfit gentil knyght." The big difference here is that we *expect* Chaucer's knight to be all these things; with Beowulf, it is the unexpected.

The puzzling things about Beowulf's life—his origin, the fact that he apparently never married and/or produced any children, his return alone from the battle that took the life of his lord, his apparent inactivity during the later Geat-Swede conflicts—these, together with the ambiguous qualities mentioned above, cease to be bothersome when one accepts the idea that, after all, his creator was a major poet trying something big and new, involving the best standards of two different ways of life, and that his concentration upon theme and mood has made of Beowulf, in places, a puzzling character. If the reader further accepts, as I do, the idea that the poet was here presenting his personal elegy for the demise of an old and in many ways admirable tradition at the moment when it was giving into and merging its best qualities with a new one, then Beowulf as a character grows less and less puzzling and begins to make very good sense indeed.

* * *

Selected Bibliography

Scholars and critics have written a great deal about *Beowulf*. For brevity's sake, I omit here most works cited elsewhere in this volume. Klaeber and Chambers have excellent bibliographies covering the earlier materials; Fry is extremely helpful through 1967. The best annual bibliography is that of the MLA Old English Group.

Starred titles are available in paperback and can be assumed quite useful for the beginning student and general reader. You will find the full titles of journals in the Abbreviations section at the beginning of this volume.

BIBLIOGRAPHIES

*Annual Bibliography: MLA Old English Group. Prepared by A. K. Brown, and distributed by the Center for Medieval and Renaissance Studies, The Ohio State University.

*Annual Bibliography: *PMLA* (June of each year; as of 1969 the OE Bibliography appears in Vol. 1).

Fry, Donald K. *Beowulf and the Fight at Finnsburh: A Bibliography*. Charlottesville, Va.: Bibliographical Society of the University of Virginia, 1969.

*Greenfield, Stanley B. "Old English Bibliography," in David Zesmer, *Guide to English Literature from Beowulf through Chaucer and Medieval Drama*. New York: Barnes & Noble, 1961.

DICTIONARIES AND GRAMMARS

Bosworth, J. *An Anglo-Saxon Dictionary*, ed. and enlarged by T. N. Toller; and Toller, *Supplement* ["Bosworth-Toller"], 2 vols. Oxford: Clarendon Press, 1908–21. A. Campbell has corrected and enlarged the *Supplement* (1972), and Oxford University and the University of Toronto are sponsoring the preparation of a new dictionary of Old English.

Campbell, A. *Old English Grammar*. Oxford: Clarendon Press, 1959.

Cassidy, Frederic G., and Richard N. Ringler, eds. *Bright's Old English Grammar and Reader*, 3rd ed. New York: Holt, 1971.

Clark Hall, J. R. *A Concise Anglo-Saxon Dictionary*, 4th ed., with a Supplement by H. D. Meritt. Cambridge: The University Press, 1960.

Marckwardt, Albert H., and James L. Rosier. *Old English: Language and Literature*. New York: Norton, 1972.

*Mitchell, Bruce. *A Guide to Old English*, 2nd ed. Oxford: Blackwell, 1968.

Moore, Samuel, and Thomas A. Knott. *The Elements of Old English: Elementary Grammar, Reference Grammar, and Reading Selections*, 10th ed. Ann Arbor, Mich.: Wahr, 1964.

*Quirk, R., and C. L. Wrenn. *An Old English Grammar*, 2nd ed. London: Methuen, 1958.

EDITIONS

Dobbie, E. V. K. *Beowulf and Judith*, vol. 4 of *The Anglo-Saxon Poetic Records*. New York: Columbia University Press, 1953.

Klaeber, Fr. *Beowulf and the Fight at Finnsburg*, 3rd ed. with Supplements. Boston: Heath, 1950.

*Thorpe, Benjamin, trans. *Beowulf Together with Widsith, and the Fight at Finnesburg in the Benjamin Thorpe Transcription and Word-for-Word Translation*, Introd. Vincent F. Hopper. Woodbury, N.Y.: Barron, 1962. Though lacking the quality of the other editions in emendations and apparatus, Thorpe's is respectable and inexpensive.

Wrenn, C. L. *Beowulf, with the Finnesburg Fragment*, 3rd ed. rev. W. F. Bolton. New York: St. Martin's, 1973.

CONCORDANCE

Bessinger, J. B., Jr. *A Concordance to Beowulf*, programmed by Philip H. Smith, Jr. Ithaca, N.Y.: Cornell University Press, 1969.

TRANSLATIONS

For a sound analysis of twelve major translations and their apparatus to 1968, see John Kenny Crane, "To Thwack or Be Thwacked: An Evaluation of Available Translations and Editions of *Beowulf*," *College English*, 32, no. 3 (Dec. 1970), 321–40.

*Alexander, Michael. *Beowulf, a Verse Translation*. Baltimore: Penguin, 1973. Mellow and haunting, but rather free.

Clark Hall, John R. *Beowulf and the Finnesburg Fragment*, ed. with Notes and Introd. by C. L. Wrenn, Prefatory Remarks by J. R. R. Tolkien. London: Allen & Unwin, 1950. An exceptionally fine, generally faithful prose version for the advanced student.

*Crossley-Holland, Kevin. *Beowulf*, Introd. by Bruce Mitchell. New York: Farrar, 1968. Lightly alliterative verse and easy to read; Mitchell's introduction covers a wide range of topics, and is especially good on OE prosody.

*Hieatt, Constance B. *Beowulf and Other Old English Poems*, Introd. by A. Kent Hieatt. New York: Odyssey, 1967. Prose version with a clear, fairly inclusive introduction.

Kennedy, Charles W. *Beowulf, the Oldest English Epic*. London: Oxford University Press, 1940. Good introduction, especially on sources; one of the best verse translations, but heavily alliterative and occasionally syntactically difficult to follow.

*Raffel, Burton. *Beowulf*. Amherst: University of Massachusetts Press, 1971; paperback by Mentor, 1963. Fairly free verse translation, and a work of art in its own right.

*Rebsamen, Frederick R. *Beowulf Is My Name*. San Francisco: Holt, 1971. Compelling free prose version narrated by Beowulf, with the "digressions" clarified.

HISTORICAL BACKGROUNDS

*Blair, Peter Hunter. *An Introduction to Anglo-Saxon England*. Cambridge: The University Press, 1962.

Chadwick, H. M. *The Heroic Age*. Cambridge: The University Press, 1912. Classic study of primitive Germanic culture.

*Gatch, Milton McC. *Loyalties and Traditions: Man and His World in Old English Literature*. Baltimore: Penguin, 1971.

Hodgkin, R. H. *A History of the Anglo-Saxons*, 2 vols., 3rd ed., with an appendix on the Sutton Hoo Ship Burial by R. L. S. Bruce-Mitford. London: Oxford University Press, 1952.

Stenton, Sir Frank. *Anglo-Saxon England*, 3rd ed. Oxford: Clarendon Press, 1971. An invaluable aid.

*Whitelock, Dorothy. *The Beginnings of English Society*. Baltimore: Penguin, 1952.

LITERARY AND CRITICAL HISTORY

Allen, Judson B. *The Friar as Critic*. Nashville: Vanderbilt University Press, 1971. See pp. 139–42 on Beowulf as a Christ-figure.

Clemoes, Peter, and Kathleen Hughes, eds. *England before the Conquest*. Cambridge: The University Press, 1971.

*Greenfield, Stanley B. *A Critical History of Old English Literature*. New York: New York University Press, 1965.

*Ker, W. P. *Medieval English Literature*. Oxford: Oxford University Press, 1912. A classic study.

*Malone, Kemp. "The Old English Period (to 1100)," in *The Middle Ages*, vol. 1 of *A Literary History of England*, ed. A. C. Baugh, 2nd ed. New York: Appleton, 1967.

Sisam, Kenneth. *Studies in the History of Old English Literature*. Oxford: Clarendon Press, 1962.

Stanley, E. G., ed. *Continuations and Beginnings*. London: Nelson, 1966.

*Wrenn, C. L. *A Study of Old English Literature*. New York: Norton, 1967.

*Zesmer, David. *Guide to English Literature from Beowulf through Chaucer and Medieval Drama*, Bibliog. by Stanley B. Greenfield. New York: Barnes & Noble, 1961.

CRITICAL ANTHOLOGIES

[*OEP*] Creed, Robert P., ed. *Old English Poetry: Fifteen Essays*. Providence, R. I.: Brown University Press, 1967. Pp. 179–325 include seven excellent essays on *Beowulf* by diverse critics.

*[*BP*] Fry, Donald K., ed. *The Beowulf Poet: A Collection of Critical Essays*. Englewood Cliffs, N.J.: Prentice-Hall, 1968.

*[*ABC*] Nicholson, Lewis E., ed. *An Anthology of Beowulf Criticism*. Notre Dame, Ind.: University of Notre Dame Press, 1963. Reprints eighteen critical essays from 1897 to 1962; a valuable addition to any *Beowulf* library.

*[*OEL*] Stevens, Martin, and Jerome Mandel, eds. *Old English Literature: Twenty-Two Analytic Essays*. Lincoln: University of Nebraska Press, 1968. Includes studies on OE versification, specific works, critical approaches, and three *Beowulf* pieces very useful for the general reader and beginner.

STRUCTURE AND METER

Bliss, A. J. *The Metre of Beowulf*, 2nd ed. Oxford: Blackwell, 1962. For the advanced student.

Bliss, Alan. *An Introduction to Old English Metre*. Oxford: Blackwell, 1962. Excellent for the beginner.

Cable, Thomas. *The Meter and the Melody of Beowulf*. Urbana: University of Illinois Press, 1975.

Isaacs, Neil D. *Structural Principles in Old English Poetry*. Knoxville: University of Tennessee Press, 1968.

*Pope, J. C. *The Rhythm of Beowulf*, rev. ed. New Haven: Yale University Press, 1966.

Sisam, Kenneth. *The Structure of Beowulf*. Oxford: Clarendon Press, 1965.

Tolkien, J. R. R. Prefatory Remarks, "On Metre," in the Clark Hall translation (see above), pp. xxviii–xliii.

SPECIAL STUDIES, BOOKS

*Bonjour, Adrien. *The Digressions in Beowulf*. Oxford: Blackwell, 1965; paperback by Humanities Press, Inc.

Brodeur, A. G. *The Art of Beowulf*. Berkeley: University of California Press, 1959.

Bruce-Mitford, R. L. S. *The Sutton Hoo Ship Burial, A Handbook*, 2nd ed. London: British Museum, 1972.

Chambers, R. W. *Beowulf: An Introduction*, 3rd ed. with Supplement by C. L. Wrenn. Cambridge: The University Press, 1963. An invaluable storehouse of information.

Cherniss, Michael D. *Ingeld and Christ: Heroic Concepts and Values in Old English Poetry*. The Hague: Mouton, 1972.

Cox, Betty S. *Cruces of Beowulf*. The Hague: Mouton, 1971. A mythological and rhetorical approach, focusing on the more difficult, critically debated sections.

*Garmonsway, S. N., and Jacqueline Simpson, trans. *Beowulf and Its Analogues*, including Hilda Ellis Davidson's "Archaeology and *Beowulf*." London: Dent, 1968; paperback by Dutton. Respectable prose translations of *Beowulf* and its OE and Norse analogues.

*Girvan, Ritchie, and Rupert Bruce-Mitford. *Beowulf and the Seventh Century*, 2nd ed. London: Methuen, 1971; paperback by Barnes & Noble.

*Grokskopf, Bernice. *The Treasure of Sutton Hoo*. New York: Atheneum, 1970.

Haber, Tom Burns. *A Comparative Study of the Beowulf and the Aeneid*. Princeton: Princeton University Press, 1931.

Jones, Gwyn. *Kings, Beasts and Heroes*. London: Oxford University Press, 1972. Enlightening general discussion of *Beowulf* on pp. 3–41.

Whitelock, Dorothy. *The Audience of Beowulf*. Oxford: Clarendon Press, 1951. A seminal study of milieu.

SPECIAL STUDIES, ESSAYS

Barnes, D. R. "Folktale, Morphology, and the Structure of *Beowulf*," *Speculum*, 45 (1970), 416–34.

Blomfield, Joan. "The Style and Structure of *Beowulf*," *RES*, 14 (1938), 396–406; rpt. in *BP*, pp. 57–65.

Bonjour, Adrien. "*Beowulf* and the Beasts of Battle," *PMLA*, 72 (1957), 563–73.

———. "Jottings on *Beowulf* and the Aesthetic Approach," *OEP*, pp. 179–92.

Britton, G. C. "Unferth, Grendel, and the Christian Meaning of *Beowulf*," *NM*, 72 (1971), 246–50.

Brodeur, A. G. "The Diction of *Beowulf*," chap. 1 of *The Art of Beowulf* (see above), pp. 1–38.

Cabaniss, Allen. "*Beowulf* and the Liturgy," *JEGP*, 54 (1955), 195–201; rpt. in *ABC*, pp. 223–32.

Cherniss, Michael D. "The Progress of the Hoard in *Beowulf*," *PQ*, 47 (1968), 473–86.

Clark, George. "Beowulf's Armor," *ELH*, 32 (1965), 409–41.

Creed, Robert P. "The Making of an Anglo-Saxon Poem," *ELH*, 26 (1959), 445–54; rpt. in *BP*, pp. 141–53.

Crook, Eugene J. "Pagan Gold in *Beowulf*," *American Benedictine Review*, 25 (1974), 218–34.

Dronke, Ursula. "Beowulf and Ragnarok," *Saga-Book*, 17 (1969–70), 302–25.

Farrell, R. T. "Beowulf, Swedes and Geats," *Saga-Book*, 18 (1972), 224–86 [includes 12 plates].

Fast, Lawrence. "Hygelac: A Centripetal Force in 'Beowulf,'" *Annuale Mediaevale*, 12 (1972), 90–99.

Greenfield, Stanley B. "Grendel's Approach to Heorot: Syntax and Poetry," *OEP*, pp. 275–84.

Gulley, Ervene F. "The Concept of Nature in *Beowulf*," *Thoth*, 11 (1970), 16–30.

Halverson, John. "*Beowulf* and the Pitfalls of Piety," *UTQ*, 35 (1965–66), 260–78.

Helterman, Jeffrey. "*Beowulf*: The Archetype Enters History," *ELH*, 35 (1968), 1–20.

Isaacs, Neil D. "The Convention of Personification in *Beowulf*," *OEP*, pp. 215–48.

Kahrl, Stanley J. "Feuds in *Beowulf*: A Tragic Necessity?" *MP*, 69 (1972), 189–98.

Kaske, R. E. "The Sigemund-Heremod and Hama-Hygelac Passages in *Beowulf*," *PMLA*, 74 (1959), 489–94.

Levine, Robert. "Ingeld and Christ: A Medieval Problem," *Viator*, 2 (1972), 105–28.

Liggins, Elizabeth M. "Revenge and Reward as Recurrent Motives in *Beowulf*," *NM*, 74 (1973), 193–213.

Magoun, Francis P., Jr. "Oral-Formulaic Character of Anglo-Saxon Narrative Poetry," *Speculum*, 28 (1953), 446–67; rpt. in *ABC*, pp. 189–221, and *BP*, 83–113.

Malone, Kemp. "Beowulf," *ES*, 29 (1948), 161–72; rpt. in *ABC*, pp. 137–54.

————. "Beowulf the Headstrong," *Anglo-Saxon England*, 1 (1972), 139–45.

Mitchell, Bruce. "Until the Dragon Comes . . .: Some Thoughts on *Beowulf*," *Neophil*, 47 (1963), 126–38.

Moorman, Charles. "The Essential Paganism of *Beowulf*," *MLQ*, 28 (1967), 3–18.

Nicholson, Lewis E. "The Literal Meaning and Symbolic Structure of *Beowulf*," *Classica et Mediaevalia*, 25 (1964), 151–201.

Nist, John. "Metrical Uses of the Harp in *Beowulf*," *OEP*, pp. 27–43.

————. "The Structure of *Beowulf*," *Papers of the Michigan Academy of Science, Arts, and Letters*, 43 (1958), 307–14.

Payne, F. Anne. "Three Aspects of Wyrd in *Beowulf*," in *Old English Studies in Honour of John C. Pope*, eds. Robert B. Burlin and Edward B. Irving, Jr., pp. 15–35. Toronto: University of Toronto Press, 1974.

Renoir, Alain. "Point of View and Design for Terror in *Beowulf*," *NM*, 63 (1962), 154–67; rpt. in *BP*, pp. 154–66.

Robinson, Fred C. "The American Element in *Beowulf*," *ES*, 49 (1968), 508–16.

Rogers, H. L. "Beowulf's Three Great Fights," *RES*, 6 (1955), 339–55; rpt. in *ABC*, pp. 233–56.

Rosier, James L. "Design for Treachery: The Unferth Intrigue," *PMLA*, 77 (1962), 1–7.

————. "Hands and Feasts in *Beowulf*," *PMLA*, 78 (1963), 8–14.

Schrader, Richard J. "Beowulf's Obsequies and the Roman Epic," *Comparative Literature*, 24 (1972), 237–59.

Sisam, Kenneth. "Beowulf's Fight with the Dragon," *RES*, 9 (1958), 129–40.

Stevick, Robert D. "The Oral-Formulaic Analysis of Old English Verse," *Speculum*, 37 (1962), 382–89; rpt. in *OEL*, pp. 62–72.

Storm, G. "Grendel the Terrible," *NM*, 73 (1972), 427–36.

Taylor, Paul Beekman. "Heorot, Earth, and Asgard: Christian Poetry and Pagan Myth," *Tennessee Studies in Literature*, 2 (1966), 119–30.

————. "Themes of Death in *Beowulf*," *OEP*, pp. 249–74.

Tolkien, J. R. R. "*Beowulf*: The Monsters and the Critics," *PBA*, 22 (1936), 245–95; rpt. in *ABC*, pp. 51–103, and *BP*, 8–56.

Wentersdorf, Karl P. "Beowulf's Withdrawal from Frisia: A Reconsideration," *SP*, 68 (1971), 395–415.

Whallon, William. "The Christianity of *Beowulf*," *MP*, 60 (1962), 81–94.

————. "Formulas for Heroes in the *Iliad* and in *Beowulf*," *MP*, 63 (1965), 95–104.

————. "The Idea of God in *Beowulf*," *PMLA*, 80 (1965), 19–23.

Whallon, William, Margaret Goldsmith, Charles Donahue, and others. "Allegorical, Typological or Neither? Three Short Papers on the Allegorical Approach to *Beowulf* and a Discussion," *Anglo-Saxon England*, 2 (1973), 285–302.

Wright, Herbert G. "Good and Evil; Light and Darkness; Joy and Sorrow in *Beowulf*," *RES*, 8 (1957), 1–11; rpt. in *ABC*, pp. 257–67.

APPENDIX I

The *Beowulf* Manuscript

First Folio of the Cotton *Beowulf*
(Reproduced by permission of the Board of the British Library)

Nothing is known of the history of the only existing manuscript of *Beowulf* before it came into the possession of Sir Robert Cotton (1571–1631). In 1731 the MS was damaged by a fire and was moved, together with the rest of the Cotton Collection, from Ashburnham House to the British Museum, where it now resides. Note the charred edges on this reproduction of a facsimile of the first page.

Here is a transliteration:

HWÆT WE GARDE
na ingear dagum þeod cyninga
þrym ge frunon huða æþelingas elle[n]
fre medon. Oft scyld scefing sceathe[na]
þreatum monegu*m* mægþum meodo setla
of teah egsode eorl syððan ærest wear[ð]
fea sceaft funden he þaes frofre geba[d]
weox under wolcnum weorð myndum þah
oð þ*æt* him æghwylc þara ymb sittendra
ofer hron rade hyran scolde gomban
gyldan þ*æt* wæs god cyning. ðæm eafera wæs
æfter cenned geong in geardum þone god
sende folce tofrofre fyren ðearfe on
geat þæt hie ær drugon aldor [le]ase. lange
hwile him þæs lif frea wuldres wealdend
worold are forgeaf. beowulf wæs breme
blæd wide sprang scyldes eafera scede
landum in. Swa sceal [geong g]uma gode
ge wyrcean fromum feoh giftum. on fæder

In modern editions of Old English verse in the original, such as those of *Beowulf* by Klaeber, Dobbie, Wrenn, and others, the lines are commonly laid out in a manner which clearly shows the poetic half-lines and the alliterative patterns:

Hwæt we Gar-Dena   in geardagum
þeodcyninga   þrym gefrunon,
hu ða æþelingas   ellen fremedon!
    Oft Scyld Scefing   sceaþena þreatum,
monegum mægþum   meodosetla ofteah,
egsode eorl[as],   syððan ærest wearð
feasceaft funden;   he þæs frofre gebad,
weox under wolcnum,   weorðmyndum þah,
oðþæt him æghwylc   þara ymbsittendra
ofer hronrade   hyran scolde,
gomban gyldan;   þæt wæs god cyning!
    Ðæm eafera wæs   æfter cenned
geong in geardum,   þone God sende
folce to frofre;   fyrenðearfe ongeat,
þæt hie ær drugon   aldor[le]ase

lange hwile;   him þæs Liffrea,
wuldres Wealdend,   woroldare forgeaf;
Beowulf wæs breme   —blæd wide sprang—
Scyldes eafera   Scedelandum in.
Swa sceal [geong g]uma   gode gewyrcean,
fromum feohgiftum   on fæder

APPENDIX II

Tribes and Genealogies†

I. The Danes (Bright-, Half-, Ring-, Spear-, North-, East-, South-, West-Danes; Scyldings, Honor-, Victor-, War-Scyldings; Ing's friends).

Scyld
|
Beow the Dane
|
Healfdene

Heorogar Hrothgar m. Wealhtheow Halga Daughter m. Onela the Swede

Hrethric Hrothmund Freawaru m. Ingeld the Heatho-Bard Hrothulf

II. The Geats (Sea-, War-, Weather-Geats)

Hrethel

Herebeald Haethcyn Hygelac m. Hygd Daughter m. Ecgtheow

Heardred Daughter[1] m. Eofor Beowulf the Geat

III. The Swedes.

Ongentheow

Ohthere Onela m. Healfdene's Daughter

Eanmund Eadgils

† From *Beowulf*, a new prose translation by E. Talbot Donaldson, pp. 57–58. Copyright © 1966 by W. W. Norton & Co., Inc. Reprinted by permission of the publisher.

1. The daughter of Hygelac who was given to Eofor may have been born to him by a former wife, older than Hygd.

IV. Miscellaneous.

A. The Half-Danes (also called Scyldings) involved in the fight at Finns-burg may represent a different tribe from the Danes of paragraph I, above. Their king Hoc had a son, Hnaef, who succeeded him, and a daughter Hildeburh, who married Finn, king of the Jutes.

B. The Jutes or Frisians are represented as enemies of the Danes in the fight at Finnsburg and as allies of the Franks or Hugas at the time Hygelac the Geat made the attack in which he lost his life and from which Beowulf swam home. Also allied with the Franks at this time were the Hetware.

C. The Heatho-Bards (i.e., "Battle-Bards") are represented as in-veterate enemies of the Danes. Their king Froda had been killed in an attack on the Danes, and Hrothgar's attempt to make peace with them by marrying his daughter Freawaru to Froda's son Ingeld failed when the latter attacked Heorot. The attack was repulsed, though Heorot was burned.

APPENDIX III

The Geography of *Beowulf*

(After Fr. Klaeber, *Beowulf*)

APPENDIX IV

Index of Proper Names

Parenthetical page references are to the Donaldson translation.

Abel. Son of Adam and Eve, murdered by his brother, Cain (3). See Genesis 4:1–8.

Aelfhere. Probably a Scylfing; kinsman of Wiglaf (45).

Aeschere. A Dane, Yrmenlaf's elder brother (24); favored retainer, battle-companion, and counselor of Hrothgar; Grendel's mother kills him and leaves his head near the mere for Beowulf and the Danes to find (23–25; 37).

Battle-Bright. Sword of Hunlaf the Half-Dane, who like his lord, Hnaef, is killed in battle by the Frisians (21, note 1).

Beanstan. A Bronding, father of the young Beowulf's swimming rival, Breca (10).

Beow. Successful Danish king, son of Scyld Scefing; father of Healfdene; Hrothgar's grandfather (1–2).

Beowulf. His father was Ecgtheow, his mother daughter of the Geatish king, Hrethel, and sister of Hygelac; hero of the poem.

Breca. A Bronding, son of Beanstan; he competes with the young Beowulf in a swimming match (10).

Brondings. The tribe of Breca and his father, Beanstan (10).

Brosings. Perhaps the fire-dwarfs of Norse mythology, they made a famous necklace worn by the goddess Freya, which Hama later stole from the Gothic king, Eormenric (22).

Cain. Son of Adam and Eve, murderer of his brother, Abel, and in our poem, evil ancestor of trolls, elves, and monsters such as Grendel and his mother (3; 23). See Genesis 4:1–17.

Daeghrefn. Beowulf kills this standard-bearer of the Hugas tribe in the same battle in which Hygelac dies (44).

Danes. Tribe of Hrothgar; also called Bright-, East-, North-, Ring-, Spear-, and West-Danes; or Scyldings ("sons or followers of Scyld"), Victor-Scyldings; genealogy (1–2); Heremod's Danish followers are called South-Danes, Honor-Scyldings, or sons of Ecgwela (16; 30); Hnaef's men are called Half-Danes or War-Scyldings; the phrase "Ing's friends" (19) seems to apply only to Hrothgar's tribe.

Eadgils. Son of Ohthere, he is a Scylfing (Swedish) prince and brother of Eanmund; Beowulf helps him win the Swedish throne from his uncle, the usurper Onela, whom Eadgils kills (42).

Eanmund. Scylfing (Swedish) prince, son of Ohthere and brother of Eadgils; he is killed by his uncle, the usurper Onela, together with the Geatish king Heardred (Hygelac's son), who had given him refuge (42, note 9); Weohstan, Onela's follower, actually kills Eanmund, and his son, Wiglaf, later uses Eanmund's sword to help Beowulf kill the dragon (46).

Earnaness. "Cape of the Eagles," the headland near where Beowulf fights the dragon (53).

Ecglaf. A Dane, father of Hrothgar's court spokesman, Unferth (9).

Ecgtheow. Beowulf's father, husband of the Geatish king Hygelac's sister (6); after Ecgtheow kills the Wylfing, Heatholaf, Hrothgar gives him refuge and pays the *wergild* (4, note 4) to the Wylfings in his behalf (9); Ecgtheow's exact tribal descent is uncertain; he seems to be a Geat more by marriage and other affiliations than by birth; for a theory on his Wylfing origin, see Joseph F. Tuso, "*Beowulf* 461b and Thorpe's *wara*," *MLQ*, 29, no. 3 (Sept. 1968), 259–62.

Ecgwela. An early Danish king, ancestor of Heremod's South-Danes or Honor-Scyldings (30).

Eofor. A Geat, son of Wonred, he is part of Hygelac's force that arrives too late to prevent Haethcyn's defeat and death in the battle with the Swedes at Ravenswood; Hygelac's army pursues the Swedish king, Ongentheow, to his citadel; after Ongentheow wounds Eofor's brother, Wulf, Eofor kills Ongentheow and Hygelac rewards him with his daughter's hand (43; 52).

Eomer. Son of the fourth-century continental Angle king, Offa, kinsman of Hemming and grandson of Garmund (34).

Eormenric. Gothic king from whom Hama stole the legendary Brosing necklace (22); Eormenric lived in the late fourth century and figures greatly in Germanic heroic legend.

Finn. Son of Folcwalda, Frisian (Jutish) king, husband of Hildeburh, sister of the Half-Dane king, Hnaef; Finn and his men kill Hnaef at Finnesburg, and Finn is later defeated and killed there by Hnaef's follower, Hengest (19–21).

Fitela. Nephew of Sigemund, the dragon-killer (16); probably the Sinfjötli of Norse mythology.

Folcwalda. Father of the Frisian (Jutish) king, Finn (20).

Franks. A powerful West German people living near the Rhine River, who conquered Gaul about 500 A.D.; they included the Hugas and Hetwares, who with their Frisian (Jutish) allies defeated the Geatish king, Hygelac, about 520 A.D. (22; 44; 51).

Freawaru. Danish princess, daughter of Hrothgar; she will be married to Ingeld, the Heatho-Bard king, in what Beowulf describes to Hygelac as an abortive attempt to abate the bloody feud between the two tribes (35–36).

Friesland. Land of the Frisians (Jutes) (20).

Frisians (Jutes). Finn's tribe (19–21); allies of the Franks who defeat and kill Hygelac (22; 41).

Froda. Heatho-Bard king, Ingeld's father (35); he was probably killed early in the Danish–Heatho-Bard feud.

Garmund. Father of King Offa the Angle (34).

Geats (War-, Weather-, Sea-). Tribe dwelling in southern Sweden, ruled successively by Hrethel, Haethcyn, Hygelac, Heardred, and Beowulf; the Scylfings (Swedes), who lived to their north, were their deadly enemies.

Gifthas. An East Germanic tribe mentioned by Beowulf as a usual source of mercenaries (44).

Grendel. A cannibalistic monster who ravages Heorot and Hrothgar's Danes by night for twelve years, his name perhaps means "grinder"; an evil descendant of the murderer, Cain (3), he is killed by Beowulf (13–15), who later cuts off his head after disposing of his mother (28–29).

Guthlaf. A Half-Dane, he and his brother, Oslaf, desiring revenge for their brother, Hunlaf, urge Hengest to turn on Finn (21, note 1).

Haereth. Father of Hygd, Hygelac's queen (34).

Haethcyn. Geatish prince, son of Hrethel; elder brother of Hygelac; he accidentally kills his brother, Herebeald, and becomes king after their father, Hrethel, dies of grief; he is later killed in battle by the Scylfings (Swedes) at Ravenswood, and Hygelac then becomes king of the Geats (43).

Halga. Danish prince, son of Healfdene; elder brother of Hrothgar, and father of Hrothulf (2).

Hama. Perhaps a Dane, he stole the precious Brosing necklace from the Gothic king, Eormenric (22).

Healfdene. Danish king, son of Beow; father of Heorogar, Halga, Hrothgar, and an unnamed daughter who marries Onela the Swede (2).

Heardred. Geatish king, son of Hygelac and Hygd, nephew of Hereric (perhaps Hygd's brother); after Hygelac's death he becomes king (41) and is later killed in battle by the Scylfing (Swedish) usurper, Onela, whereupon Beowulf succeeds him (38–39).

Heatho-Bards. Germanic tribe dwelling probably on the South Baltic coast; ruled by Froda and later by his son, Ingeld, to whom Hrothgar will marry his daughter, Freawaru, in an attempt to abate the deadly feud that results in the destruction of Heorot (35–36; 2, note 9).

Heatholaf. A Wylfing killed by Beowulf's father, Ecgtheow; Hrothgar pays the Wylfings Heatholaf's *wergild* (4, note 4) on Ecgtheow's behalf (9).

Heathoraemas. Tribe dwelling where Breca swims ashore after his swimming match with the young Beowulf (10).

Helmings. Tribe of Wealhtheow, Hrothgar's queen (11).

Hemming. Kin or forebear of the fourth-century continental Angle king, Offa (34).

Hengest. A Half-Dane who succeeds Hnaef, whom he later revenges by killing Finn (19–21); he may be the same Hengest who traditionally was among the first Germanic mercenaries to arrive in England ca. 450 A.D.

Heorogar. Hrothgar's elder brother whom he succeeds as king of the Danes; the grateful Hrothgar gives his armor to Beowulf, who gives it to Hygelac (2; 9; 38).

Heorot. Means "hart"; elaborate Danish hall built by Hrothgar; construction, foreshadowing of its destruction by Ingeld (2–3); Grendel's first attack (3); Beowulf's arrival (8); Beowulf's fight with Grendel (13–15); Grendel's mother's attack (23–24); for the significance of the hart or stag, see William A. Chaney, *The Cult of Kingship in Anglo-Saxon England* (Berkeley: University of California Press, 1970), pp. 130–32.

Heoroweard. Danish prince, son of Hrothgar's elder brother, Heorogar (38); it is not mentioned in *Beowulf*, but Heoroweard will defeat Hrothulf and become king after Hrothulf kills Hrothgar's son and heir, Hrethric.

Herebeald. Son of King Hrethel the Geat; brother of Hygelac; accidentally killed by his other brother, Haethcyn, in an archery match (43); a contrasted version of the Cain-Abel story.

Heremod. Early ruler of the South-Danes (Honor-Scyldings), a prototype of the evil king; he kills rather than rewards his companions (30), and then seeks refuge among the Jutes, who kill him (16).

Hereric. A Geat perhaps, Hygd's brother possibly; uncle of Hygelac's son, Heardred (39).

Hetware. Frankish tribe allied with the Hugas and Frisians when they defeat Hygelac and his Geats (41; 51).

Hildeburh. Daughter of the early Danish king, Hoc, and sister of Hnaef; her husband, Finn, king of the Frisians (Jutes), is killed by Hnaef's follower, Hengest (19–21).

Hnaef. King of the Half-Danes, son of Hoc, brother of Hildeburh; killed by Finn and his Frisians (Jutes) (19–20).

Hoc. Early Danish king, father of Hnaef and Hildeburh (19–20).

Hondscioh. One of fourteen Geats who accompany Beowulf to Hrothgar's court; killed by Grendel (13; 36).

Hreosnabeorh. Geatish area raided by the Swedish king, Ongentheow, and his sons prior to their defeat at Ravenswood (43).

Hrethel. Geatish king, son of Swerting, father of Herebeald, Haethcyn, Hygelac, and Beowulf's mother; grandfather, guardian of Beowulf, whom he raises from age 7 (7; 42–43); dies of grief after his son Haethcyn accidentally kills his own brother, Herebeald (43).

Hrethric. Danish prince, son of Hrothgar and Wealhtheow, brother of Hrothmund (21; 32).

Hronesness. "Cape of the Whale," the site of Beowulf's funeral pyre (54).

Hrothgar. Danish king, son of Healfdene; brother of Heorogar, Halga, and the wife of Onela the Swede; father of Hrethric, Hrothmund, and Freawaru; builds Heorot (2); rewards Beowulf (18–19; 32–33); gives Beowulf advice ("Hrothgar's Sermon") (30–31); plans to betroth his daughter, Freawaru, to Ingeld, the Heatho-Bard (35–36).

Hrothmund. Danish prince, son of Hrothgar and Wealhtheow, younger brother of Hrethric (21).

Hrothulf. A Dane, son of Hrothgar's brother, Halga (21); the cousin of Hrothgar's sons, Hrethric and Hrothmund, he will later kill Hrethric after Hrothgar's death and be defeated and slain in turn by Heoroweard, his cousin, son of Hrothgar's elder brother, Heorogar (38).

Hrunting. Sword Unferth lends Beowulf for use against Grendel's mother; despite its heroic pedigree it, like Unferth, is little help against monsters (26–29), but the characteristically magnanimous Beowulf later thanks Unferth for its use (32).

Hugas. Frankish tribe; in alliance with the Hetware and Frisians they defeat and kill Hygelac; Beowulf kills their hero, Daeghrefn (44; 51).

Hunlaf. Danish warrior, brother of Guthlaf and Oslaf, killed in Hnaef's fight with the Frisians (21).

Hygd. Geatish queen, daughter of Heareth; wife of Hygelac, and mother of Heardred (33–34); Beowulf gives her the necklace Hrothgar gave him (38); she offers Beowulf the kingdom after Hygelac dies (41), and may have been the "Geatish woman" who speaks at Beowulf's funeral (54–55).

Hygelac. Grandson of Swerting (22), son of Hrethel, and king of the Geats; Beowulf's uncle and lord, and husband of Hygd (33–34), he dies in defeat at the hands of the Franks and others during an aggressive expedition (22; 41); gives Beowulf Hrethel's sword (38), and dies wearing the necklace Beowulf got from Hrothgar (23).

Ing. Legendary Danish king (19).

Ingeld. Son of Froda and king of the Heatho-Bards (35); Hrothgar will attempt to abate the deadly feud between Danes and Heatho-Bards by giving Ingeld his daughter, Freawaru, in marriage; Beowulf predicts that the plan will fail (35–36), and the *Beowulf* poet also alludes to this (2, note 9).

Jutes. Or Frisians, ruled by Finn (19–20); they and their allies, long after Finn's death, defeat and kill Hygelac (22; 41); the evil Danish king, Heremod, dies among them, perhaps in exile (16). For a view that some of the references to the Jutes may actually be to giants, see R. E. Kaske, "The *Eotenas* in *Beowulf*," OEP, pp. 285–310.

Merewioing. Merovingian, or Frankish (51).

Modthryth. A queen contrasted with Hygd (34); probably the wife of Offa the Angle, famed fourth-century continental king.

Naegling. Sword used by Beowulf to kill the Hugas hero, Daeghrefn, at Hygelac's defeat (44); it is useless, however, against the dragon (47).

Offa. Fourth-century continental Angle king, son of Garmund and father of Eomer, husband of Modthryth (34). A theory is that *Beowulf* was composed at the court of the famous Anglo-Saxon king, Offa of Mercia (reigned 757–96 A.D.), a descendant of the Offa praised here. (See J. Earle, *The Deeds of Beowulf* [Oxford, 1892], pp. lxxv–c; and Dorothy Whitelock, *The Audience of Beowulf* [Oxford, 1951], pp. 58–64.)

Ohthere. Scylfing (Swedish) king, son of Ongentheow; brother of Onela, who usurps the throne from Ohthere's sons, Eanmund and Eadgils (42).

Onela. Swedish (Scylfing) king, husband of Hrothgar's sister (2); he usurps the throne from Eanmund and Eadgils, his elder brother Ohthere's sons and heirs, and slays Heardred, whereupon Beowulf becomes king of the Geats; he is later defeated and slain by Beowulf and Ohthere's son, Eadgils (42).

Ongentheow. Swedish (Scylfing) king, father of Ohthere and Onela (34); defeats and kills Haethcyn near Ravenswood (51), and is shortly afterward defeated by Hygelac and killed by Eofor (52).

Oslaf. A Half-Dane and brother of Hunlaf (21, note 1).